British civilians
in the front line

Manchester University Press

British civilians in the front line

Air raids, productivity and wartime culture, 1939–45

HELEN JONES

Manchester University Press
Manchester and New York
distributed exclusively in the USA by Palgrave

Published by Manchester University Press
Oxford Road, Manchester M13 9NR, UK
and Room 400, 175 Fifth Avenue, New York, NY 10010, USA
www.manchesteruniversitypress.co.uk

Distributed exclusively in the USA by
Palgrave, 175 Fifth Avenue, New York,
NY 10010, USA

Distributed exclusively in Canada by
UBC Press, University of British Columbia, 2029 West Mall,
Vancouver, BC, Canada V6T 1Z2

British Library Cataloguing-in-Publication Data
A catalogue record for this book is available from the British Library

Library of Congress Cataloging-in-Publication Data applied for

ISBN 0 7190 7290 5 *hardback*
EAN 978 0 7190 7290 1

First published 2006

15 14 13 12 11 10 09 08 07 06   10 9 8 7 6 5 4 3 2 1

Typeset in Sabon with Gill Sans display
by Graphicraft Limited, Hong Kong
Printed in Great Britain
by Biddles Ltd, King's Lynn

Contents

Figures

Acknowledgements

I should like to thank Elizabeth Harvey, Michael Hill, Kate Lowe and Eugene McLaughlin for their helpful comments on an earlier draft of the manuscript. I also benefited from discussions following seminar presentations at the universities of Oxford, London and Liverpool.

I am grateful to all those who generously provided written and oral memories of their experiences of air raids, and to Michael Griffith for allowing me to use his father's papers.

Every effort has been made to trace copyright owners, but this has not always been possible.

I am grateful to all those libraries, record offices and archives listed in the Bibliography, in particular: British Library, National Sound Archive; Syndics of Cambridge University Library; Churchill Archives Centre, Churchill College, Cambridge; Imperial War Museum; David N. Andrews to quote from Sylvia M. Andrews's diary; Graham Simons to quote from G. D. Simons' papers; Clerk of the Records, House of Lords Record Office; Modern Records Centre, University of Warwick; Portsmouth Museums and Record Service; Southampton City Council Oral History Unit, and Archives. In addition I thank all those libraries, archives, record offices and copyright holders who have granted access to their holdings and permission to use material in their possession without a fee.

1

Introduction: 'The front-line runs through the factories' (Winston Churchill)

Origins

In the Annual Report of the Chief Inspector of Factories for 1940, I came across an account of workers' behaviour during air raids. The Chief Inspector observed that when large-scale air attacks began on Britain, workers spent long periods in air-raid shelters; thus productivity slumped at the very moment when the output of munitions and aircraft was vital to the country's survival. In order to deal with the problem, a system of individual warnings given by look-outs (known as raid or roof spotters) posted on works/factories was adopted, and workers were urged to continue working after the siren, until the spotters gave the warning of imminent danger. These arrangements, which the Chief Inspector claimed were highly successful, originated and were carried out by means of consultations between employers and workers, without any legal compulsion.[1] This account recalled stories that I was told as a child growing up in Plymouth, a city that had been heavily and repeatedly blitzed: the public siren warned of an air raid, but, if the dockyard siren also sounded, people knew that the raid would be a heavy one, for even those in the dockyard took cover. Slotting these comments together, I was struck by the fact that the behaviour of civilians in air raids seems to have been strongly influenced by the nature of their work.

These comments did not fit easily, however, with many of the dominant accounts and images of civilians in wartime: evacuees, people demanding safe shelters; adults and children running to shelters on the sound of the siren; and shelterers camped out for hours on end – with which I was also familiar. The thought of workers carrying on after the public siren until a works' warning sounded, and so presumably running additional personal risks, did not seem to fit with accounts of wartime workers standing up to management, and of a government forced to listen and respond to a more assertive working class. I started to look for more evidence of people in industry carrying on with their work after the public siren sounded, and, to my surprise, I found patchy references in histories of the war, as well as fairly consistent contemporary evidence, that this was a widespread practice. I also discovered that, during the Battle of Britain, top politicians and senior civil servants had been gripped with the problem of people stopping work on the sound of the siren and thus holding up production.

While the eyes of historians have been trained on the skies over Britain during the summer of 1940, at that time many people were just as concerned with what was happening on the ground. I quickly understood why Whitehall was desperate for workers in industry, especially the aircraft industry, to carry on after the siren sounded, but this did not answer two fascinating and linked questions: why were many thousands of workers willing to ignore the public air-raid siren, and what did the experience of working after the public siren mean to people? It soon became apparent that the answers were complex and strayed well beyond the confines of industry and docks, and would involve unearthing the reasons behind people's behaviour after the siren sounded in a host of situations. Workers in industry during air raids are, nevertheless, at the heart of this study because of the importance of their contribution to the war effort and the centrality of their behaviour in air raids to productivity and the production of munitions of war. The reaction of industrial workers in air raids was the government's initial concern, its reason for taking up the issue and for undergoing a dramatic policy U-turn, and industrial alarm schemes and roof spotting were first developed with industrial workers in mind. Workers in industry were central to the whole question.

This is not a general history of civilians during the war, or an overall account of civil-defence workers, firefighters, ambulance drivers and firewatchers, although they inevitably feature. It is not concerned with people who tried to avoid heavy raids by moving away from target areas, or who trekked out of the cities at night and returned during the day to work. It does not deal with the Home Guard and anti-invasion plans, and it is not a general study of production, only one particular aspect of it (although a full appreciation of that aspect does have implications for our understanding of wartime culture, by which is meant people's attitudes and beliefs, and the way in which these were manifested in behaviour and language).

This book is concerned with understanding people's behaviour in air raids, especially when they were at work; the media reconstruction of that behaviour; the language used to describe behaviour in air raids, and to promote certain types of behaviour; the impact of the experience of air raids; the relationship between the personal, workplace, local and national experience; wartime identities, choices and priorities; and current memories of behaviour in air raids. Historians have not systematically or comprehensively tackled these issues, despite the huge number of publications on the Second World War in Britain and a seemingly insatiable popular interest in the war. Historians have shown surprisingly little interest in analysing civilians as direct physical targets of the enemy, 'in the front line', yet it is important to study civilians in air raids for a number of reasons.

Air raids were the most direct, physical and violent feature of the civilians' war. Air raids killed and maimed in ways that other aspects of the war on the Home Front – rationing, evacuation, direction of labour – did not. The government and the media believed at the time that people's attitudes towards, and behaviour in, air raids was vital to avoiding defeat and winning the war. When people experienced air raids, especially the early ones and the blitzes, they were people's overriding preoccupation.[2] Air raids not only altered the physical cityscape, but also the personal mental landscape of those who experienced raids. The meaning that people gave during and after the experience of air raids indicates the intensity of that experience: people viewed their experience of air raids as so important that it was as if their lives before and after were lived in parentheses. While it is not possible to separate completely the experience of air raids from the immediate post-raid experience, the focus here is on the actual raids.

Historiography

Not long after the end of the war, Richard Titmuss reinforced a view of the Second World War that had already taken root. Titmuss was interested in evacuation, provisions for the homeless, hospitals, local government and welfare services. He rightly pointed out that it was much easier to assess the physical and material effects of air raids than people's reactions to them and their 'states of mind'. In his detailed and long study he made only a few, generalised and speculative comments about people's behaviour in raids. He suggested that East Enders' 'coming to terms' with, and 'adjustment' to air raids was made possible by their family relationships and sense of belonging within the family; and by them pursuing 'ordinary' activities, because these symbolised 'normal' life.[3]

Titmuss's emphasis on family relationships does not explain people's ability to cope when not with family; it assumes that the family was the core unit of people's lives, but, by the time that the air raids began, many men had been conscripted, so family structures were already lopsided. An explanation that focuses on the family fits suspiciously neatly with stereotypes of close-knit East End families, but the importance of relationships is one that should not be dismissed.

Titmuss argued that the war changed attitudes and led directly to welfare legislation. He claimed that evacuation and bombing of homes stimulated enquiry and proposals for reform. The mood of the people and values changed: if dangers were to be shared then resources should also be shared. In the months following June 1940, decisions were taken and policies shaped that sustained the health and working capacity of the population during the war and the social reconstruction after it.[4] Titmuss's interest in the relationship between war and social reform remained central to much of the debate about the nature of wartime experiences. Many historians have looked at wartime developments in order to explain aspects of post-war society.[5] Although there are some notable exceptions, historians have been less interested in examining policies that were developed during the war solely to deal with the war situation on the Home Front.[6] David Thoms mentioned the policy of working after the siren, but did not analyse its significance or the national and local negotiations that accompanied it.[7] We still lack insights into the way in which policies relating to air raids were developed.

Historians, have, nevertheless, analysed specific aspects of wartime society, such as industrial relations, crime, health, and the reception of evacuees, and in doing so have mounted a challenge to the once all-pervasive view of social solidarity and cross-class unity.[8] They have shown much less interest in children who were not evacuees but lived through heavy raids, the well-being of those who experienced raids, and work-place practices in raids. The relationship between war and social change, which has fascinated historians, focuses in part on the role of women in society and relationships between women and men,[9] yet we do not know whether there were gender differences in the life-and-death decisions that people took over what to do in air raids.

While historians who examined issues such as industrial and gender relations were challenging the notion of wartime unity, other historians were reassessing the nature of party politics in wartime.[10] A whole host of academics threw themselves into the fray, and there is now a veritable mountain of books and articles arguing over the definition of consensus and the extent to which it existed during and after the war, but historians analyse consensus primarily in terms of party politics and attitudes towards welfare reforms, rather than in relation to wartime behaviour.

Arguments over national unity, a breakdown in class barriers, high morale, a commitment to fair shares, cross-party consensus over post-war planning and the creation of the welfare state, appeared in numerous books and form part of some highly influential studies. These studies analyse national events, examine major cleavages in society, such as class and gender, and general attitudes in society.[11] Film historians have produced some of the most interesting work on national identity (as well as on class and gender), but although regions, countries and classes were all represented in wartime films, local identity was, on the whole, absent, so some of the most interesting work of historians on national identity has failed to explore local identity.[12]

Relatively little attention has been paid to local nuances and identity. Angus Calder wrote of the importance of local pride in air raids, although he was interested in this from the point of view of morale,[13] and David Thoms has shown that local and regional variations in the blitz experience were recognised at the time, and that local factors affected attitudes and behaviour *after* raids.[14] Although historians typically consider wartime identity in terms of national identity,[15] local identity was also significant; the local experience of war was part of people's experiences and identity in wartime.[16]

In an analysis of national identity, Sonya Rose has shown that a single national identity was shot through with gender and class contradictions and tensions, but she does not explore local identities. Rose is interested in the nature of the wartime national community, and the way in which it was depicted. She argues that national identity was constructed not only with reference to an external enemy, but also to an internal one, which comprised those who pursued their own personal interests. Those best representing Britain were deemed to be those active citizens, 'doing their bit', although this again was never gender-blind.[17] Rose does not explore the fact that, for the government, one of the most urgent needs, particularly in 1940 and 1941, was for people to 'do their bit' by maintaining production in air raids.

What went on at the workplace has been analysed in both class and gender terms.[18] Work defined one's contribution to the war effort, and industrial productivity was central to the civilian contribution to avoiding defeat. Work was a major theme of wartime literature and propaganda.[19] Historians, however, have devoted little attention to the active contribution of civilians to the Battle of Britain in 1940; their focus, not surprisingly, has been on the RAF.[20]

Historians have become more questioning of generalisations about the war and, informed by developments in related subjects, have explored the way in which the war was constructed and presented at the time, through for instance the BBC and cinema, and the way in which the process of writing the histories of the war has been constructed.[21] Sian Nicholas has shown that the BBC in particular played a central role in many people's lives. Almost everyone had access to a radio, and its appeal cut across class, gender, regional and age lines. When the BBC claimed that people were 'carrying on' and that 'Britain can take it', its message was made more credible by the fact that this was what the BBC did in air raids and when bombed. As Sian Nicholas has stated, the BBC not only reported but also experienced the blitz.[22] Film historians have analysed films that contain scenes of air raids, although, as these scenes are (with certain notable exceptions) normally incidental to the films' main themes, they have not been closely analysed. One exception is an analysis of *Fires Were Started*, which shows the way in which firefighters, each with their own individual strengths, worked together, and the importance of their relationships with each other.[23] This study builds on the work of those who have already written about reconstructions of people's behaviour in air raids and the language used to describe it on the BBC and at the cinema.

As part of the reassessment of received opinion on wartime unity, the events of 1940–41 have been critically reconsidered. Clive Ponting argued that, as a result of heavy air raids, morale was low, although it did not 'crack', not because of British courage and resilience – for no society subjected to massive bombing has disintegrated – but because people lacked an alternative.[24] The problems with this argument are that Ponting's evidence of low morale is highly selective and there is not much of it. He does not explore what social disintegration might have looked like, in particular he does not consider the way in which heavy and remorseless raids and firestorms led to short-term breakdowns in civil society in cities such as Hamburg, Dresden and Nuremberg. Rapid social reintegration, as well as Nazi propaganda that downplayed atomised existences, may help to explain Ponting's assumptions.[25] Reactions in Britain were not a forgone conclusion.[26] There were different options and strategies that people could have chosen.

Angus Calder argued that there are certain key features in accounts of the blitz, such as heroes and the victory of good over evil, which are used to explain a fact, the defeat of Nazism. These features are typical of myths, by which he was not suggesting that aspects of the account are not necessarily true, but rather that they follow a particular template. Calder raised a number of important issues about people's experiences of air raids. He asserted that by the end of August 1940 the bombing was not as bad as people had expected, and that people generated responses and reactions that would be useful later; that by the time most cities were heavily bombed the reported behaviour of Londoners had fixed the 'cheerful cockney' as a model for others to follow; that local pride was strongly involved in post-raid reactions and in proving that one's city was as brave as London; and that photographs established the 'normality' of good morale.[27] Calder mentioned but did not analyse these factors or explore the meanings behind them; neither did he analyse the experience of air raids throughout the war. He was primarily interested in the way in which the history of air raids has formed part of the 'myth', rather than in unpacking reconstructions of the myth at the time, actual behaviour and reasons for that behaviour. Numerous historians have mentioned the effects of air raids in passing. Arthur Marwick, for example, proposed that on the whole air raids toughened civilian morale and created social unity, but he devotes a mere two pages to the subject in a book covering nearly seventy years, so inevitably he cannot analyse the reasons behind these claims.[28]

Historians who look at air raids typically consider behaviour *after* blitzes. Angus Calder emphasised panic, defeatism and looting after big raids. Andrew Thorpe, writing on wartime morale, argued that morale did not crack in air raids for a number of reasons: they were not as heavy or concentrated as planners anticipated; shelters and trenches offered protection; post-raid services helped people; revenge attacks lifted people's spirits; and people adjusted and were resilient. Thorpe was unable in a single chapter, which also dealt with morale generally in the war, to explain the precise relationship between these factors and behaviour in air raids; the processes at work were complex and contained a number of contradictions and caveats that Thorpe did not have the space to explore. Beaven, Thoms and Griffiths identified the symbolic importance of the city centre, recreational facilities and other aspects of working-class community to post-raid morale, but did not examine behaviour during raids.[29]

In the 1970s, Tom Harrisson discussed behaviour during raids, pointing out how little air raids disrupted production, and indeed the whole thrust of his argument was to show the senselessness of bombing civilians, precisely because it did not undermine morale or hit production.[30] What Harrisson did not adequately explain was *why* so many people were willing to continue, especially *at work*, and not take cover. This is a crucial question, for during the Battle of Britain the output and repair of fighter aircraft was a government obsession, and was closely linked with workers' behaviour in air raids. People's attitudes towards air raids, when they were at work, was vital to the prosecution of the war.

Harrisson maintained that learning to live with the blitz had no knock-on effect, in that people did not learn anything from the experience, so it was wholly negative. In contrast, it will be argued here that the experience of air raids gave many people a strong sense of local pride and an enhanced sense of local identity, and a great sense of personal achievement, unrelated to the usual competitive and hierarchical yardsticks of money, education and lasting family relationships by which society normally judges achievement. To have experienced air raids and survived them was taken as a personal success in itself. As the working class were more likely to have experienced heavy raids, and also more likely not to 'succeed' in terms of accumulating money and educational achievement, one might speculate that members of the working class gained most in terms of a personal sense of achievement.

Harrisson, with hindsight, was keen to emphasise how little air raids disrupted production, and thus their worthlessness and senselessness. At the time, however, the media and politicians were greatly exercised by the effects of air raids on production; precisely because civilians' work was regarded as crucial to the war effort, politicians and the media likened the role of civilians at work in air raids to that of the Armed Forces. Harrisson did not make the link between ideas of civilian and military behaviour; neither did he explore gender differences, or the way in which risk was perceived.

While Harrisson discussed behaviour during air raids, his focus was on post-blitz conduct, which he linked to questions of morale, although he never quite defined his term beyond 'keeping up spirits', and 'feelings'. Starting from the point of 'morale' is problematic, anyway, as it is a concept that during the war was, and has been since, difficult to define and measure. During the war, the government often equated high morale with cheerfulness, although it was quite possible to be grumpy but absolutely committed to the war effort. There has been a long-running debate ever since over what is meant by morale and how good it was during the war.[31] This book avoids walking that well-worn path, and instead focuses on fresh questions.

As well as books with written texts, the history of the war has been presented in numerous books with photographs, in films and in museum exhibitions. Post-war British feature films set during the war have tended to concentrate on the Armed Forces (prisoner of war camps, naval dramas, RAF derring-do and commando raids) or resistance in occupied Europe, rather than on civilians in Britain. Robert Murphy has argued that from the 1970s there was a shift from violent action to intimate romance, and a greater willingness to question received wisdom about the war.[32] Nostalgia, however, did not disappear; in John Boorman's popular and well-made 1987 film *Hope and Glory*, air raids are portrayed through the eyes of a child as an adventure and an opportunity.[33] While the behaviour of a child in *Hope and Glory* resonates with much wartime evidence about children's behaviour, children and adults did not necessarily react in the same way, and the experience seen through the eyes of a child can, therefore, only be a partial one. Popular films still treat the war with nostalgia and sentimentality, which cannot challenge or redirect thinking.[34]

While there have been some shifts in emphasis and treatment as well as continuities over the years, it is important to remember that because of the frequency with which older films are shown on the television, and the common use of video recorders so that no film need be missed, many people will see older images of the war far more frequently than any current interpretation. Relatively few British wartime feature films showed scenes of air raids, and those that did do so only used them as incidental to the plot. They are unlikely now to change received wisdom about people's behaviour in air raids. The television is not the only way in which presentations of the war remain relatively static.

Local museums hold and display the material culture of air raids – sirens, gas masks and shelters – that have become the symbols of the civilian experience of war. These materials are about the system in place for protecting the population, and the population protecting itself. The other side of the coin, that of people eschewing protection, ignoring the siren and not taking cover, has not left material evidence, and cannot therefore be displayed. It is the visual remains of the war that have become icons of the war, yet gas masks were never used and often not even carried; shelters were frequently inadequate and not used; and sirens were used less after the initial outburst of warnings, and often ignored, but frequency of use and attitudes towards their use cannot be gleaned by their display. These wartime material icons offer a less-complete narrative of evidence than written documents, newsreels, feature films, newspapers, photographs and memories. Historians have to analyse a range of sources, not only the visually ubiquitous and iconic, which they then interpret as evidence in order to contextualise remaining material culture.[35]

The most frequently visited display of Second World War memorabilia is at the Imperial War Museum London, which also contains 'The Blitz Experience', which is essentially about civilians taking cover in shelters, and has been thoroughly critiqued by Lucy Noakes.[36] It involves sitting on a bench, which slightly shudders, in the dark for a few minutes with sounds of bombs exploding in the background and a cheerful cockney providing a commentary, interspersed with community singing. Visitors then walk out of the shelter into a mock-up of a bombed street. Among its many problems, there is no way of knowing from 'The Blitz Experience' that most people did not take cover in shelters or that many people were at work in air raids.

Aims and argument

The research for this book set out to answer a number of crucial and related questions: how did people at work react to the direct risks and dangers of air raids, and what determined their behaviour? To what extent did people's behaviour vary according to whether they were at work or not, and what motivated people to behave in certain ways in air raids, whether or not they were at work? What was the impact of these experiences on people's feelings and identities? In answering these questions it was discovered that once air raids began, the government policy of protecting civilians, the details of which had slowly developed over time, suddenly and dramatically switched. Now, the government actually encouraged civilians at work not to take cover but to carry on after the air-raid siren sounded – often at risk to life and limb. The government, fearful of the country's reaction to this extraordinary demand, embarked upon an unprecedented exercise in popular consultation and democratic decision-making. In chapter 2, for the first time, the thinking behind this policy and the local and national negotiations that accompanied it, are revealed. We already know that people were initially very frightened in air raids and that Air Raid Precautions (ARP) were often incomplete and inadequate, but in chapter 3 these restraints on people working after the siren are set alongside local circumstances, particularly at work. Despite all the problems of 'carrying on', there is a huge amount of varied evidence, amassed here for the first time in chapter 4, that many people did indeed continue with what they were doing after the air-raid siren sounded, whether at work, at home, in shops or in the cinema, and when people did take cover, for example when there were direct raids overhead, it was not usually in a public air-raid shelter. Even during the blitzes, there were those, such as firemen and ambulance crews (men and women), who did not take cover. Yet, the dominant image that we now have of civilians in air raids is as shelterers, for example, in the well-known shelter drawings of Henry Moore on permanent display in the Tate Britain Art Gallery, London. These drawings present the reactions of women and children in particular as negative and passive. Although there are powerful images of women in the workplace, taking on men's jobs and joining the auxiliary forces, these are not images of women at direct risk in air raids, and generally they relate to a slightly later period of the war, when the worst of the raids were, for the most part, over. People's behaviour at work was affected by influences well beyond the factory gates; workers were also parents, shoppers, cinema-goers and sports fans, and chapter 4 shows how people in a wide variety of situations behaved in air raids and how the media represented them. In chapter 5 we move on to an in-depth analysis of the work situation.

In order to encourage people to carry on at work, a system of look-outs or roof/raid spotters sprung up across the length and breadth of the country. These people reflected and contributed to the wartime obsession with aircraft. Popular interest in aircraft and the way in which people tried to identify personally with the air battle are the context in which people enthusiastically took up roof spotting; this needs to be appreciated in order to understand how and why roof spotting swept the country and was transformed from a fun hobby into a serious job of national significance. The crucial role of roof spotters, and the cultural context in which they operated, has until now been virtually ignored by historians. While roof spotters, unarmed and non-uniformed, played a proactive role in prosecuting the war, it is civilians in uniform and fire-watchers who are still publicly remembered and commemorated. Yet, as we reveal, at the time, roof spotters were embedded in national culture and frequently represented in the media. The story of roof spotters and the industrial alarm schemes that grew up around them, shows rational responses to decisions that were in part technical ones, but people's behaviour at work needs to be understood in a wider context of wartime culture, of which the media was an important part.

The language and images used to try and influence behaviour are closely analysed in chapter 6. While the media reconstructed attitudes and behaviour in air raids, as driven by abstract and national factors, we unravel the multiple day-to-day, concrete and local influences on people's behaviour in air raids at times of almost unimaginable danger, risk and uncertainty. We will see that while relationships were important to people in coping with raids, these relationships were not necessarily familial ones. Finally, chapter 7 draws together a number of themes, in particular the role of the media and the concept of 'front line' civilians.

Sources

Contemporary writings

Historians all too often do not reflect in print on the nature of their sources unless they are writing methodological guides to 'doing history', but it is particularly important to do so here, as an unusually varied range of different sources for a single book on Britain in the Second World War has been used. The evidence deployed in this study comes from a wide array of contemporary sources, written and visual, as well as memories, written and oral, collected up to sixty years after the events described.[37]

One of the most interesting sources of information for people's feelings about – and behaviour in – air raids is the Ministry of Information's weekly reports on public opinion compiled from 1940 until the end of the war, from a wide range of sources, including Chief Constables, Granada cinema managers, local newspapers, Citizens Advice Bureaux,

Mass-Observation, people listening in queues or at bookstalls to conversations, listening-in to telephone conversations, or opening letters (120,000 in the first week alone).[38]

Mary Adams, 1898–1984, was Director of Home Intelligence at the Ministry of Information between 1939 and 1941, and it is reasonable to assume that she influenced the nature of the early reports. Her *DNB* entry describes her as a socialist and romantic communist, an atheist, and a strong advocate of humanism and common sense. According to Calder, she was a key authority in government circles, enjoyed a wide range of contacts (her husband was a Conservative MP), and brought academic and scientific caution to her work. Two assessors produced abstracts and summaries and compiled a report from the material that they received. The assessors then wrote a final report, in consultation with Adams.[39] Public opinion was thus interpreted and reinterpreted. Sometimes the views of the compilers come across strongly, although it is not always easy to tell at what point interpretation is overlaying original comments. The original reports that were sent to the Ministry of Information no longer survive – only the reports compiled from them. Although the reports are second or third hand, they draw on a range of sources, they were compiled at the time, and they present a varied picture of events and experiences, so they are a guide to what some people were thinking, saying and doing. While in the early years at least, Mary Adams may have wished to present a particular picture of the working class to the rest of Whitehall, we simply do not know how far editing skewed the overall tone and content of the reports. We do know that the reports offer insights into a range of feelings, reactions and concerns.

There is separate unpublished contemporary material amassed by Mass-Observation, founded in 1937 by Tom Harrisson, an anthropologist; Charles Madge, a South African poet; and Humphrey Jennings, a documentary film-maker. Tom Harrisson, 1911–76, was born to British parents in Argentina, where he spent periods of his childhood. As a young man he went on organised expeditions to study exotic plants, birds, animals and people. He then applied this anthropological approach to Britain, and, along with Madge and Jennings, set up a group that observed everyday life in real situations; they recorded what they saw in reports, photographs and paintings; others wrote down their own experiences in diaries. Mass-Observation recruited volunteers through newspaper advertisements and by word-of-mouth. They tended to be young, lower middle class and left wing; just under half were women. David Mellor has argued that Harrisson and Madge's expatriate detachment gave them a viewpoint of British culture from an imagined 'exterior', alien, territory. Mass-Observation drew on anthropological and ethnographic work that was part of the European documentary movement of the 1930s. Anthropology, market research, opinion polls, social surveys and investigative reportage all influenced Mass-Observation's methods.[40]

Mass-Observation really came into its own during the war, when a huge amount of material was collected on virtually every aspect of wartime life. Part-time and untrained volunteers, as well as a small group of full-time, trained Mass-Observers either reported their observations in response to specific 'directives' (open-ended questions), or kept detailed diaries. In the case of material collected during and immediately after air raids, mass-observers would have experienced the raids, so they were not outsiders looking in, and their own personal experiences must have affected the commentaries that they wrote on other people's behaviour. Mass-Observers put people into social-class categories, even if they were observing people unknown to them. Inferences about the behaviour of different social classes were sometimes drawn from these classifications.[41] As this appears fundamentally unreliable, no Mass-Observation generalisations about differences between social classes are used here. Unsubstantiated claims about people's courage according to class, age and gender are also ignored.[42] On occasions, Mass-Observers wrote about the 'feelings' that they had about people's motives,[43] but again this is unreliable evidence. Some observers wrote about their impression of morale, but 'impressions' and 'morale' are such slippery concepts that it seemed best to avoid relying on such material.[44]

The inevitable subjectivity of the material means that we learn about the attitudes of those collecting the material. There was no training given to those who volunteered for the project, and no attempt was made to distinguish subjective from objective recordings. Indeed, subjectivity ran throughout Mass-Observation.[45] Mass-Observation has been criticised for being 'unscientific' 'inchoate and uncontrolled', but other diarists, letter writers and autobiographers could all be dismissed on the same grounds. Along with novels, they are all a mixture of experience, observation and imagination, and they are all forms of the genre of narrative. The material comprises stories within a story (anecdote) and is significant for the interpretation of personal experience.[46] Other historians have used both the home intelligence reports and Mass-Observation extensively,[47] although not always critically.

Before the war started, government planners feared widespread panic, and this concern with panic is reflected in the way in which early studies of people's reactions to air raids were conducted.[48] When people expected a panicky response to air raids, an absence of panic was worthy of comment; by the later stages of the war, when people assumed that others would react calmly in raids, any evidence to the contrary was seized upon.

During the war, a good deal of material was published about people's experiences in air raids. The general tone of this material was upbeat; it frequently indulged in generalisations; it was living up to an image that had already been created and to which it, in turn, was contributing. In much published and unpublished material at the time and since, there is a tendency to relay amusing anecdotes and to highlight the surreal.[49] There was, too, a common language that was used to describe the way in which people behaved, which followed a template and was formulaic: people were described as 'carrying on'. The historian needs to unpick the different elements of this seemingly straightforward term. It was used to refer to carrying on with exactly the same activity when the air-raid siren sounded, with the same activity during an air raid, with activities after a raid, with daily routine in wartime, and with a host of war-related activities that were not necessarily taking place during a raid. The historian has to be constantly alert to the timing of statements, where they are made, and their different meanings. One has to distinguish between the use of language and actual behaviour, and between aims and outcome. It was the socially acceptable thing to claim that one was 'carrying on'; the BBC presented people as 'carrying on',[50] and the press claimed that people were 'carrying on' in order to encourage others to do so.

Newspapers reconstructed people's behaviour in air raids so as to provide readable human-interest copy and to exhort readers. Newspapers, read by a substantial proportion of the population, are an important source.[51] A range of national and local newspapers has been consulted. Among the national press, three newspapers, *The Times*, the *Daily Herald* and the *Daily Express*, were subjected to detailed scrutiny.[52] How far individual newspapers reflected genuine or widespread public concerns is not always easy to ascertain. One cannot assume that opinions expressed in a newspaper, or the type of issues that newspapers focused upon, reflected more than a particular editor's preoccupation.

Newspapers carried a huge amount of copy about air raids: graphic descriptions of the bombing, people's brave behaviour in raids, and physical destruction, often accompanied by carefully selected pictures. Indeed, selection was crucial to the press's reporting of air raids, because of the strict wartime censorship. Every detailed report was submitted to the censor, because only sparse details could be freely published. The name of the place or building bombed could not be mentioned for a month, and then only without a precise date. Businesses could not be named for ten days, and then only without a date. There were restrictions on the way in which casualties could be mentioned. Details of heavy raids and casualties were often not published until many months later.[53]

An analysis of the media is especially pertinent to this study. The media is a collection of texts that are thought to affect the way in which people understand themselves and the way in which they lead their lives.[54] All media entails a process of senders, messages and receivers. It is the task of the historian to try and unravel all three, although they are not equally accessible; analysis of receivers and reception can be especially difficult and often dependent on speculation and informed guesses. What the historian is analysing in the media are representations, which are not the same as mirror-images or reflections. Instead, they are a construction of images or categories that are a way of labelling or presenting aspects of our identities.[55]

The reasons why something is written will affect its content. So, material that emphasised how well people were coping was not only a public device used by newspapers for encouraging people to cope, but also a more personal one used by letter-writers for reassuring the recipient, and countering fears that may have been unleashed by newspaper reports of heavy bombing. In such cases, there is no way of telling the 'real' fear of the sender or the recipient, but such letters are indicative of the need that some felt to reassure others of their safety and ability to cope.[56] It is worth pointing out at this point that what people said that they felt and what they actually felt at any one moment may not always have been the same. One psychiatrist claimed that when it was said of someone that he was not afraid of the raids, what this usually meant was that he got over his fright in a few minutes or hours, or by the next morning.[57]

While Piette sees a clear-cut division between public and private stories of writers and poets, no such binary opposites have been detected in the sources used here.[58] Letters crossed the divide between public and private, as did other sources such as diaries. Diaries written for Mass-Observation most clearly have a 'public' element to them, even though they were not published at the time. It has been suggested that the questions from Mass-Observation gave diaries their shape; they were an interactive performance that can be detected in their language and self-analysis.[59] Diaries written for Mass-Observation were written in the knowledge that others would definitely read them, and occasionally entries refer to, or are directed explicitly at, Mass-Observation, for example, when one woman sent 'Greetings' to the organisation in her diary.[60] Some diarists not writing for Mass-Observation intended others to read them.[61] Diaries show, chronologically, the links between national events and the war, and the private individual. The writing process, however, alters and filters the original experience, for, once thoughts are committed to paper, they take on a new form and significance, which may or may not be intentional. The process of writing can change feelings. One woman found writing a diary for Mass-Observation to be therapeutic, so the activity itself modified feelings and attitudes.[62] A man wrote in his diary (not for Mass-Observation) 'I lack my customary buoyancy of spirits . . . But the very act of writing these notes, as I travelled, attested to the unreason of my gloom and slowly medicined me to a more cheerful frame of mind.'[63] Intense emotions may not be written about at all, as for instance when the same diarist wrote nothing in the period following his wife's death, because diary entries would have been 'forced and unworthy'.[64]

Two wartime diary writers in particular are worth mentioning here. In September 1939, in response to a call from Mass-Observation, Nella Last started a diary that she kept up for thirty years. When war broke out she was a middle-aged housewife living in Barrow-in-Furness, Lancashire, with her husband, who was a joiner and shop-fitter. She had two grown-up sons. Nella Last was active in the Women's Voluntary Service (WVS) and wrote about her experiences of daily life in wartime, which included aerial bombardment. She sent her diary in instalments to Mass-Observation; in 1981 an edited version from the war period was published. She wrote at great length and, of all the Mass-Observation diary writers, she was the most regular and persistent. She analysed her personal feelings and relationships, and wrote about the local and national events that touched her life. However, we do not know why she wrote for Mass-Observation or what she personally gained from it.

Colin Perry, an eighteen-year-old Londoner, wrote a diary between March and November 1940. In 1969 he gave what he had kept of the unpublished diary to the Imperial War Museum. Although it was not published until 1972, it is clear that Perry had hopes of writing material for publication at the time, and the flowery style suggests a self-conscious attempt to write in a literary fashion. He certainly does not write as he would have spoken, for example 'I must partake of this beautiful evening in a crisp walk on the common.' At one point we read that he wanted to write about a trip he had made 'as a piece of literature.' Perry destroyed some of the manuscript in 1945, just before he married, for fear that his wife would read and ridicule it. The diary is a detailed account of the feelings of an eighteen-year-old, and records what his experiences meant to him at the time. When the diary was published in 1972, Perry wrote: 'As it was my own composition, intended for no person other than myself, the words flowed rapidly for they were no more than the tangible expression of what was going on in my mind and of the sights I saw about me'. In fact, the diary is rather more complicated than this prologue suggests.

Perry's diary was a multi-purpose document. Perry used it to communicate: he showed extracts to a friend and sent snippets as part of letters to a girl in Australia. He also sent off sections of the diary to the USA, in the hope of publication. Parts of the diary read now as if they were written as an exercise in writing, so possibly he saw the diary as a writing practice or basis for other things that he might want to write. (He hoped to write a story.) So, the writing was not an end in itself, but was expected to take on a life of its own as it sailed around the world. Perry, although angry that he could not apply to fly in the RAF because he did not possess a school certificate, repeatedly identifies himself with London, with the nation and with the empire. There are parallels between Perry sending his thoughts around the world, Britain's role in the world, and his joining the merchant navy at the end of the diary and sailing around the world. Indeed the diary is framed by external events: wartime developments, Perry's day-to-day life in wartime London, and the media reconstruction of these events, which Perry then uses in his personal diary reconstruction. Perry conscientiously reads newspapers, cuts out pieces that he likes, and uses them in writing his diary. He is conscious of the way in which stories circulate in the press: he includes in his diary extracts of a cable sent to the USA about Britain and then returned to Britain and published in the London *Evening Standard*. Perry uses the language and sentiments of the press. He is aware of aspects of observation, memory and the writing process; on one occasion he provides three different accounts of the same event. He writes in the language, and expresses the emotions, that he has heard on the BBC or read in the newspapers. Just as diaries and letters can express the emotional significance of events at the time, memories can convey their longer-term significance.

Memories

Contemporary sources are supplemented by written and oral memories. Many people, from all walks of life, have subsequently written about their wartime experiences. This material also has its limitations. There is a problem in knowing whether what people say they did and why is what they really did or what they would like to have done, and how far they are collapsing their own and others' experiences into a single, common experience.[65]

In order to convey the drama of the moment, direct speech is sometimes included in later accounts. In the mid-1960s, a journalist who had lived in Pembroke Dock at the time of the raids later wrote an account, which he admitted was almost entirely from memory, that included strings of direct quotations.[66] While it is possible that he may have remembered the occasional comment, it is unlikely that he could have remembered numerous conversations verbatim. Here are a series of reconstructions:

the author is turning memories of situations into direct speech, the reader then turns the direct speech into new images, and at each turn the original event becomes more distant – not only because it is further and further away in time but also because of the series of changed modes of expression and understandings that it goes through.

All the contemporary material was created without historians' intervention, whereas the interview memory material only exists in the public domain because of intervention by an historian. The material is therefore different in the nature of its creation, in the relationship between historian and material, and thus in the 'evidence' it provides for interpretation. In some cases the sources confirm each other, but often they provide contrasting evidence. The contemporary evidence gives a greater sense of carefully reasoned responses, of formal systems and of organisations playing an important part in a rational decision-making process. Memories tend to downplay the formal and organised.

Events and experiences are not embalmed in the amber of memory. Personal testimonies given in interviews to historians are not the same as people's experiences and views at the time that they occurred. Alexandro Portelli has argued that oral history tells us less about events than about their meaning: they tell us about what people wanted to do, what they believe they were doing, and what effects they think an event had on them.[67] The best oral history now explores the relationship between discourse and subjectivity. Penny Summerfield has argued that personal testimonies draw on the generalised subject available in discourse to construct the particular personal subject.[68]

There are huge problems with asking people, sixty years after the event, why they behaved in certain ways. We know that people may form perceptions of risk as an *ex post facto* rationale for their behaviour.[69] Most people interviewed for this study were rather vague on chronology and dates, and often could not distinguish one period of the war from the other, although it was usually possible to work this out. It can be difficult or impossible to reconstruct original feelings and experiences, especially when interviewees may say what they want the interviewer to hear or what they think he or she wants to hear. The difficulties of interpretation of memory evidence mean that it is used in this book primarily to explore how the past is being reconstructed in the present. Summerfield categorised her interviewees into 'stoic' and 'heroic' respondents; no clear-cut contrasts emerged from the oral material analysed here. People's testimonies varied according to the event or experience they were describing and according to the nature of the interview: the interview proved easier to categorise than the interviewee. Interviews varied according to where they took place, the length of time they lasted, the rapport between interviewer and interviewee, and the age of the interviewee and the sharpness of their recall.

People frequently used language and images that Britain's public history and culture have come to associate with the war, and interviewees often used this language when talking in general terms about their experiences, but, when talking specifically, it often became clear that the meaning varied.[70] Since the Second World War, the British have experienced strong and repetitious public images and histories of the war, in films, in newspapers, at commemorative events and on television. In many cases public images and personal experiences have slowly blended into private 'memories' of the past. People rummage through those images and articulate them, sometimes at the prompting of historians, as personal memories of their own experiences. How do we know this to be the case? People repeat post-war clichés and frequently present public images that are not always in accord with contemporary evidence. Some people do, however, challenge received wisdom, and others, while repeating general clichés, also offer specific comments that contradict them. Historians then feed the stories they have collected from interviews back into their public histories. The process is not a circular one, for at each stage elements are added on or picked off. Oral history is not a single event, but rather part of a process of moulding our understanding of the past, and constructing and reconstructing what the past now means. The oral material collected by historians, like other sources, is selective. It will depend on who is willing to be interviewed; historians then sift the material collected, using the most articulate and pertinent comments for their projects. Historians will typically select lively, vivid, 'telling' material, for they – like those interviewed – make assumptions about listener and reader response.

Contemporary evidence was essential for chronology; one of the main problems with people recalling events fifty-five or sixty years ago was that often they could not remember the chronology of events. In some cases, people had prepared what they would say in an interview, as they thought it would help them remember and prevent them rambling. In fact, these more careful accounts tended to be more cliché-ridden. A further problem with memory accounts is that some people freely mixed views on current events with memories of their views on wartime events, and it could be difficult to disentangle the two. Memories did, nevertheless, provide evidence not available in the records; in particular, they underlined the importance of the informal and personal in formal and public processes, and they were an indication of what people now regard as significant. As memory plays an important part in our public and private history, a range of memory sources were tapped.

Interviews have limitations not only because of the interviewees, but also because of the interviewer. Interviewees, with one or two exceptions, were contacted through free and local newspapers and then by word of mouth. Some ex-aircraft workers were also interviewed at Brooklands, where Vickers and Hawker's had aircraft factories during the war, and where old aircraft are now restored. As none of those being interviewed had been public figures but were freely and generously sharing their memories, it was not appropriate to cross-question and point to contradictions in what they said, or to conflicts with other evidence; when people did not want to talk about a particular event or question, they were not pursued. Everyone tried to be helpful, and this inevitably created a relationship with the material collected that does not exist with contemporary sources. Oral history usually focuses either on those who have held positions in public life, such as politicians and senior civil servants, or on people's private, day-to-day lives. The interviews conducted specifically for this project, and those used from oral history archives, aimed to explore memories of private individuals whose daily lives in wartime were intertwined with government policy for national survival. The interviews aimed to explore the connection between state power and memories of risk, patriotism and self-interest among private individuals when day-to-day living collided with extraordinary events.

Finally, memory evidence has contributed to the skewing of the age profile of wartime histories. Memory evidence and post-war public history privileges the experiences of those who were young in the war, because older people did not live as long to tell their tale. One effect of this biological clock has been that the evacuation of children has received a huge amount of attention in oral histories. Older people are less-attractive subjects, and children, who are so quintessentially vulnerable, are appealing subjects of wartime studies.

In conclusion, it should be made explicit that the memory evidence needed the contemporary evidence for context as well as breadth, depth and complexity of evidence; the contemporary evidence is not so dependent, but it is enhanced by the memory sources. All the sources used in this book have been sifted and interpreted. Sources with internal inconsistencies are given less weight than those without contradictions. Clichés are given less weight than nuanced and complex comment, but interpretation is also built up from a series of simple statements. Contemporary and memory material is clearly distinguished in the text. There is a good deal of direct quotation from contemporary sources. It is important that the reader sees the language that contemporaries used to express their experiences at the time; direct quotation underlines the subjectivity of the source, and it gives some indication of the narrative nature of the sources. The quotations are contextualised and form part of an overall analysis. All the sources, contemporary and memory, written and visual, are used as evidence in the argument and story that unfold in the following chapters. We begin in the uncertain days following the retreat from Dunkirk and the first German air raids over Britain.

Notes

1 Parliamentary Papers 1940–41, vol. iv, Annual Report of the Chief Inspector of Factories for 1939 and 1940.
2 National Archives, Kew (formerly Public Record Office, hereafter PRO) INF, 1/292, weekly home intelligence reports, 30 September–9 October, 4–11 November 1940.
3 Richard Titmuss, *Problems of Social Policy* (HMSO, 1950).
4 Richard Titmuss, *Problems of Social Policy*, pp. 337–50, 508.
5 For example, Keith Middlemas, *Politics in Industrial Society: The Experience of the British System Since 1911* (André Deutsch, 1979); Correlli Barnett, *The Audit of War* (Macmillan, 1986).
6 I. McLaine, *Ministry of Morale: Home Front Morale and the Ministry of Information in World War II* (Allen and Unwin, 1979); Sian Nicholas, *The Echo of War: Home Front Propaganda and the BBC* (Manchester University Press, 1996); Ina Zweiniger-Bargielowska, *Austerity in Britain: Rationing, Controls and Consumption, 1939–1953* (Oxford University Press, 2000).
7 David Thoms, *War, Industry and Society: the Midlands 1939–45* (Routledge, 1989).
8 Harold L. Smith, *Britain in the Second World War* (Manchester University Press, 1996); Edward Smithies, *Crime in Wartime: A Social History of Crime in World War II* (George Allen and Unwin, 1982); Richard Croucher, *Engineers at War* (Merlin Press, 1982); Helen Jones, *Health and Society in Twentieth-Century Britain* (Longman, 1994), chapter 5; John Macnicol, 'The evacuation of schoolchildren', in Harold L. Smith (ed.), *War and Social Change: British Society in the Second World War* (Manchester University Press, 1986). Tony Lane has also challenged the notion of the 'people's war' and of the British character manifesting itself in wartime: Tony Lane, *The Merchant Seamen's War* (Manchester University Press, 1990).
9 Arthur Marwick, *Britain in the Century of Total War: War, Peace and Social Change, 1900–1967* (Penguin, 1970); Arthur Marwick, *War and Social Change in the Twentieth Century: A Comparative Study of Britain, France, Germany, Russia and the US* (Macmillan, 1974); Penny Summerfield, *Women Workers in the Second World War: Production and Patriarchy in Conflict* (Croom Helm, 1984); Philomena Goodman, *Women, Sexuality and War* (Palgrave, 2000).
10 Stephen Brooke, *Labour's War: The Labour Party during the Second World War* (Clarendon, 1992).

11 Paul Addison, *The Road to 1945: British Politics and the Second World War* (Pimlico, 1994); Harold L. Smith, *Britain in the Second World War* (Manchester University Press, 1996).
12 In particular, see Jeffrey Richards, *Films and British National Identity* (Manchester University Press, 1997), p. 109.
13 Angus Calder, *The Myth of the Blitz* (Pimlico, 1991).
14 David Thoms, 'The blitz, civilian morale and regionalism, 1940–1942', in Pat Kirkham and David Thoms (eds), *War Culture: Social Change and Changing Experience in World War Two* (Lawrence and Wishart, 1995), pp. 5–11.
15 Most recently, Sonya Rose, *Which People's War? National Identity and Citizenship in Britain 1939–1945* (Oxford University Press, 2003).
16 For a discussion of definitions of 'local' and the importance of local history, see Sally Sokoloff, 'The home front in the Second World War and local history', *The Local Historian*, 32 (2002).
17 Sonya Rose, *Which People's War?*
18 Richard Croucher, *Engineers at War*, Penny Summerfield, *Women Workers in the Second World War* and David Thoms, *War, Industry and Society: the Midlands 1939–45* are examples of historians' interest in the workplace. Ernest Bevin has also received attention, for example, Alan Bullock, *The Life and Times of Ernest Bevin. vol. 2. Ministry of Labour 1940–1945* (Heinemann, 1967), p. 12. Ernest Bevin (1881–1951), an ex-trade-union leader and Minister of Labour and National Service 1940–45, is seen as the architect of an integrated wartime industrial-relations strategy which involved an input from both sides of industry. Starting late in ill-starred circumstances, Bevin's mission had the clear aim of increasing productivity. Concentrating on Bevin's integrated policy, however, ignores the disjointed aspects of policies for industry and the problems of co-ordination across departments, while too great an emphasis on central government misses important regional and local relationships that were of special wartime significance.
19 Alan Munton, *English Fiction in the Second World War* (Faber, 1989), p. 28. Examples of wartime novels focusing on work: J. B. Priestley, *Daylight on Saturday* (Heinemann, 1943); Henry Green, *Caught* (Hogarth Press, 1943); John Strachey, *Post D* (Victor Gollancz, 1941).
20 For instance, Paul Addison and Jeremy Crang (eds), *The Burning Blue: A New History of the Battle of Britain* (Pimlico, 2000) do not discuss the role of civilians.
21 Sian Nicholas, *The Echo of War*; Malcolm Smith, *Britain and 1940* (Routledge, 2000).
22 Sian Nicholas, *The Echo of War*, p. 127.
23 Anthony Aldgate and Jeffrey Richards, *Britain Can Take It: The British Cinema in the Second World War* (Edinburgh University Press, 1994).
24 Clive Ponting, *1940: Myth and Reality* (Hamish Hamilton, 1990), pp. 163–5, 171.

25 Neil Gregor, 'A *Schicksalsgemeinschaft*? Allied bombing, civilian morale and social dissolution in Nuremberg, 1942–1945', *Historical Journal*, 43:4 (2002), pp. 1051–70 for discussion of atomisation and breakdown in community ties.
26 Robert Mackay, *Half the Battle: Civilian Morale in Britain During the Second World War* (Manchester University Press, 2002).
27 Angus Calder, *The Myth of the Blitz*, pp. 125–9, 142.
28 Arthur Marwick, *Britain in the Century of Total War*, pp. 297–8.
29 Angus Calder, *The People's War: Britain 1939–1945* (Panther, 1971); Andrew Thorpe, 'Britain', in Jeremy Noakes (ed.), *The Civilian in War* (Exeter University Press, 1992), pp. 22–3; B. Beaven and D. Thoms, 'The blitz and civilian morale in three northern cities, 1940–42', *Northern History Journal*, 32 (1996) pp. 195–203; B. Beaven and J. Griffiths, 'Mass-Observation and civilian morale: working-class communities during the blitz 1940–41'. Mass-Observation Archive Occasional Paper no. 8, 1998, University of Sussex Library.
30 Tom Harrisson, *Living Through the Blitz* (Penguin, 1978), pp. 302–4.
31 Most recently, Robert Mackay, *Half the Battle*. See PRO INF 1/292, 25 November–4 December 1940.
32 Robert Murphy, *British Cinema in the Second World War* (Continuum, 2000), pp. 233, 262. Three television films, first shown between 1978 and 1984, *Licking Hitler*, *The Imitation Game* and *Rainy Day Women*, as Murphy has pointed out, depicted a dirty war in which the government was devious and unscrupulous, and distorted truth in the name of national security; the men are not brave or heroic, and the women are abused and exploited.
33 Also nostalgic are *Yanks* (1979) and *Land Girls* (1998).
34 For a discussion of films and British collective memory of the Second World War, see Geoff Eley, 'Finding the People's War: film, British collective memory, and World War II', *American Historical Review*, 106 (2001), pp. 818–38.
35 Another way in which the war is presented and kept in public view in a fairly unchanging fashion is through popular local studies of the war. Academic historians rarely draw on local studies. Often it is difficult to trace the sources of unreferenced local studies, but they should not be ignored, as they bear witness to the continuing importance of the war experience at the local community level. They are an indication of the way in which the meanings of wartime experiences are expressed, the way in which personal, local and national histories are woven together, and popular history constructed.
36 Lucy Noakes, *War and the British: Gender, Memory and National Identity* (I. B. Tauris, 1998), pp. 39–45.
37 I do not discuss every single type of source here, just the most problematic.
38 Other historians have used these reports, although they do not always acknowledge their limitations.
39 Angus Calder, *The Myth of the Blitz*, pp. 121–2. Mary Adams had a degree in botany from University College, Cardiff, and she had lectured at the

University of Cambridge. In 1930 she joined the BBC, and, from 1936, worked on the new television service until it shut down at the outbreak of war, after which she joined the Ministry of Information.

40 David Alan Mellor, 'Mass-Observation: the intellectual climate', in Jessica Evans (ed.), *The Camerawork Essays: Context and Meaning in Photography* (River Orams Press, 1997), pp. 133–7.

41 University of Sussex, Mass-Observation Archive, Air Raids, TC, 23/5/B, H. P., 16 August 1940.

42 Mass-Observation Archive, Air Raids, TC, 23/8/J, Bromley, 21 October 1940.

43 Mass-Observation Archive, Air Raids, 23/10/F, Oxford, 28 September 1940.

44 Mass-Observation Archive, Air Raids TC/65/3.

45 British Library, National Sound Archive, C 459/43/5. In 1937, Tom Harrisson had persuaded painters and the photographer, Humphrey Spender, to work unpaid for him. A range of methods of collection, rather than the soundness of any one of the methods, seems to have been important to Harrisson. Spender later commented on the 'odd' characters who may not have been very reliable, working for Mass-Observation, and the shortage of volunteers to annotate, store and analyse the material. The archival problem was resolved when Mass-Observation found a home at the University of Sussex, where it had its own archivist.

46 Dorothy Sheridan, Brian Street and David Bloome, *Writing Ourselves: Mass-Observation and Literary Practices* (Hampton Press, 2000); Mary Chamberlain and Paul Thompson (eds), *Narrative and Genre* (Routledge, 1998).

47 For example, Anthony Aldgate and Jeffrey Richards, *Britain Can Take It: The British Cinema in the Second World War*; Robert Mackay, *Half the Battle*.

48 Mass-Observation Archive, Air Raids, TC 23/8/A. For instance, in July 1940 the Economic League undertook a survey of people's reactions to air raids, in which they focused on the absence of panic.

49 For example, H. R. Pratt Boorman, *Hell's Corner: Kent Becomes the Battlefield of Britain* (Kent Messenger, 1942).

50 Sian Nicholas, *The Echo of War*, p. 109.

51 Louis Moss and Kathleen Box, *Newspapers: An Inquiry into Newspaper Reading Amongst the Civilian Population* (Wartime Social Survey for Ministry of Information, June–July 1943); P. Kimble, *Newspaper Reading in the Third Year of the War* (George Allen and Unwin, 1942). During the middle years of the war, 77 per cent read a morning paper every or most days; 50 per cent saw an evening paper, which would have been a local one; 46 per cent regularly saw a local weekly or bi-weekly paper; and 87 per cent saw a Sunday paper. Men were more avid newspaper readers than women – often reading more than one paper; women typically read only one paper.

52 *The Times* was chosen as a broadly middle-class paper; the *Daily Herald* as a broadly working-class, left-wing paper; and the *Daily Express*, as a

right-wing popular paper (owned by Lord Beaverbrook, who was Minister of Aircraft in Production 1940–1).

53 George P. Thomson, *Blue Pencil Admiral* (Sampson Low, Marston & Co. 1947), pp. 77–81.

54 Adam Briggs and Paul Cobley (eds), *The Media: An Introduction* (Longman, 1998), p. 277.

55 Adam Briggs and Paul Cobley (eds), *The Media*; Gill Branston and Roy Stafford, *The Media Student's Handbook* (Routledge, 1996), p. 125.

56 University of Leeds, Liddle Collection 1939–45, 038 Nancy Sands, Letters from Jean to Nancy, 21 September 1940, not dated, but October 1940, and subsequent diary entries. Over the summer and autumn of 1940, a woman living in north London repeatedly wrote reassuring letters to her sister who had been evacuated with her firm to Torquay, with phrases such as: 'We are getting quite used to it', and 'This tells you that in spite of the newspapers saying that London has been suffering from its worst raids we are still very much alive and kicking'.

57 Melitta Schmideberg, 'Some observations on individual reactions to air raids', *International Journal of Psychoanalysis* 23:3 and 23:4 (1942), p. 164.

58 Adam Piette, *Imagination at War: British Fiction and Poetry, 1939–1945* (Papermac, 1995), pp. 4–5.

59 Roger Bromley, *Lost Narratives: Popular Fictions, Politics and Recent History* (Routledge, 1988), p. 166.

60 Mass-Observation Archive, ES diary 5420. 21 December 1940. See also: 'The diary of Muriel Green 29 October 1939, 28 December 1939, 6 February 1940, 8 March 1940, 23 March 1940', in Dorothy Sheridan (ed.), *Wartime Women: A Mass-Observation Anthology 1937–45* (Phoenix Press, 2000), pp. 57, 62, 80, 85–6, 89.

61 Peter Donnelly (ed.), *Mrs Milburn's Diaries: An Englishwoman's Day-to-Day Reflections* (Harrap, 1979); Colin Perry, *Boy in the Blitz: The 1940 Diary of Colin Perry* (Sutton Publishing, 2000). First published by Leo Cooper 1972.

62 Mass-Observation Archive, ES diary 5420, 8 May 1941.

63 Art McCulloch (compiler), *The War and Uncle Walter: The Diary of an Eccentric* (Doubleday, 2003), p. 109, 6 March 1940.

64 Art McCulloch, *The War and Uncle Walter*, p. 199, 11 January 1942.

65 Robert Perks and Alastair Thomson (eds), *The Oral History Reader* (Routledge, 1998), p. 67; Oliver Sacks, writer and neurologist, published a memoir of his childhood in which he graphically described two incidents during the war when a 1,000 bomb fell in the neighbour's garden and when an incendiary bomb fell behind his house. A few months after the book's publication, he explained in an interview in the *Guardian* newspaper that writing the book confirmed his belief that there is 'no such thing as fixed memories, only the act of remembering'. After the memoir was published, his brother, Michael, said that Oliver could not possibly remember a particular bomb dropping on their home, because he was not there at the

time. Sacks continued 'I can hear the hissing of the metal, I can see it now. Why? Because I was sent a very vivid letter about it'. Oliver Sacks, *Uncle Tungsten: Memoirs of a Chemical Boyhood* (Macmillan, 2001), p. 23; Oliver Sacks, 'Inside story Sacks appeal', *Guardian*, (10 May 2002) tabloid section, p. 4.

66 W. L. Richards, *Pembrokeshire Under Fire: The Story of the Air Raids of 1940–41* (J. W. Hammond, 1965).

67 Alessandro Portelli, 'The peculiarities of oral history', *History Workshop Journal*, 12 (1981), pp. 99–100.

68 Penny Summerfield, *Reconstructing Women's Wartime Lives* (Manchester University Press, 1998), p. 16.

69 Paul Slovic, *The Perception of Risk* (Earthscan, 2000), p. 221.

70 Penny Summerfield, *Reconstructing Women's Wartime Lives*, p. 189. This accords with Summerfield's findings as, for instance, when women used the language of national unity with phrases such as 'we were all in it together', but this referred specifically to the group of women with whom they worked, not the country at large.

2

'A present to Hitler': policy and persuasion

German tactics

From the early summer of 1940, when Germany began bombing Britain, civilians were increasingly vulnerable to attack. In early June 1940 the German *Luftwaffe* started bombing southern ports and convoys in the English Channel. For the rest of June and throughout July there were intermittent air raids scattered across the country; in early August the bombing raids intensified. The *Luftwaffe* concentrated on radar stations and RAF airfields, but also hit industrial, dock and urban areas. The tactic was to knock out Britain's air defences so that German troops could cross the Channel, scramble up the beaches, or parachute down and land on British soil without being bombarded from the air. On 4 September, possibly as a result of the RAF's attacks on Berlin – but more likely the failure of the *Luftwaffe* to deliver a knock-out blow to the RAF, the German commanders' failure to appreciate the importance of radar to British defences, and Hitler's underestimation of the RAF – the Germans modified their tactics. Instead of focusing on immobilising the RAF, German bombers concentrated on British cities and industries; on 7 September the East End of London was heavily bombed. This was a development rich in consequences, for the shift away from airfields gave the RAF breathing space, and by the end of October 1940, the immediate threat of invasion had passed; the Battle of Britain was over. Although it was not known at the time, despite many subsequent air raids and blitzes on British cities, no Nazi jackboot would leave its ugly imprint on British soil.[1]

'A present to Hitler'

British civilians had a direct part to play in averting invasion and avoiding defeat, by maintaining the production and repair of aircraft for the RAF and keeping up productivity in other firms producing goods and material directly for the war, whether for the RAF, the Royal Navy or the army. Throughout the summer and autumn of 1940, the rate at which aircraft could be built and repaired was the War Cabinet's top priority.

In mid-October Churchill told the War Cabinet 'The A1 priority must remain with Aircraft Production.'[2]

Herein lay the key to the civilian contribution to the Battle of Britain: the British had to find ways and means of maintaining and increasing productivity, at a time when radar stations and the Observer Corps' spotting of German aircraft over the south coast of England triggered air-raid warnings across a far wider area than was actually at risk of bombing, and workers, including those in aircraft and other war-related industries, were dashing and darting for cover, and staying holed up in air-raid shelters, sometimes for hours on end, with their machines silent and unproductive. Hour after hour of vital time was being lost. These hours were, in the words of Leslie Hore-Belisha, Liberal MP for Plymouth Devonport, 1923–45, 'a present to Hitler'.[3]

During the Battle of Britain and subsequent air raids, civilians played a vital, and largely unsung, role in avoiding defeat – a role that was only made possible by them overthrowing previous assumptions, and government overturning existing policy on the protection of civilians from aerial bombardment. In the 1930s, politicians had gradually formulated domestic policies for a future war. When war broke out, experience from the First World War led to rationing, conscription and the designation of reserved occupations. Politicians had responded to expert opinion and newsreels of bombing in the Spanish Civil War by developing Air Raid Precautions (ARP), later known as civil defence. ARP – including the blackout, shelters and evacuation – had involved forward planning (although this is not to deny a degree of chaos and a series of mistakes).

In the period leading up to war, and in the early months of war before bombs were dropped, government policy prioritised maintaining calm and order among civilians, by protecting them as far as possible within a war situation. Hence, plans were drawn up, and then implemented, to evacuate the cities, and to put ARP in place. In practice, not all target cities were evacuated, and many local authorities and firms were tardy in building adequate shelters. The government nevertheless aimed to protect civilians, especially women and children.

Government thinking was represented in an ARP recruitment poster, *Serve to Save*, which was heavy with symbolism. A male civilian is shielding, with body language and with an ARP shield, a mother and baby. His size, way out of proportion to them and to the homes in the background, emphasises the force of his protection. His facial expression denotes strength, determination and bravery, and is in stark contrast to the fearful, cowering mother. The image of the man protecting mother, child and home is a traditionally gendered wartime one, but the powerful male civilian image is non-traditional. The poster is not depicting a real-life

ARP warden but an imaginary one, so inviting men to imagine themselves in the role. The poster may have been produced as a counter to the rather low esteem in which ARP wardens were initially held. It survived throughout the war, in one form or another, finding its way on to at least one warden's log book (see figure 2.1).

At the outbreak of war, but before the Germans started bombing Britain, the government urged civilians to stay inside or in shelters in the event of air raids or indeed of invasion. They produced leaflets on taking cover in air raids, and warning photographs of what people should not do (which was to stand outside watching aircraft in air raids) (see figure 2.2). All those in the picture are men, and indeed there is some evidence, or at least a belief at the time, that men were more likely to stand watching dogfights than women, so the picture's targets may well have been men. All the men are respectable, with one in army uniform and another in the Home Guard, and are carrying gas masks. The photograph looks as if it were taken for the specific purpose of getting the government's message across, because it appears to be posed. However, it is also rather interesting and alluring: the viewer wants to see what the men are all staring at so intently, which suggests that it may not have been very effective in meeting its purpose. Whether anyone who enjoyed watching enemy aircraft would have been dissuaded by this – or any other – photograph is doubtful. We know that people continued to watch enemy action in the skies until experience or heavy raids changed their minds.

Typical of government advice was that given by Harold Butler, Regional Commissioner for Civil Defence Southern Region, when he spoke at Banbury Town Hall on 'The civilian in total war'. He urged his audience to 'Try to master your curiosity. Don't go out to see what is happening; that is the way to manufacture casualties'. In air raids or in the event of invasion, people were to stay inside.[4]

Once bombing began, the government took a number of measures to minimise the disruptive effects of air raids on production: air-raid warnings became less frequent; factories and plant were dispersed away from industrial areas; and some factories moved underground (a slow and expensive process, and therefore not common). Some offices carried on their work in basements. Barrage balloons and anti-aircraft batteries (Ack-Ack) aimed to divert bombers; and the best-known defence, British fighters, attacked both German bombers and their fighter escorts. Experiencing the sound and fury of aerial bombardment depended on where people lived and worked.

Air raids were not the only cause of lost production, but they were an important source of lost production during the Battle of Britain. The

2.1 Serve to Save

2.2 Air-raid warning. A lesson in pictures. What not to do in an air raid

disruption to work caused by air-raid sirens was most acute during the summer of 1940, when Germany dropped bombs by day; once the *Luftwaffe* shifted the bulk of its bombing to evenings and night-time raids, the problem became less acute, but nevertheless remained throughout the war, not least because shift work continued around the clock. At the time of the Battle of Britain over the summer of 1940 and then the blitzes on Britain, 1940–41, air raids' disruption of work was a key problem for productivity. Blitzes of industrial and dock areas became less frequent, but in 1942 there were the 'Baedeker raids' on less-industrialised cities. In 1943 there was a decrease in bombing, but from June 1944 the enemy sent over V1s, and then V2s for which no warning was possible. Over the years a growing range of factors – tiredness due to lack of sleep because of night-time air raids; a shortage of labour, especially of people with appropriate skills; a scarcity of materials; a lack of adequate plant; poor industrial relations, including unofficial strikes; absenteeism due to illness, accidents and day-to-day domestic demands, as well as transport and housing problems for workers – came to play an increasingly important role in productivity. For all these problems on the domestic front, the government was constantly developing policies.

Experience and seasoned advice were the hallmarks of domestic policies in the early part of the war (and the peacetime norm), with one remarkable exception. Whitehall and industry suddenly, and without preparation, thought outside the box and framed a policy that a couple of months earlier would have been unthinkable. Although the negotiations were perceived to be slow at the time, over the summer of 1940 a brand-new policy – which stood all previous thinking on its head – had the support of the elephantine organisation of central government, trade unions and employers' organisations.

According to some historians, Churchill – who had just replaced Neville Chamberlain (dogged by poor form and fortune) as Prime Minister – identified the problem, and then devised and implemented a solution. Indeed, this is the impression that Churchill gave in his history of the Second World War. While there is no doubt that Churchill, who recognised the seriousness of the problem and was keen for a quick solution, kept a sharp eye and firm hand on the problem, it was not Churchill's personal insight and policy alone. Industry and Whitehall all identified the problem of lost production after the siren sounded and the solution of putting people on roofs to look out for approaching enemy aircraft, so that work could continue after the public siren; the implementation of the policy involved much negotiation.[5] Roof spotting was, nevertheless, closely associated with Churchill. It was common currency in the press, including the *Daily Express*, owned by Churchill's friend, Max Aitken (Lord Beaverbrook, Minister of Aircraft Production 1940–41), that Churchill dreamt up the nickname 'Jim Crows'.[6] The *Yorkshire Post* explained that Churchill probably got the name by associating spotters with a ship's crow's nest. 'He has had two spells at the Admiralty, remember'.[7]

Background to negotiations

When the air was thick with talk of invasion, when air-raid sirens were disrupting war production, and when bombs were falling on urban, industrial and dock areas, the government's priority shifted from civilian safety to balancing civilian safety with maintaining productivity. The government wanted workers in war-related industries to ignore the public air-raid siren and only take cover when enemy bombers were immediately overhead.

Lord Beaverbrook as Minister of Aircraft Production was directly responsible for providing the RAF with planes and repairing damaged ones. He could not wait for formal negotiations to take place over working after the siren. In his typically unorthodox fashion he asked Jennie

Lee (1904–88) a journalist, and a Labour MP from 1929 to 1931 (and subsequently from 1945 to 1970) to visit aircraft factories and impress on people the need to work after the siren. We learn from Lee's autobiography about the role that she felt she played. Lee threw herself into the job enthusiastically, even joining a roof spotter on the roof of an aircraft factory in the Midlands after the air-raid warning had sounded. She spoke to shop stewards and at factory meetings. Lee believed that her Labour movement background meant that she was not seen as the stooge of the Ministry, and that the personal touch, coupled with Beaverbrook's disregard for red tape, got results. She cited the example of an aircraft factory that she visited at Reading: it had good shelters but when the siren sounded the men bolted home across the fields because their wives and children lived in flimsy houses with no shelters. Lee promised to get them shelters and, despite a severe shortage of cement, Beaverbrook delivered her promise.[8] We do not, however, have a record of the male aircraft workers' view of a woman from the Ministry of Aircraft Production, or of how far her visit contributed to a change of heart. Individual and informal efforts may have had their place, but the issue was a complex one, involving tens of thousands of workers in life-and-death decisions, and more formal, albeit slower, negotiations were meanwhile taking place.

With air-raid sirens wailing and bombs dropping, discussions quickly took place across Whitehall. The importance of the issue is indicated by the fact that Churchill, the War Cabinet, numerous ministries and both sides of industry were all involved in thrashing out a solution. At the end of June, the War Cabinet began discussing the problem of air-raid warnings leading to lost production, and it continued to discuss the issue on a regular basis until October. So desperate were ministers to maintain production, that they even considered abandoning air-raid warnings altogether. The involvement of numerous individuals and interests added to the complexity of the problem and slowed down a formally agreed solution. Negotiations were fraught, and despite the presence of Ernest Bevin, Minister of Labour and National Service and member of the War Cabinet 1940–45, with his trade-union ties and long experience of negotiations, there were misunderstandings between government, industry and the RAF.

National negotiations

While Whitehall traditionally operated within discrete, and often competitive, departmental boundaries, and air-raid warnings were formally the responsibility of the Ministry of Home Security, the problem cut across departmental boundaries, as air-raid warnings leading to lost production disrupted large swathes of industry and had knock-on effects on the fighting capacity of all three Services. The mooted solution was, anyway, far too sensitive for one department to handle. On 22 June the Ministry of Supply, alarmed at the loss of production in vital war factories, rang the Ministry of Home Security. Over the previous few nights some key factories had lost three to four hours of production a night because workers had gone to the shelters when the air-raid siren sounded. The Ministry of Supply wondered if some, or all, workers would continue to work through the public siren; the two departments decided that this was too big a question to resolve themselves and that it should go to the Civil Defence Committee (a Cabinet Committee of all ministers whose departments were potentially involved in civil defence).[9]

Churchill instantly recognised the significance of the problem, and immediately grasped the importance of overthrowing received governmental wisdom on air-raid warnings and of changing people's attitudes towards them. Part of the strategy for encouraging people to work after the siren was to downplay the abnormality of air-raid sirens and so promote 'normal' behaviour. On 26 June Churchill told Duff Cooper, the Minister of Information, 1940–41, that journalists should be asked to handle air raids in a 'cool' way, for 'The people should be accustomed to treat air raids as a matter of ordinary routine . . . Everyone should learn to take air raids and air raid alarms as if they were no more than thunderstorms.'[10]

On the same day, 26 June, the loss of production due to air-raid warnings came up at the War Cabinet. It was agreed that Arthur Greenwood, a member of the War Cabinet and Minister without Portfolio, so not burdened by departmental responsibilities, should meet with various government ministers and draw up recommendations. By the standards of interdepartmental co-operation, Greenwood worked like lightning. The following day he contacted the Minister of Aircraft Production, the First Lord of the Admiralty, and the Minister of Supply, for details of the effects of bombing on war production. Beaverbrook hastily informed Greenwood that many thousands of working hours had been lost that week alone, not from bombs but from air-raid sirens sending workers to shelters. He told Greenwood in his forthright style: 'This is very serious and in my opinion you must stop it'. Beaverbrook claimed to have evidence that both management and workers wanted each factory to have the right to continue work after the siren. On 2 July the War Cabinet discussed Greenwood's recommendations. It was agreed that workers would be told that they should continue work after an air-raid warning sounded 'until they heard the sound of bombs or gunfire'.[11] No time was lost in publicising the decision; on the same day, Sir John Anderson, the Home Secretary and Minister of Home Security, 1939–40, told the House of Commons that, in order to defeat the enemy's efforts to dislocate production in war industries, workers – as far as local conditions allowed – should be encouraged to continue work after the public air-raid warning, until it was clear that an attack was imminent in the area.[12]

Detailed negotiations in order to gain widespread agreement for working after the siren were under way. On 3 July the Civil Defence Committee approved a proposal from Bevin for him to issue instructions to employers and workers. Two days later, representatives of the Admiralty, Air Ministry, Ministry of Home Security, Ministry of Supply and Ministry of Transport met to discuss maintaining production during air raids. They agreed that employers should be encouraged to appoint an observer at every factory or shipyard, who would receive some training from the Air Ministry, and who would then be responsible for deciding when shelter should be taken and when work resumed. At mines there should be an observer, somewhat analogous to a checkweightman, at the top of each pit. No decision was made about docks, railways or road transport, but negotiations were taking place between ministers and these industries. The agreement then went to the Production Council while the British Employers' Federation (BEF) and TUC were consulted. On 9 July the War Cabinet agreed to proposals for a 'lights' warning in the air-raid warning system (so that the distance and direction of enemy aircraft were colour coded), and asked the Home Secretary, in conjunction with Sir Hugh Dowding, AOC-C, Fighter Command, how best to restrict the warning without undermining confidence. The War Cabinet was also informed that a plan to maintain production during air raids had been agreed between the BEF and the TUC,[13] but this proved to be premature.

While trade unions had just lost many of their peacetime rights at work (the right to strike, the right to move jobs and the right to exclude unskilled workers from jobs that through custom and practice were designated skilled ones), central government was consulting the unions and incorporating them into the policy-making process as never before. The trade unions saw an eye for the main chance and used the negotiations over working after the siren to press for changes in a different area of ARP, and one that would not normally come within their ambit. They linked a question of grave concern to many people, that of the inadequacy of shelters, with the unrelated issue of working after the siren. In so doing, they drew a distinction between men at work (not using shelters) and women and children at home (requiring safer shelters). In 1940 a division of labour between men in paid work and married women in the home held true for many but not all families, but this changed as the war continued; the view that men should take risks while women and children should be protected may have been widespread in 1940, but the difference became an increasingly false one as the war progressed. In 1940, focusing on the distinction served a useful purpose in discussions, for it linked an outcome – working through the siren and higher productivity – desirable to the government, with an outcome – better shelters – demanded by many who were not represented in these negotiations. On 10 July Bevin reported to the Civil Defence Committee that agreement had been reached in principle to continue work after the 'red' warning. Three days later, at a meeting held at the Ministry of Labour, trade unions expressed a willingness to take responsibility for a system of roof spotters to give local warnings, although they again raised the issue of shelters. On 17 July Bevin reported to the Civil Defence Committee that the responsibilities of roof spotters had not been settled: the question of shelters was being examined, workers were anxious for there to be more 'red' warnings so that their wives and children had plenty of opportunity to take cover, and he was arranging a campaign of education for the workers. On 20 July it was decided to have a standing consultative body, representing trade unions, employers, production departments, the Ministry of Labour, the Ministry of Home Security and the air staff, to make recommendations about policy as conditions changed. Until now, only ARP had been on the agenda at the Ministry of Labour meetings with trade unionists and employers' organisations. On 24 July the Civil Defence Committee decided that wider publicity should be given to the working of the warning system, and the next day Bevin agreed that the Ministry of Home Security should summon a conference to discuss the policy of having more 'red' warnings.[14]

Both the TUC and the BEF already had industrial ARP committees from which they could draw representatives, and in early August the two sides of industry visited factories to observe their systems for ARP and working after the siren.[15] On 6 August discussions resumed at the Ministry of Home Security between employers' organisations, trade unions, various ministries, the air staff and Fighter Command. It was agreed that managers and workers in every works vital to the war should consider how work could continue after an air-raid warning. They agreed – although some employers were not very keen, as they felt that it imposed too great a responsibility on them for their employees' safety – that if the management and workers approved, a factory could adopt a roof spotter system to warn of an impending attack. Some issues, such as whether workers who had taken cover would return from the shelters before the all clear sounded, remained unresolved.[16]

Churchill was taking a close interest in developments. On 1 September he composed a memorandum that set out the need for a change in the warning system, with various suggestions on the way in which it should work. He argued that an alert should not interrupt the normal life of an area, but when there was an alert there should be look-outs posted at all factories engaged on war work; the alarm should be the order to take cover and for the full staffing of ARP positions. He did not think that in government offices in London anyone should be forced to take cover until actual firing began and the siren ordering the alarm had been sounded. He concluded, 'No one is to stop work merely because London is under Alert conditions.' The next day the War Cabinet discussed what changes could be made to the air-raid warning system.[17]

Churchill wanted the matter resolved, and on 3 September 1940 another meeting between government and industry was held at the Ministry of Home Security, chaired by William Mabane, Parliamentary Secretary at the Ministry of Home Security, 1939–42, with the TUC, employers' organisations, Squadron-leader J. H. Harris, and civil servants from the Ministry of Aircraft Production, Ministry of Supply, Ministry of Labour and the Mines Department. They discussed how production and morale could be boosted, and casualties minimised. There were two proposals on the table: either a warning should be given when an attack was almost certain; or the public warning should be sounded, but essential workers in industry should continue to work until an attack in the vicinity of the factory was imminent. Both sides agreed that they preferred the latter system. Employers had initially been mistrustful of posting watchers on roofs to look out for approaching enemy aircraft, but now they acquiesced, as Fighter Command offered to provide instruction for roof spotters. It was agreed in principle, therefore, that key workers would continue to work after the public air-raid siren, and would only take cover when bombers were in the immediate vicinity. Leaflets explaining the system would be drafted and, it was suggested, Churchill would write the foreword. Fellow workers, trained to spot approaching enemy aircraft, would give the warning: the 'roof spotter' was officially born.[18]

Many firms were already working after the siren and using roof spotters before national negotiations had been concluded.[19] The need for the practice to become the national norm meant that much effort was devoted to persuading workers that they should work after the siren. Some firms had already adopted roof spotters in order to maintain production after the siren sounded; in other firms roof spotters were used for a different reason. Detecting approaching enemy aircraft was not always easy, especially when some broke away from the main formation and were not picked up by radar. Over the summer of 1940, bombs fell on firms in Norwich before the air-raid siren sounded, and lives were lost. In order to avoid this happening in future, a number of firms pooled their resources and employed roof spotters to give them warnings, irrespective of whether the public siren had sounded. These same spotters were also used to enable workers to continue working after the public siren had sounded.[20]

While some firms were already working after the siren, this was not universal. On 4 September Beaverbrook left the War Cabinet in no doubt about the gravity of the situation. He related how on Saturday 31 August, 700 workers had left an aircraft factory making Spitfires at Castle Bromwich at lunchtime 'without authorisation' and a further 700 had left at 5 p.m. Over the weekend, 3,500 employees had remained at work, but there was a marked disinclination on the part of the employees to continue working after an air-raid warning. Production had fallen and Beaverbrook urged prompt action to avert a further deterioration in productivity levels; he wanted the air-raid warning system scrapped – a possibility the War Cabinet discussed along with using existing powers to compel men in aircraft factories to remain at work. The War Cabinet agreed that changes were needed, but it could not agree over the extent of those changes, so on 4 September it decided to leave the changes in the system to the agreement reached the day before at the Ministry of Home Security.[21] Throughout September the War Cabinet continued to mull over the problem, although it never deviated from the policy of working after the siren, with roof spotters, subject to local agreements.[22]

Even though working after the siren was without doubt a high priority for government, industry was frustrated at the slow rate of progress. The TUC felt that the government let matters drift and did not call enough meetings over the summer, and that the government was too slow in distributing leaflets about the air-raid warning and spotter system. Indeed, a few months later, Walter Citrine, General Secretary of the TUC, claimed that it was the TUC and employers' organisations that had originally initiated discussions about working after the siren, not the government. Employers certainly wanted closer liaison between government and industry. (The Ministry of Home Security defended its tardy distribution of leaflets, on the grounds that the printers it used had been bombed.)[23]

While the BEF was negotiating on behalf of employers, some firms expressed their disquiet about – and suggestions for – roof spotters. In September 1940 the general manager of a firm in Staffordshire wrote to the BEF that roof spotters should not be selected from among a firm's own employees, but should be trained and provided by government. It was not fair, he maintained, to expect a man to do his duty to the firm and to fellow workers who, in many cases, may be his own relatives. Another firm in Middlesex wrote that the speed of approaching enemy aircraft made it impossible for roof spotters to identify bombers in time, and instead, industrial observer posts, staffed by trained observers, should pass information on to roof spotters across London. These were not isolated concerns, and both employers and trade unions demanded that the government should train roof spotters and direct them to individual firms. The government would not budge; it maintained that such a system would be too slow and difficult to put into practice: firms had to provide their own roof spotters.[24] In private, Beaverbrook was far from happy with the system.

Beaverbrook had no inkling of how to work as part of a team, only of how to issue orders, which were on occasions unrealistic and time wasting. Although it had been agreed – without much enthusiasm – that spotters should be volunteers from their own factory, Beaverbrook believed that it was essential to have men in uniform acting as spotters, in order that workers would have faith in them. On 22 September he imperiously demanded that Sir Archibald Sinclair, Secretary of State for Air and Leader of the Liberals, 1940–45, should supply him with fifty RAF officers to act as roof spotters at aircraft factories:

> I want men in uniform, and I want them now. The psychological effect on the workers of having Air Force officers to watch for them will be immense. And it is the effect on factory morale that is important. An indifferent spotter with a uniform will do more good than a trained spotter without one . . . the aircraft industry is the life blood of the Royal Air Force. And I should much prefer that it were the prestige of the Air Force uniform that enabled aircraft factories to remain at work at the hour of danger.

On 26 September Sinclair replied to Beaverbrook, listing a number of reasons for turning down his request: the warning system was not the responsibility of the RAF 'Our job is to fight'; if the RAF were used they would not be RAF personnel in anything other than their newly acquired uniform; the system commended recently by the Prime Minister, Minister of Labour and various other ministers was for people to look after themselves and appoint their own spotters; and the roof spotter had 'a very limited utility', their main function being to support the morale of workers who would otherwise 'shrink from working during an air-raid warning under the threat of bombardment'. It was not fair therefore to put the onus on the RAF. Sinclair maintained that although Sir Hugh Dowding was training roof spotters, he refused to accept any responsibility for the warnings given by roof spotters, and he believed that they should be recruited from members of a firm in whom workers and management had confidence. Dowding himself told Sinclair on 27 September that Beaverbrook's proposal was 'preposterous', but if Beaverbrook wanted anything done he would turn his own ideas upside down in order to do it, partly because Beaverbrook always did anything that Dowding asked him to do, and partly because he 'gets magnificent results by bold departures from precedent'.[25] Dowding's reason for being less dismissive of Beaverbrook's 'preposterous' demand than Sinclair was both political and personal. There was no more love lost between Dowding and the Air Ministry than between Beaverbrook and the Air Ministry, and although they were very different characters, a strong fellow feeling existed between Dowding and Beaverbrook, for they both had sons who were RAF pilots.

Beaverbrook's relations with Sinclair were tense. Beaverbrook's demand for RAF roof spotters came at the end of a stream of requests to the Air Ministry, which Sinclair had turned down (and of which Beaverbrook, tetchily, had kept a record).[26] Beaverbrook really wanted to pursue his goals unencumbered by the priorities and needs of other departments, exercising the sort of freedom he was used to as a newspaper proprietor: 'it is my view that I should have complete authority over aircraft and that I should not be obstructed in my business either by debates in the Cabinet or by difficulties from the Air Ministry.'[27]

Churchill and Beaverbrook were old chums (Churchill was enormously impressed with Beaverbrook's achievements at MAP, as he was not slow to tell him), and Churchill sided with Beaverbrook in his spats with Sinclair (also a longstanding pal of his). On 26 September, when Beaverbrook had just made yet another demand on the Air Ministry, Churchill told Sinclair, 'I earnestly trust you will see that his wishes are met fully and immediately . . . I really could not endure another bickering', but even Churchill could not always get his own way. John Colville, Assistant Private Secretary to the Prime Minister, noted in mid-December, 'The interminable wrangle between MAP and the Air Ministry goes on, like The Brook, for ever.'[28]

When air staff agreed to train roof spotters, it was assumed that the RAF would give direct instruction on a wide basis. In fact, the RAF offered only limited training to a group who were then paid to train other roof spotters. Fighter Command provided two separate three-day courses at Hendon in North London, each attended by seventy-five people who were already ARP instructors. These 150 then returned home and taught roof spotting to others from local firms. Priority was given to training roof spotters from firms producing war-related materials. Courses lasted three to five days, with thirty people per course, so roughly 4,000 roof spotters were trained in a week. Neither the TUC nor the employers' organisations were happy with the arrangement, but the RAF insisted that they did not have the resources to run further courses themselves.[29]

Persuasion

Throughout the war, the government used ministers' speeches, posters, advertisements, pamphlets, films and BBC broadcasts – which combined slogans, straightforward messages as well as civilian role models – in an effort to stimulate a commitment to the war and behaviour that would assist the war effort.[30] Over the summer and autumn of 1940, politicians across the political rainbow, from the Prime Minister down, tried to encourage workers to carry on after the siren sounded and to rely on roof spotters to warn them of imminent danger. Politicians did this through clear and direct appeals and warnings, stating explicitly that the production of materials for the war was vital in order to avoid invasion, and that defeat would follow if civilians did not maintain output.

Propaganda thrives on figurative language, and politicians quickly adopted a wartime metaphor by referring to civilians who carried on after the siren as Armed Forces in the front line. It was language that was already in common usage, so did not jar or ring false notes; military metaphors abounded in daily speech: on the warpath, in the wars, battling through crowds, plan of action, war of nerves, live to fight another day, and up in arms. (The Ministry of Food used a military metaphor in some of its advertisements when it urged 'Eat Wisely to Keep Fighting Fit'.)[31] It flattered civilians when they were mentioned in the same breath as RAF pilots – the most glamorous men in the country. The concept of the civilian in the front line was a political construction. Civilians had been in the thick of wars in the past, but now the language of the front-line civilian was used to harness civilians to the war effort; it was a device for waging war. The use of this metaphor reinforced the message that the role of civilians was essential to avoiding defeat. It was easily understood, for the centrality of the Forces to the outcome of war was self-evident. It tried to engender certain types of behaviour widely associated with the Armed Forces, such as duty, sacrifice, bravery, following orders, teamwork, and loyalty to King and country. The use of military metaphors was inclusive; it challenged the notion of a gulf between the civilians at home and the military, a concept that had been such a widespread assumption in the public memory of the First World War.

Churchill spoke in all-inclusive language of the contribution that civilians in production were making to the war. He made an explicit link between the civilian in the factory and the fate of the country. On

19 May 1940 he warned that 'If the battle is to be won, we must provide our men with ever-increasing quantities of the weapons and ammunition they need. We must have, and have quickly, more aeroplanes, more tanks, more shells, more guns.' Such a link had been made in the First World War, but in the rhetoric of the Second World War it was the risk entailed in working after the siren that created the notion of the British civilian in the front line, taking similar risks to the troops: 'There will be many men, and many women, in this island who when the ordeal comes upon them, as come it will, will feel comfort, and even a pride – that they are sharing the perils of our lads at the front . . . – and are drawing away from them a part at least of the onslaught they have to bear.'[32] On 14 July 1940 Churchill proclaimed 'This is a War of the Unknown Warriors' and, in contrasting the First World War and the Second World War, a month later he claimed, 'The front line runs through the factories'.[33] In the adjournment debate on 19 December 1940, when Churchill did extend the metaphor beyond those working during air raids, he made a subtle shift in his language by depersonalising it and only referring to the organisation:

> The organisation of shelters, the improvement of sanitation, and the endeavour to mitigate the extremely painful conditions under which many people have to get their night's rest – that is the first task of the Government at home. The Air-Raid Precautions, the Home Office, and the Ministry of Health are just as much in the front line of the battlefield as are the armoured columns which are chasing the Italian columns about the Libyan desert.[34]

Churchill personally endorsed the system of spotters: 'In this way we can combine the maximum industrial output with the greatest possible protection for those at home'.[35] He also set an example by going out into raids and watching them, which the press in Britain and the USA helpfully reported.[36] (Indeed, sections of the US media provided lively reports of all Britons carrying on during air raids.)[37] When the brightest star in the political firmament stood watching the night sky light up, his actions spoke even louder than his stirring messages: it was the word made flesh.

Herbert Morrison, the Labour Minister of Supply in 1940 (subsequently Home Secretary, 1940–45), referred to 'the great army of workers' in armaments firms.[38] He was one of the few politicians who linked attitudes and practices over the summer of 1940 with the post-war world. When he paid tribute to those co-operating in government and private armaments factories, he claimed that these were seeds for social and industrial advancement after the war. So, he was not actually making any concrete promises, but rather suggesting that out of wartime work practices, wider social changes could grow.[39]

Sir Archibald Sinclair publicly linked workers carrying on through air-raid warnings with victory: 'every worker who stays at his post when the red warning goes and when danger threatens . . . is driving so many nails into Field-Marshal Göring's coffin.'[40]

Ernest Bevin emphasised the need for the production of munitions for as long as possible during an air raid. He linked civilians who produced munitions with Spitfire pilots, admitting that there was a risk in working after the siren, but pointing out that the danger was no greater than for the man in the Spitfire. He spoke of production as a means of defence and security, and offered the carrot of financial reward when he stated that those who took risks to keep production going were 'entitled' to generous treatment by the state.[41]

When Beaverbrook exhorted workers in aircraft factories to work once the siren had gone off, he did not talk the language of negotiation and voluntary choice, but rather emphasised that it was 'imperative' that workers 'must' carry on working, for it was their 'duty' to supply men on the fighting front with all the aircraft they required.[42] On the same day, Ellen Wilkinson, Parliamentary Secretary at the Ministry of Pensions, with responsibility for paying civilian compensation, emotively warned that 'any needless stopping of work is an act of surrender'.[43] The government produced a leaflet in which it admitted that working after the siren carried risks, and although roof spotters could reduce these risks, all engaged on vital production were 'front-line troops'.[44] On 8 October Leslie Hore-Belisha criticised armaments' workers who went to shelters during work time: 'The implication of the statement that we are all in the front line is that we ought to behave as if we were in the front line.'[45]

In addition to exhortations in Parliament, which were then relayed in the press, politicians took their message out of London to the people that they most wanted to influence. For numerous reasons (see chapter 3), South Wales dockers were among those most reluctant to carry on after the siren. Politicians could not get down to South Wales fast enough. The fact that they were Labour Party members (apart from Lewis Jones, a Liberal National MP), must have made it easier for them to preach to staunch trade unionists than for Conservative colleagues in the Coalition government (who would have been burdened with a stereotypical image of Tory grandees venturing forth from their safe piles in the country, in order to encourage workers to run risks to save the skins of the most protected sections of society). David Rhys Grenfell, Parliamentary Secretary, Department of Mines, 1940–42, spoke in Swansea at a meeting arranged by the Ministry of Information. His tactic seems to have been to try and shame the dockers into taking risks. He drew attention to the fact that miners' work carried an inherent danger; more miners had been killed in South Wales in the previous fourteen months than people killed by enemy action in the whole of Wales, but that did not stop the miners from going down the pits and hewing coal. He added a note of moral pressure on those who were not taking risks: 'all workers should make the same sacrifice when the nation [is] struggling for freedom'. If people were not willing to work, he did not think that they should expect the Armed Forces to go in their name. His message was backed up by the local Swansea West Liberal National MP, Lewis Jones, 'Idle mills and idle factories and furnaces in times like this [are] an act of desertion to the valiant men who [are] fighting for us'.[46]

The press reported these politicians' speeches verbatim, which gave them a wide circulation and directness as well as extra gravitas and importance; the papers reinforced the politicians' messages by their own explicit support. Information and explanation were closely welded to exhortation. Initially, when the government had urged civilians to take cover on the sound of the siren or to stay inside, the press across the country had endorsed the policy and adopted a censorious tone towards those who shunned the shelter. An *Oxford Mail* editorial opined 'the real duty of the individual is to prevent himself or herself from becoming a casualty, and the risks are tremendously increased when sections of the population go out of doors.'[47] A City of London newspaper referred to 'foolhardy' young people who chose to clamber up on roofs rather than take cover, and warned that 'Casualties give trouble to others': such people were 'not brave but foolish'.[48] The *Yorkshire Post* told its readers in an editorial that 'The essential duty for civilians in air warfare is to take diligent measures for the protection of their homes, their children and themselves'.[49] When the government changed its tune, so did the press.

Front-page headlines appeared such as 'Minister Explains Raid Sirens Policy – Wars Can Not Be Won Unless Risks Are Taken. Playing Into Enemy Hands If All Work Stops For One Plane'.[50] The *Daily Express* explained, and supported, the system of working after the siren and of roof spotters, both explicitly and by carrying stories of roof spotters.[51] Local newspapers supported the government's shift towards fewer air-raid warnings, even though it entailed greater risks. The *Hackney Gazette*, following the bombing of Croydon before the siren sounded and the ensuing outcry about restricted warnings, argued explicitly in support of the government's policy, 'as the Home Secretary pointed out yesterday, the public must be ready to take this risk as part of the price to be paid in order to defeat the enemy's purposes'. It argued against too many air-raid warnings, which the paper described as sounding like 'the wail of souls in torment', on the grounds that they would cause 'unnecessary and serious interruption of industry and transport, undue interference with ordinary activities, and at night-time constant loss and disturbance of sleep – effects which would, of course, elate the enemy.'[52] The provincial press wrote patriotically about the importance of working through air raids. Local newspapers' editorials urged workers in essential industries to work after the siren.[53] Weekly news magazines carried the same exhortation as the dailies. *The New Statesman and Nation* concluded as early as August 1940 that 'We shall have to get used to working through periods of possible danger'.[54]

The press took up the theme of civilians in the front line, although the meaning shifted depending on the context. In early September 1940, *The Times* maintained that 'all engaged in vital production are front-line troops'.[55] Churchill was placed firmly in the front line, with headlines such as 'Premier in Front Line' when reporting his inspection of defences along the south coast of England.[56] The *Daily Express* stretched the term to snapping point, however, with 'Brokers (Now in Front Line) see Gilt-Edged Spurt'; it went on to announce that 'heartened' by Churchill's speech there had been a near-boom in gilt-edged securities on the Stock Exchange, such that middle-aged stockbrokers, who had been secretly grieving for weeks that their job was so unimportant, were now feeling relief that they were 'in the front line'.[57]

As well using the language of the front line, the national press also merged civilians and the Forces with language such as 'Every worker is a soldier'. After the first heavy raids on London, as East Enders trekked off to find alternative accommodation, the press claimed that the 'civilian population is taking its Dunkirk', which also gave a bleak story a positive spin.[58] In explaining the system of working after the siren, *The Times* claimed that the desire of the industrial workers to be 'treated as soldiers, who do not lightly leave their posts', was 'practically unanimous', the only misgivings being over whether people forfeited their rights to legal compensation for injury which, *The Times* assured its readers, the government had stated would not happen.[59]

Local newspapers, like national ones, used the same military metaphors as politicians, with claims such as 'Workers' readiness to brave the risks of the battle' and 'We are all in the front line now, whether we are soldiers, sailors, airmen, farm workers, or workers in any industry'.[60] The *Wimbledon Borough News* linked working after the siren with front-line battle, and went on to quote Kipling as addressing every man working for victory.[61] The local Exeter newspaper, the *Express and Echo*, despite criticising successive governments' indifference to civilian protection and shelters,[62] threw its weight behind the government policy of restricting air-raid warnings, and the practice of not rushing to shelters on the sound of the siren. It exhorted and praised its readers in equal measure.[63] Taking risks, acting like soldiers and displaying courage were integral to the civilian's role in avoiding defeat, a role, the paper made clear, that involved continuing with work after the siren sounded. It warned 'Wars cannot be won without taking risks . . . We are all soldiers now, and must accept a soldier's risks as philosophically and as cheerfully as we can'. Working after the siren was essential, for 'In this way British workmen will foil the Nazi raiders'. It was by working after the siren and thereby running the risks of war that civilians were transformed into front-line troops, 'We are "doing our bit" on the Home Front, which just now is the Front Line'.[64]

The language of the 'front-line civilian' appeared not only in politicians' speeches and the press, but in a range of media. The BBC attempted to instil in civilians a sense of their role as a 'fighting front'; it referred to workers 'in the front line' and broadcast talks that emphasised that 'Britain could take it'.[65] J. B. Priestley in his Sunday evening *Postscripts*, broadcast on the BBC between June and September 1940 and listened to by roughly one-third of the population; the 1940 Ministry of Information film *Britain at Bay*, which Priestley wrote and narrated; government campaigns on various aspects of wartime life; national-savings campaigns; and even novels, all used military metaphors and likened civilians to front-line troops, although in these cases all civilians, not just those working after the siren, were included.[66] Newsreels also used military metaphors, for example, in September 1940, one announced 'Forty-Five Million Heroes Can't Be Wrong!' and 'Everyone in the Front Line'. When direct shellfire from across the Channel hit Dover, it too was in 'the front line'.

Government tried to implement the policy of working after the siren by exhortation, example and explanation, which is a far cry from Clive Ponting's description of the government in 1940 as 'instinctively repressive',[67] and it raises the question of why the government did not attempt to impose a practice that it perceived as crucial to the war effort. The answer lies in the political fog of 1940. Government and industry thrashed out the policy at a time when some members of the government were highly suspicious of the willingness of the workforce to support the war effort. Within Whitehall, worried ministers and civil servants weighed up the potential threat that the Communist Party posed to production. Over the summer of 1940, they mulled over the desirability of introducing regulations forbidding 'attacks on authority', but in the end decided that the threat was not great enough.[68] The Communist Party was at the forefront of hot and furious criticisms of government over the lack of attention paid to ARP: cheap blackout curtains and blinds in factories and workshops that meant appalling lighting and ventilation; low levels of ARP pay, but above all the inadequacy of shelters and the need for deep, bomb-proof shelters.[69] The Communist Party's paper, *Worker*, supported roof spotters until Churchill endorsed them, and then the paper criticised them.[70] In this atmosphere of uncertainty, an attempt to impose a blanket policy of working after the siren could only have fuelled the flames of Communist Party agitation, and given more cause for grievance, which was exactly what the government was trying to avoid. This suggests that the Communist Party had an influence beyond its strength, because of the government's uncertainty over the extent of its support; and, as a result, a huge and rapid exercise in industrial democracy swept the country. Following national negotiations and high-profile pronouncements by ministers, which the press eagerly seized on and endorsed, the government did not shrink from debate, but took its argument to workers across the country.

Local negotiations

Initially, negotiations between unions and employers over air raids had concerned payment for time lost during air raids.[71] Towards the end of September 1940 the National Arbitration Tribunal laid down payment for time lost during air raids: in respect of time lost up to two hours on any shift and not exceeding eight hours in any week, compensation was paid to time-workers at full normal-time rate, and, for any additional time lost, the compensation was to be at half that rate. Piece-workers had an equivalent compensation. When time lost was due to interruption, workers had, if required (subject to the 1937 Factory Act) in the same or following week, to make up the time lost up to two hours before or after an ordinary shift. They could be asked to work for up to eight hours to make up lost time. A worker who declined 'without good reason' to make up the time lost was not entitled to compensatory payments.[72] Once the focus of discussions swivelled away from payment for time lost, there were no cash-induced lubricants to smooth the decision-making process.

In September 1940 the British Federation of Master Printers, the Newspaper Society and the Printing and Kindred Trades Federation began negotiating to cover general printing and provincial newspapers working after the alert until danger was imminent, but in the meantime they agreed that essential work should continue with roof spotters – subject to agreement between management and the local trade-union branch.[73]

Trade unions and individual train companies negotiated working after the siren. In October 1940 the unions agreed in principle with the four major train companies that train and signal staff would remain at their posts throughout an air raid, booking offices would issue tickets, and that all other staff would continue to work until trained roof spotters gave a warning of imminent danger. Trains were meant to slow down in air raids, so as to give the drivers more control in an emergency, but anecdotal evidence suggests that trains often speeded up – presumably to move away from the area under bombardment.[74]

When the TUC had linked working after the siren with air-raid shelter protection for families, in their negotiations with the government, they reflected one of the demands that miners were making. Miners made a point of coupling what they did in air raids with the protection afforded their families. Back in July 1940, the miners had called for air-raid shelters for mining communities and for fellow miners to support ARP and the Home Guard; they even asked to be armed, presumably in order to repulse invading troops from key coalmines or to defend their families from the enemy; there is no evidence that this request was conceded. It was agreed that South Wales miners would not be told of air raids when they were underground, but if a miner's house or family were affected, he could go home as soon as the all clear sounded. When miners were kept underground because of an air raid at the end of a normal shift, no payment was made for time spent waiting for the all clear, but concessions were made if miners were late to work because of an air raid.[75] On 1 September 1940 a miners' conference in Cardiff approved a scheme for collieries in South Wales to continue working until roof spotters gave warning of danger. Men in key positions were to have shelters and to carry on working through a raid. The winding of coal was to cease during a raid, and all surface machinery, except that required for ventilating or lighting the mine, would stop. Despite this agreement, miners continued to protest against the inadequate air-raid shelters for their women and children.[76]

As well as negotiations between employers and employees, local employers discussed the issue among themselves. In Southampton, for instance, the local Chamber of Commerce discussed whether firms with roof spotters should hoist a flag when danger was imminent, in order to warn others – a practice that worked in other areas but was criticised here on the grounds that warnings should be the responsibility of government, not the civil community or individual employers. There were also suggestions for local rather than national co-ordination of the Observer Corps, and for people not to 'play too much for safety' as this lost many hours of work; after all, the ARP and other services did not wait for the all clear. This last point underlines the way in which behaviour was frequently placed in the context of what others were doing.[77]

Local negotiations for working after the siren were unusual for their speed; for their involvement of ministers from different departments; and for taking place in different arenas, which included trade-union meetings, public meetings in cities, and meetings at individual firms. At a time of unparalleled restrictions and regulations, the key players in war production created a forum for unfettered dialogue. Once government, trade-union leaders and representatives of employers' organisations had agreed that, in principle, work should continue after the siren, they all worked closely together to arrange meetings and conferences in munitions and other key centres: London, Birmingham, Bristol, Cardiff, Coventry, Derby, Glasgow, Leeds, Liverpool, Manchester, Middlesbrough, Newcastle, Sheffield, Southampton, and Swansea. The conferences were not only to persuade workers, but also to find out how different firms coped with working after the siren. Between 8 and 15 November, government spokesmen, including two of the most senior Labour ministers, Ernest Bevin and Herbert Morrison (the new Home Secretary and Minister of Home Security, 1940–45), urged local firms to adopt the system of roof spotters.

The government encouraged those making speeches to connect civilians with the RAF in the defeat of Hitler, and to link behaviour on the shop floor with the defeat of Hitler's strategy of disrupting production. Herbert Morrison toured South Wales. In Newport he did not mince his words. 'We have to beware of looking for 100 per cent safety for the civil population . . . If we hide ourselves and are unwilling to take any risks, if we want to go off our job directly the siren goes whether aircraft are about or not, it means that our strength is to be decreased, and the striking force of the enemy will be increased and we shall be whacked'.[78]

As well as warning of the dire consequences of not taking risks, praise was showered where praise was due. On 23 November 1940, at a trade-union conference in Cardiff, Ernest Bevin invested a docker, Tim O'Brien, with a certificate and medal for industrial heroism. In the summer he had rescued several of his mates after the bombing of a ship on which they were working. (He had already received the *Daily Herald* Order of Industrial Heroism on the recommendation of the Transport and General Workers' Union.)[79]

In Southampton, where Supermarine produced Spitfires, the link between the willingness of these workers to carry on after the siren and the fighting capacity of the country was made not only by William Mabane, but also by Air Marshal Sir Arthur Barrett, when addressing a conference of employers and employees at the Civic Centre. That such a meeting was necessary and that it did not take place until November, shows that those workers whose work after the siren was most crucial were not necessarily the quickest to change their practices.[80] Evidence from Bristol reinforces this view. At J. S. Fry and Sons, each department decided whether to work after the siren, and those that did agree chose their own roof spotters; at Bristol Aeroplanes discussions were still going on a fortnight after Fry's had settled their system.[81]

Local production defence committees were set up – with two trade-union representatives, employers' organisations, the Regional Commissioner's Alarm Officer, Regional Raid Spotters' Training Officer and a Factory Inspector – where conferences had been held, and in Bradford, Glasgow, Halifax, Huddersfield, Hull, Leicester, Plymouth and Preston, to promote joint works conferences on production.[82] The production defence committees surveyed the way in which local firms engaged in war production worked after the siren; promoted joint works conferences to explain the system of roof spotters and other ways of receiving warnings; offered advice to firms engaged on war production; and reported to the Ministry of Labour's Consultative Committee. The unions' initial experience of these committees was that they did encourage greater co-operation from employers.[83]

On his appointment as Minister of Labour, Ernest Bevin had instituted procedures for consulting with industry; a ban on strikes and lockouts followed discussions with representatives of both sides of industry. What the talks over working after the siren presaged, however, were consultations on a range of issues affecting people at their workplace at all levels of industry not just with representatives of the two sides. Bevin wanted to make active participation in the industrial democratic process his trademark, and, while the reality often fell far short of this ideal, he presented it as part of what distinguished Britain from enemy countries, where, he claimed, compulsion and threats were the order of the day.[84] It is possible, moreover, that the effect of air raids was generally to subvert managerial control over work, since the question of the amount of time to be spent at work was open to discussion, and rigid hours of work had to be eased. Time not spent at the workbench was time that could be spent in political discussion or in trade unions recruiting new members.[85]

Conclusions

It is often assumed that government in the Second World War learnt from the mistakes of the First World War, and was thus able to organise the country for war more effectively and quickly; the delivery of labour, material and services all benefited from earlier experience. The relatively low incidence of air raids in the First World War meant that this experience was of little use to planners in the 1930s.

Historians have pointed to conflicts in the policy-making process over differing long-term visions and plans.[86] This chapter has revealed that disagreements also existed over immediate, wartime domestic policies, as indeed one might expect in the highly charged atmosphere of the summer of 1940. Squabbles and misunderstandings within and between Whitehall, the RAF and industry, nevertheless, paled into insignificance alongside the overarching common goal of avoiding invasion and defeat. Policy was not 'owned' by a particular individual or government department, and it was not the influence of any one individual or group that shaped it. Individuals were not representing a single interest, such as their department or trade union, but a host of interests, both personal and public. The policy could influence whether enough aircraft were made, spare parts found and damaged aircraft repaired, in order to ward off the expected German invasion. Everyone was a potential winner if they got it right, and a loser if they got it wrong. Conflict was not simply a matter of personality clashes, party differences or territorial ambitions. Few policies can claim to have had so many of the policy-makers' interests at heart.

Not unusually, those involved in the policy-making process were male, although the decisions affected both men and women at work. Agreements were reached in 1940 at a time when there was fear and even expectation of invasion, British forces had retreated from continental Europe and had yet to savour the sweet taste of victory, the country was isolated in Europe, there was a new and largely untried government, and great uncertainty; yet, decisions taken in these extraordinary circumstances affected practices for the rest of the war. Many thousands of workers, both men and women, subsequently entered industry, but it was those people in employment in 1940 who shaped workplace practices on working after the siren for the rest of the war. Later, other factors crowded in to affect productivity, but none was solved with such a dramatic policy U-turn or extensive democratic exercise.[87]

Historians have analysed the workings of Whitehall during the war, and have dissected the personalities and powers of ministers. This chapter has revealed a policy-making framework with tentacles reaching far beyond Whitehall, into every nook and cranny of production, and involving an unheard-of degree of direct democracy. In London a principle was established but it was up to every individual firm in the country to create the practice. Although Parliament debated working after the siren, no new legislation was required, and the process, although involving local authorities in their role as employers, did not need their support either. In many areas of domestic policy that involved the protection and welfare of citizens, central government passed permissive legislation, which meant that it was left up to local authorities to adopt it if they chose to do so. It was certainly not government practice to offer a local democratic forum independent of local authorities. Here was a policy that needed the active approval of civilians because of its risk to civilians, and because of government uncertainty over the willingness of civilians to run that risk. Politicians were asking people to carry on at work after the public air-raid siren sounded, at a time when there were a number of very good reasons for them not to run additional risks. The broad social and cultural – as well as specific workplace – hurdles that people needed to leap over in order to change their behaviour are unravelled in the following chapter.

Notes

1 The Germans did, however, invade and occupy the Channel Islands.

2 Cabinet Papers, 66/12, 15 October 1940, Winston S. Churchill: Note, in Martin Gilbert (ed.), *The Churchill War Papers. vol. II. Never Surrender, May 1940–December 1940* (Heinemann, 1994), p. 947; J. B. Priestley vividly expressed the importance of aircraft production in his novel *Daylight on Saturday*, set in an aircraft factory: 'It is a termitary out of which come rolling great winged creatures. It is a power house. Take away these drawing offices, these toolmakers' sheds, these long rows of machines, these workers on assembly, and within ten days the whip is at your back. All the brave drilled men, willing to rush towards death, all the flags and national anthems, all the patriotic speeches, cannot rescue a people now. Without such factories as this, they are lost or dependent. Where these factories are, there is power. Without them we could not survive in wartime . . .' J. B. Priestley, *Daylight on Saturday* (Heinemann, 1943), p. 3.

3 *Hansard*, vol. 365, col. 319, 8 October 1940, Leslie Hore-Belisha.

4 *Oxford Mail* 21 June 1940.

5 Henry Pelling, *Winston Churchill* (Pan, 1977), p. 456; Angus Calder, *The People's War: Britain 1939–45* (Panther, 1971), p. 195; Winston S. Churchill, *The Second World War. vol. 2. Their Finest Hour* (Cassell, 1949), pp. 310–11.

6 *Daily Express* 19 September 1940.

7 *Yorkshire Post* 18 September 1940.

8 Patricia Hollis, *Jennie Lee: A Life* (Oxford University Press, 1997), pp. 93–4; Jennie Lee, *My Life With Nye* (Jonathan Cape, 1980), pp. 130–1; Anne Chisholm and Michael Davie, *Beaverbrook: A Life* (Hutchinson, 1992), p. 384.

9 National Archives, Kew, previously Public Record Office (hereafter PRO) HO 186/216, 22 June 1940, unsigned note.

10 Winston S. Churchill, *The Second World War. vol. 2*, p. 151.

11 PRO T 230/117, Effect of air raids on production generally in factories; CAB 65/8 191 (40) 6, 2 July 1940, War Cabinet.

12 *Hansard*, vol. 362, col. 660, 2 July 1940, Sir John Anderson.
13 PRO T 230/117, Effect of air raids on production generally in factories; CAB/8 198(40)6, 9 July 1940, War Cabinet.
14 PRO HO 186/1784, Memorandum air raid warning system, signed F. C. J., 26 July 1940.
15 University of Warwick Library, Modern Records Centre (hereafter MRC) FBI archive 200/F/3/S1/22/31/46, 14 August 1940.
16 PRO HO 186/1784, Ministry of Home Security air raid warning system and industry. Note of meeting held at the Home Office on 6 August 1940; MRC, TUC archive MSS 292, TUC Industrial ARP 883.212/6, 6 August 1940.
17 Martin Gilbert (ed.), *The Churchill War Papers. vol. II*, p. 756; PRO CAB 65/9 239 (40)4, 2 September 1940, War Cabinet.
18 PRO HO 186/1090, Ministry of Home Security air raid warning system and industry. Note of meeting held at the Home Office, 3 September 1940.
19 *Express and Echo* (Exeter) 30 September 1940. Over the summer of 1940 many in the south-west of England were willing to take the risk of carrying on with their work after the siren sounded: firms introduced roof spotters before national agreements were concluded or official roof spotting courses introduced.
20 PRO ZLIB 10/40, Air raid 'spotting' 1940–1945. The failure of air-raid sirens to sound in Norwich created a political storm within Norwich and between Norwich and the Ministry of Home Security. See PRO HO 199/63.
21 PRO 65/9 241 (40) 3; 65/9 242 (40), 4 September 1940, War Cabinet.
22 PRO CAB 65/9 245 (40) 2, 9 September; 249 (40) 7, 13 September; 255 (40) 6. 20 September; 256 (40) 5, 23 September; 270 (40) 4, 14 September 1940.
23 PRO HO 186/1784 Conference with TUC and employers, 1 October 1940. Notes for Home Secretary; TUC, *The TUC in Wartime: An Informal Record of Three Months' Progress* (TUC, January 1941). This is rather different from the impression created in David Thoms, *War, Industry and Society: The Midlands, 1939–45* (Routledge, 1989), p. 119, that the government imposed the system.
24 MRC FBI archive 200/F/3/S1/22/32/5–7 and 36.
25 PRO AIR 19/182. Beaverbrook to Sinclair, 22 September 1940; Sinclair to Beaverbrook, 26 September 1940; Dowding to Sinclair, 27 September 1940.
26 House of Lords Record Office (hereafter HLRO), BBK D/29, 30 August 1940.
27 HLRO BBK D/29 Beaverbrook to Halifax, 4 September 1940. (Letter probably not sent.)
28 Martin Gilbert (ed.), *The Churchill War Papers. vol. II*; Winston S. Churchill to Archibald Sinclair and Sir Cyril Newell (Churchill Papers, 20/13), 26 September 1940, p. 874; John Colville diary (Colville papers), 15 December 1940, p. 1239 (cited in Gilbert). Colville is making reference to the last verse of Tennyson's poem 'The Brook'.
29 PRO HO 186/1784, Ministry of Home Security air raid precautions in industry. Note of meeting held at the Home Office on 1 October 1940. Item 2:

Arrangements for the training of roof spotters; MRC MSS TUC 292.883, The Roof Watcher system, not dated.

30 Robert Mackay, *Half the Battle: Civilian Morale in Britain During the Second World War* (Manchester University Press, 2002), pp. 142, 172–3.
31 *Westminster and Pimlico News* 27 September 1940.
32 Randolph S. Churchill (compiler), *Into Battle: Speeches by the Rt. Hon. Winston S. Churchill PC, MP* (Cassell, 1941), pp. 211 and 231.
33 Randolph S. Churchill (compiler), *Into Battle*, pp. 251, 253.
34 Martin Gilbert (ed.), *The Churchill Papers: vol. 11*, p. 1264.
35 *The Times*, 11 September 1940.
36 *Express and Echo* (Exeter) 24 September 1940, quoting the *New York Times*.
37 William Shawn (ed.), *Mollie Panter-Downes London War Notes 1939–1945* (Farrer, Straus and Giroux, 1971). All the material originally appeared in the *New Yorker* between 1940 and 1945.
38 *Daily Herald* 3 July and 30 August 1940.
39 *Daily Herald* 26 July 1940.
40 *The Times* 19 September 1940.
41 *The Times* 19 September 1940.
42 *The Times* 23 September 1940.
43 *The Times* 23 September 1940.
44 *The Times* 11 September 1940.
45 *Hansard* vol. 365, col. 319, 8 October 1940, Hore-Belisha.
46 *Western Mail* 21 October 1940.
47 *Oxford Mail* 25 June 1940.
48 *The City Press* 23 August 1940.
49 *Yorkshire Post* 20 June 1940.
50 *Bristol Evening Post* 22 August 1940.
51 *Daily Express* 3 July, 11, 19, 20 September.
52 *Hackney Gazette* 23 August 1940.
53 *Wandsworth Borough News* 15 November 1940.
54 *New Statesman and Nation* 24 August 1940.
55 *The Times* 11 September 1940.
56 *Daily Express* 3 July 1940.
57 *Daily Express* 20 June 1940.
58 *Daily Express* 19 June and 9 September.
59 *The Times* 20 September 1940.
60 *Croydon Times* 28 September 1940.
61 *Wimbledon Borough News* 11 October 1940.
62 *Express and Echo* (Exeter) 25 September 1940.
63 *Express and Echo* (Exeter) 8 November and 15 November 1940.
64 *Express and Echo* (Exeter) 22 August, 30 September, 1 October.
65 Sian Nicholas, *The Echo of War* (Manchester University Press, 1996), pp. 7, 120, 125.
66 *Western Evening Herald* 7 October 1940; J. B. Priestley, *Postscripts* (Heinemann, 1940); GPO Film Unit, Ministry of Information, *Britain at*

Bay, 1940; Nigel Balchin, *Darkness Falls from the Air* (Collins, 1942), p. 202; Nevil Shute, *Most Secret* (Heinemann, 1945).
67 Clive Ponting, *1940: Myth and Reality* (Hamish Hamilton, 1990), p. 138.
68 PRO HO 45/25552.
69 Communist Party of Great Britain, *Party Organiser*, April 1940.
70 Angus Calder, *The People's War, Britain 1939–1945* (Panther, 1971), p. 282.
71 *The Times* 28 August 1940. In August 1940, the National Union of Boot and Shoe Operatives was pressing the employers for payment or compensation for time lost during air raids.
72 *The Times* 25 September 1940.
73 *Western Mail* 20 September 1940.
74 PRO RAIL 258/303/5 Board of Directors GWR, 25 October 1940; 29 November 1940; *Western Mail* 8 October 1940.
75 *Daily Herald* 18 July, 22 July 1940.
76 *The Times* 2 September 1940.
77 *Southern Daily Echo* 24 October 1940.
78 *Western Mail* 15 November 1940.
79 *Western Mail* 25 November 1940; *Daily Herald* 8 August 1940.
80 *Southern Daily Echo* 15 November 1940.
81 *Bristol Evening Post* 11 September 1940.
82 *Hansard* vol. 367, cols 923–4, 11 December 1940, Ralph Assheton.
83 TUC, *The TUC in Wartime* (January 1941).
84 Alan Bullock, *The Life and Times of Ernest Bevin. vol. 2. Minister of Labour 1940–1945* (Heinemann, 1967), p. 21; Keith Middlemas, *Politics in Industrial Society* (André Deutsch, 1979), p. 275; Ministry of Labour *Gazette* October 1940.
85 Richard Croucher, *Engineers at War* (Merlin Press, 1982), p. 111. No examples are given to support the point.
86 Kevin Jefferys, *The Churchill Coalition and Wartime Politics 1940–45* (Manchester University Press, 1991).
87 While David Thoms in *War, Industry and Society. The Midlands 1939–45* (Routledge, 1989), refers to a 'significant shift of policy which changed the balance of interest between production and personal security', he does not analyse the policy in detail or convey the drama and the unusual nature, and thus significance, of the policy shift.

3

Restraints on working after the siren

Introduction

Politicians were asking people to run additional risks in air raids after years of horror stories and shocking reports about their devastating impact. People were already fearful of raids before they experienced them. The dread of bombardment was confirmed in early bombing raids, when people were extremely frightened. Both in the early raids and throughout the war, people were killed at work: carrying on at work after the siren sounded and during an air raid was a less-safe option than being in a shelter. Defences against air attack, such as barrage balloons and Ack-Ack, particularly in the early part of the war, were inadequate at work, as elsewhere. Poor industrial relations, as well as trade unionists who defended their members' safety, initially created pockets of resistance to working after the siren, but for much of the war the issue disappeared from the agenda. Only towards the end of the war when the Germans sent over pilotless planes (V1s – popularly known as doodlebugs), did an unwillingness to carry on after the siren again arise, but this was more from war-weariness among Londoners than from industrial disputes. No siren warning was possible for V2s. Some of the material in this chapter will already be familiar to historians of the war, but it needs restating here, in order that the hurdles many people had to overcome in order to carry on working can be fully appreciated.

Pre-war views of the coming war

In the 1930s experts and the public believed that in a future war, enemy aircraft would drop bombs that would devastate civilian populations. It was assumed that there was no defence against such bombers; Stanley Baldwin, when Prime Minister, warned that 'the bomber will always get through'. So, governments prioritised the production of bomber aircraft, rather than fighters to take on enemy bombers and their fighter escorts. It was not until the late 1930s that Hugh Dowding, who was to be Air Chief Marshal during the Battle of Britain, persuaded the government to put more faith in fighters, and to build as many as they could, as quickly as possible. It was also assumed that the enemy would drop not only bombs but also – and far worse – poison gas, which would devastate large sections of the population. Popular fiction before the war graphically described the horrors of gas attacks on civilian populations.[1] Even so, novels did not catch the public's attention as much as newsreel footage and commentaries – which reached a far wider audience than books – of the effects of aerial bombing of civilians in Spain during the Civil War. Newsreels of Guernica in April 1937, and of other bombed cities, along with women and children evacuees, especially Basque children who came to Britain, were juxtaposed with news of Britain's rearmament, of factories making gas masks and of air-raid precautions. Cinema audiences saw on the screen the horrors of aerial bombardment and what might be in store for them.[2]

Those reporting the effects of air attacks on Spain focused on the worst aspects of bombardment. One man, for instance, visited Barcelona to inspect air-raid precautions under war conditions and, on his return, wrote a pamphlet in emotive language, which would have put the wind up the sturdiest of characters, while tucking in an easily overlooked point that his most graphic descriptions referred to only a minority of the population:

> In aerial attack death and destruction arrive in an instant.
>
> Whether by day or night, without warning men, women, and children are hurled into eternity.
>
> Life verily hangs by a thread.
>
> This is perhaps the supreme characteristic of mass terrorism from the air against the defenceless population of a great city . . .
>
> To some it was like waiting in the death cell for the hour of execution. Others were affected as much by the noise of the anti-aircraft guns as by the explosion of the bombs . . .
>
> Some people were affected less by the sight of the dead than by the agony and groans of the living . . .
>
> To the more highly strung their imaginative terrors were more terrible than the actual sight of dismembered limbs and spreading pools of blood . . .
>
> And yet, . . . mass panic and hysteria [had] little general effect.[3]

Cinema images and reports from Spain mingled with memories or stories, oral and written, of life in the trenches and of the horrors of gas during the First World War. Policy-makers drew on the calculations of experts, who erred on the side of the worst possible scenarios. From the mid-1930s, as the government began planning air-raid precautions, the issuing of gas masks to every woman, man and child was thought to be essential, and, of all the half-prepared measures, this was the most comprehensive by the time that aerial attacks began. Great anxiety was aroused by government forecasts and popular anticipation of a war in which aerial bombardment of civilians was a central strategy.[4]

Fright

Initially, the very sound of the siren frightened people. Its 'banshee wailing', in Churchill's words, was noisy, unpleasant and associated with expectations of suffering, death and destruction. People were frightened by its sound.[5] They halted in their tracks, packed up work, stopped whatever they were doing, and bolted for cover or the shelters.[6] On 23 October 1939, before experiencing air raids, Richard Brown, an Ipswich engineer and ARP warden, noted in his diary that the siren 'certainly does make one's ticker and tummy work overtime. Its wail is a little terrifying though I wouldn't have it otherwise.'[7] One psychologist reported from his research that, 'Bodily effects of fear such as muscular incoordination, cessation of digestion and sexual appetite, and the "sinking feeling", were noticeable during early raids, and occasional instances of panic among crowds were reported.'[8] Anticipation and initial reactions were similar: people were frightened.

People continued to be frightened when they experienced the blitzes or their homes were destroyed, and this fear usually returned during the following few raids. Nella Last recorded in her diary 'a night of terror' in May 1941, when land mines, incendiaries and explosives were dropped. Most of her windows were blown out, the metal frames strained, the ceilings down, the walls cracked, doors were splintered and off their hinges, the house rocked and there was dirt from the chimney. During the raid, she and her husband cowered under an indoor shelter, which was showered with plaster. The next day she was very sick. She described the mix of emotions that she had felt during the raid: on the one hand, she calmly accepted that this was 'the end', but on the other hand she was full of regret that she had not opened a tin of fruit for afternoon tea (a real treat)![9]

The sounds in air raids were terrifying. One man in Bristol noted on 24 November 1940,

> The sky is now lit up with different coloured flares; the barrage is terrific, and the air is filled with the constant drone of Jerry planes, the scream of falling bombs and the thunder of their explosion . . . Glory be! It's the all clear. What a marvellous sound, and what a reprieve from hell. I never expected to hear it again.[10]

Nella Last wrote in her diary of 'Screaming bombs, planes we did not hear until the bombs dropped, dog-fights overhead, machine-gunning, rattling and splattering, so dreadful, so frightening.'[11] Although the writer Alan Sillitoe only experienced one heavy raid in Nottingham, it was the sounds and uncertainty of raids that remained with him when later he wrote,

> Few bombs fell on our area, but the piercing whistle of one descending will remain: and all the time in our frail shelter, whenever German planes were overhead, the consciousness that the next second might be our last never quite gave way to dumb endurance.[12]

As well as frightening sounds, there were terrifying sights among the dead and injured, and the smell of fire lingered in the nostrils.[13] All the senses were engaged in experiencing the fright and horror. People described the effects of raids on all their senses: the sound, the sight, the smell, the physical reverberations, and the taste of dust. Early raids appeared to confirm the assumption that there was no defence against bombers.

Dangers

Continuing work during air raids carried great dangers. People died while at work in aircraft factories, docks, hospitals and offices, and on trains.[14] Others died in civil-defence duties during air raids. Well before negotiations had been finalised for working after the siren, there were workers who were dying at their post during air raids.[15]

On two occasions people were killed when the BBC's Broadcasting House was bombed. The importance of the BBC to the war effort has been well demonstrated.[16] It was the key means of instant communication within Britain. As well as a practical function, the BBC also had a symbolic one, as it spread from the heart of London into almost every home in the country. By 1939 the BBC had become the way in which rulers communicated news of national significance to the public: in 1937 Edward VIII had publicly revealed his abdication on the radio, and in September 1939 when Neville Chamberlain announced to the country that Britain was at war, he too took to the airwaves. The cost of continuous broadcasting during air raids was a high one. Although there was a roof spotter on Broadcasting House, his warnings (Look Out! There's A Big One Coming!) afforded only limited protection, and none at all to those who did not leave their work stations whatever the danger. On the evening of 15 October 1940 Bruce Belfrage was reading the summary preceding the news. In the middle of a sentence, millions of listeners heard a muffled sound of an explosion in the distance. Belfrage paused momentarily. The studio was still vibrating when a voice said 'It's all right' over the microphone, and Belfrage continued. The news in German, which was going out simultaneously, was also uninterrupted. Here was the supreme example of the stiff upper lip, of steady calm when there was crashing all around. BBC staff in Broadcasting House died at their posts. During an air raid on the night of 8/9 December Broadcasting House was damaged, staff were injured, including the Controller of Programmes, B. E. Nicholls, and a policeman was killed in the street.[17]

The risks of injury and death in an air raid were not evenly divided. Those in paid work, especially those in war-related work, were more likely to be casualties than other groups of civilians. Adults were more likely to be casualties than children, and men were more likely to be casualties than women. Over the summer of 1940 German bombers targeted factories and docks in the daylight raids. More men worked in factories and docks, and more men were, therefore, air-raid casualties. Working after the siren thus affected male civilians more than female ones. During night-time raids in 1940 there was little difference in the ratio of female to male casualties. By 1941, however, as more men were working at night in civil-defence jobs, as firemen, as part of rescue crews, and as fire-watchers, as well as on night shifts in factories, there was a higher proportion of male than female casualties in night-time raids. The practice of working after the siren therefore affected more men than women, although there is no evidence that, among men and women at work, men were any more willing to carry on than women.[18] Away from work, there is no evidence of differences between women and men in their attitudes towards air raids, or that women were more nervous than men.[19] Indeed, women in civil defence worked alongside men in the heat of the blitzes, as air-raid wardens and ambulance drivers. While men and women risked their lives working in civil defence, they could not offer full protection to the rest of the population in an air raid, and in the early raids protection was at its least effective.

Air Raid Precautions (ARP)

From the late 1930s government introduced measures, known as ARP, to reduce the dangers of aerial attacks and dampen the population's fears. The 1937 Air Raid Precautions Act required local authorities to put ARP in place, for which central government would pay nine-tenths of the costs. Initially, it was difficult to recruit enough people for ARP; and many who joined before the air raids started had to face public hostility. People grumbled that full-time civil-defence personnel were a waste of money, after easy jobs, and bossy because their main job appeared to be telling people off for not complying with the blackout (blacking out light that could attract enemy bombers). Such criticism must have contributed to a feeling that the training and waiting was hardly worthwhile. Among the general hostility, two groups in particular – women, and Afro-Caribbean men living in London – had a difficult time at the outset, although there is no evidence that this hostility continued throughout the war. We know about women and Afro-Caribbean men who fought against prejudice and eventually gained respect; we do not know how many others walked away.[20] Prejudice against volunteers on the grounds of gender or colour must have undermined the effectiveness of ARP, especially as appropriate personnel were in short supply. Other, organisational, problems also hindered ARP. Barbara Nixon, an air-raid warden, provided her personal explanation of the initial storm and shock experienced by Londoners. When the heavy raids began in London, Ack-Ack was not fired, so that people felt defenceless; air-raid wardens' training was, she believed, inadequate, and there was poor co-ordination between the civil-defence services.[21]

The 1939 Civil Defence Act gave the government powers to requisition buildings for shelters, and it placed an obligation on the owners of factories and shops to adopt ARP. Many firms and local authorities complied only slowly and tardily. Firms were confused over what government was asking them to do, and what precisely would meet the requirements of the Civil Defence Act. Many of the plans that were drawn up for air-raid shelters, which were seen as underpinning safety measures in case of bombing, did not meet government requirements and had to be revised. The blackout; barrage balloons; camouflaging factories; and works' Home Guard units were all seen as essential to protect those works that were considered particular targets for bombing or invading troops. Putting such protection in place and maintaining it was not risk free for the workforce.

For at least a year prior to the German invasion of Poland, government had been urging managers of factories – often to no avail – to take precautionary steps against bombing in the event of war. Consequently, the declaration of war was followed by frenzied activity, as firms desperately tried to make up for lost time: in September 1939 alone there were 129 fatalities at work. With no time for putting up proper blackout material at windows, pots of black paint were daubed on windows; men toppled off roofs in the rush to protect factories against bombardment; workers put in excessive hours and paid scant attention to the risks to life and limb; and the lesson learnt at great cost in the First World War that more haste means less speed was forgotten. The initial stages of war were characterised by frenzied and often inappropriate action.

Countless lives had been lost before there was sight or sound of a German bomber.[22]

There was good reason, even without the added hazard of air raids, to regard work as a risky business, and the air-raid shelter as a protection from more than enemy bombs. A blackout to protect from one kind of danger increased the risks from other ones. The blackout made ventilation worse, increased the risks of gassing, and raised temperatures in workrooms, especially foundries. Not surprisingly, people found the absence of street lights and the blackout of natural light from homes and businesses depressing and dangerous: the death rate on the roads and at work jumped. Most of the increase in accidents occurred in firms with war-related contracts. By 1940 there had been a 33 per cent increase in accidents at engineering factories, a 47 per cent increase in accidents at factories making machines and motor vehicles, a 21 per cent increase in accidents at chemical firms, and a significant increase in shipbuilding accidents. The biggest leap in wartime accidents overall for men occurred between 1939 and 1940, when the accident rate leapt from 41 accidents per 1,000 men to 49 accidents per 1,000 men. By the time that government ministers turned their attention to the deaths and injuries caused by the blackout and production drives, much damage to life and productivity had already occurred.[23] The Inspectors of Factories tried to get as much natural light in workplaces as possible, and from 1941 specific requirements about the amount of light required for work were laid down.

The war intensified the dangers of work; workers who were brought in fresh to processes with which they were unfamiliar were more likely to have an accident; and longer hours and night work left workers tired and so more accident-prone. As in the First World War, it was during the initial stages of war that the hazards of work were greatest. Although the lessons of the First World War were learnt in some areas of life, most of industry operated in total ignorance of the research into industrial health undertaken between the wars.[24] Fortuitously, the implementation of the 1937 Factory Act meant that new standards of health and safety had recently come on stream – a process that had quickened the interest of many trade unions and employers' organisations in safety, health and welfare.

In the last two years of the war, the accident rate did improve. New workers had time to settle down and adjust to the dangers; there were fewer workers unaccustomed to factory work; most people put in less hours of work a week; and in 1944 many workers took their first real holiday since the outbreak of war; people could enjoy a break from the strain and monotony of war work. Even so, there is little evidence that the much-heralded 'welfare' work had a significant influence on the protection of war workers, and in many cases the war actually delayed general improvements in amenities. There was a serious deterioration in upkeep and cleanliness; there were leaky roofs, makeshift repairs and a general air of dilapidation.[25]

In 1939 there was bewilderment over whether volunteers should enrol for ARP duty at work as well as with the local authority, or just one of these, and, if they enrolled at work, whether the firm had sole call on their time. The employers' view was that if they had paid for their employees to receive ARP training, those workers should be available to firms full-time. Even after the outbreak of war there was confusion over what firms would require from those with ARP training. The position, unclear to many at the time, was that employers had first call on workers during normal working hours.[26]

There was also uncertainty over the calls that local authorities could make on firms to release workers for general civil-defence duties. Local authorities could not direct management, and managements could not order an employee to undertake civil-defence duties, except fire watching. Even when civil-defence workers gained know-how in air raids, private firms and local authorities did not share their experiences. The issue was never resolved and problems of co-ordination between industry and civil defence continued.[27] At the start of 1940, Sir John Anderson, the Home Secretary, delivered a sharp rebuke to local authorities and employers when he reminded them that civil defence was not a competition between them.[28] His words fell on stony ground, for when the government arranged courses on ARP in 1943 it still found confusion, lack of training in industry and an absence of information; tensions between factories and local authorities over the division of responsibilities and a lack of machinery for co-operation; anomalies; problems in disseminating information; and, in some factories, no civil defence at all. By 1943 fears of invasion had subsided, so civil-defence measures were not thought so imperative, but worries still existed over the possibility of gas attacks.[29]

Co-operation between firms and local authorities was often weak, although this varied from area to area. Collaboration in London was inadequate throughout the war. Letters were sent and meetings were held, but to little avail. There was a lack of information and a shortage of data flowing in both directions. ARP organisation in London was highly atomised, despite its geographical concentration. As late as 1944, arrangements for co-operation were still being thrashed out.[30] In contrast, Luton, a town just north of London, was held up as a paragon of collaboration and integration, yet, even there, there were problems.[31]

Money often lay at the heart of disagreements. In Cornwall there was a quarrel between the County Council and a firm, over who should pay for the sounding of a works' siren that also acted as a public siren. On other issues, however, such as council training of industrial ARP personnel on decontamination courses, anti-gas measures and how to deal with bombs, there was no disagreement, because financial responsibilities were clear cut and not contested.[32]

On occasion the lack of co-ordination between firms and local authorities spelt disaster, as happened in July 1940 when Hall Russell's in Aberdeen was bombed. The first-aid people at the factory were ignorant of the city's ARP scheme, and there was no link between the head of the firm and the city's ARP. Chaos ensued: the injured did not receive basic first-aid treatment on the spot, but were transported in heavy vehicles at great speed; the rapid and rough transportation worsened their shock and injuries. The dead and the dying were all transported together, and those with appalling wounds were in full view of anyone on the street who looked at them. As a result of this macabre incident, the government sent a circular to every firm in the country about the importance of them knowing about local authority ARP schemes, firms and local authorities co-ordinating their efforts, and the need for agreed plans.[33]

As well as difficulties between firms and local authorities, there were six different government departments trying to get messages across to industry, and as late as 1945 they had different views on civil-defence training.[34] Balancing the need to disseminate information with avoiding information somehow falling into enemy hands was a perennial problem. It was never satisfactorily resolved how to warn factory managers that fire was a far more serious hazard from air attacks than high-explosive bombs.[35]

The unpredictability of war meant that much effort was devoted to problems that never materialised. Fears of what aerial attack might involve meant that time and effort had to be spent on aspects of ARP and post-raid services that, thankfully, were never required. All local authorities had to distribute gas masks, and make provision for decontamination in case of gas attacks. Anti-invasion committees were set up the length and breadth of the country. Once Germany had invaded France, parts of the country, such as Cornwall, which it had been assumed would be safe from air raids or invasion, found themselves potential targets and suddenly had to put new ARP in place. Even small villages boasted anti-invasion committees, undertook exercises in case of invasion, and ran first-aid courses. Disruption and war organisation were not confined to the cities.[36]

Businesses that had put ARP in place before war broke out often had to change them once experience had been gained from the reality of war.

So, for instance, originally it was assumed that air-raid shelters should be within seven minutes of the workplace, but once bombing raids began and many workers did not take shelter as soon as the alarm was sounded, shelter had to be found closer to the work. As workers joined the Armed Forces and transferred to other work so some of those initially trained in ARP were lost; training had to be ongoing.[37] Initial misjudgements in an entirely new situation meant that there was a good deal of frantic improvisation and adaptation once war was declared, and again once Germany started bombing Britain. Responsibility fell on the owners of properties to provide adequate shelter for employers, but in cases where firms rented property this could lead to disputes and even court appearances.[38] The difficulties of adopting wartime measures; the varied pace at which even those works most crucial to the war effort managed to put facilities in place; and the lack of national uniformity is well illustrated by the case of Vickers.

Vickers[39]

Vickers was a powerful armaments firm, with sites the length and breadth of the country: it built battleships, cruisers, destroyers, carriers and submarines in Barrow and the naval yard at Newcastle; Spitfire fighter planes at Supermarines in Southampton and Castle Bromwich; Wellington bombers in Weybridge, Chertsey and Blackpool; tanks in Elswick; and munitions of every description in Barrow, Crayford, Chertsey, Dartford, Elswick, Manchester and Scotswood; it also owned English Steel in Sheffield.[40] It was a truly 'national' firm, with every site a strategic target for enemy bombers.

Vickers' ARP and practices for working after the siren were as varied as the works it owned. Despite the centrality of all Vickers' employees to the prosecution of the war, the rate at which protection for these vital workers was put in place varied enormously. There was no national pattern to the speed with which shelters were built, the circumstances in which they were used, or the systems for working after the siren sounded.

ARP, including shelters, varied from works to works. By the end of 1939, shelters had been built for Barrow's workers and they had been trained in ARP. Yet, the naval yard, undertaking similar work to Barrow, was well behind in ARP. Scotswood had completed its ARP, but Palmers-Hebburn was still digging trenches and putting ARP in place.[41] In the early months of 1940 Barrow continued to build up its ARP; Chester now had adequate ARP, shelters and a decontamination station, but the naval yard was improvising, and assuming that the ships the men were building would provide them with shelter in the case of an attack.[42]

At Manchester the shelters were still incomplete when air raids began over Britain, and the naval yard was still building shelters after bombs had fallen in the area.[43] As firms adapted their works, took on more workers, and shifted their priorities, so they had to adjust their ARP. Although Barrow had been one of the first of Vickers' works to build shelters, when it expanded in 1940 it had to build a further deep shelter for 600 workers, and later, at the end of 1942, it needed additional shelters as more workers moved into the submarine dock.[44]

Local circumstances could at one and the same time make a works especially vulnerable and hard to protect. Supermarine in Southampton was particularly vulnerable: it was building Spitfires, it was on the coast so warnings of approaching enemy planes often came at the last moment, and the Germans had dropped mail in the area before the war, so its lay-out was well known to the enemy. The vulnerability of Supermarine was confirmed on 26 September 1940, when the Woolston and Itchen works were both seriously damaged.[45] Supermarine's vulnerability was compounded at the Itchen works, because there was no suitable ground in the immediate vicinity for building underground shelters (the ground was only just above sea level, so underground shelters would have flooded at high tide); instead surface shelters were built, with access through a tunnel under a railway line.[46]

The decision to carry on working once the siren had sounded was not a straightforward choice between being safer in the shelter or more at risk at the workbench or on the production line. Once raids began, it was discovered that running for a shelter could be as dangerous as staying put. At Southampton it was often difficult to give much advance warning of approaching enemy aircraft, and people could be streaming up to the shelter just as the bombers arrived.[47] Although attitudes towards working after the siren changed, this took time, and over the crucial summer of 1940 when Spitfire production was essential to avoiding defeat, the attitude of those building Spitfires was, allegedly, far from urgent. According to one contemporary source, everyone rushed to the shelters with great alacrity when the siren sounded, but dawdled back on the all clear, causing tensions between the military guarding Supermarine and the civilians employed there.[48]

Even when workers were willing to continue working after the siren, the practice could not be implemented overnight: if shelters were not close enough for people to run to at the last minute, shelters had to be relocated.[49] At Elswick they had to modify their shelters and lighting at the same time as roof spotters were being trained. Only gradually could all the shops work through the siren.[50] In Barrow a direct telephone line from the local ARP defence centre to the works ARP control centre was laid, and a continuous connection was maintained in order to warn the works of any enemy aircraft in the area. The question of roof spotting was discussed at the works committee and agreed upon. By the time the system was up and running, the roof glass of most of the important shops, in which some shelter was available, was protected. It was then necessary to maintain power and lighting up to an imminent attack, which in turn required a considerable amount of extra blackout. Shelters that were easily accessible were also required, but they took six months to build, so some were not able to work after the siren until the worst of the air attacks were over.[51] At Palmers Hebburn a number of measures had to be taken for people to carry on working after the siren: protection against flying glass; training for spotters; and the building of a spotters' tower. Even so, some chose to ignore the siren before the work was completed.[52]

Putting adequate protection in place was not always easy when there was a shortage of materials. Wire netting, for instance, which was used to prevent shattered glass flying in all directions, became like gold dust, holding up protective work at Palmers Hebburn, Barrow and the naval yard.[53]

For all the efforts, some dilatory, some inadequate, some comprehensive and some efficient, to protect people and plant, there was no getting away from the fact that certain plants, docks and railways were prime targets for the enemy to bomb. Taking cover in an air-raid shelter was no guarantee against injury or death, but not taking cover carried greater risks. ARP could not offer full protection, although it could often lessen the impact of falling debris, dust and flying glass.

Industrial relations

Although there is no evidence that poor industrial relations held up agreements for working after the siren at Vickers, there is evidence that some trade unionists did not believe that they or their families received adequate protection, and that poor industrial relations hampered agreements to work after the siren sounded. While the majority of trade unionists supported the national agreement that the TUC had reached, there were discordant voices. Workers did not unthinkingly take the government's cue. Trade unionists complained about the inadequate levels of compensation under the Personal Injuries Scheme, and anomalies between it and Workmen's Compensation; the alleged unwillingness of managements to co-operate; danger from flying glass when windows were blown out; and transport difficulties.[54]

At the TUC annual conference in October 1940 three delegates, two of whom were from the Amalgamated Engineering Union (AEU), criticised the agreement and the system of roof spotters. Indeed, the AEU appear to have been the most critical section of workers, at odds with the TUC leadership and, it would seem, the bulk of other workers.[55] A. E. Eyton, of the AEU, who worked in Birmingham, insisted that the TUC should not have agreed to the system, because many firms did not provide adequate shelter. H. Kanter, of the Tailor and Garment Workers, worked in the East End of London as a roof spotter. He asserted that the system was not practical because of clouds. He told the conference that the previous week he had been on a roof with a couple of other spotters; the public alert sounded but the factory continued working. The spotters heard the drone of planes but could not see anything. Suddenly, a German plane dived down below the clouds, dropped two or three bombs in the immediate vicinity, and flew off. Kanter pressed the button to warn workers to go to the shelter, but the damage was already done. Those bombs, he warned, could easily have fallen on his factory.[56] It has also been claimed that later in the war many shop stewards were 'seriously perturbed' at the spotter system.[57]

Even where unions had agreed to work after the siren, not all members were willing to follow the union line. In parts of north-west England and in parts of Yorkshire, workers held out for safeguards. Employers and employees in factories engaged on war work were concerned that production would suffer because of transport problems, which suggests not only differences between different areas, but also between different groups of workers in the same area. In Manchester, Salford, Stockport and Leeds, workers went against their union. The men who would not continue after the siren claimed that it was because of concerns for their families not themselves, but some doubted the adequacy of government compensation should they be permanently injured. In an effort to win doubters around, some areas provided road/raid spotters for transport. The unwillingness of those men who would not continue needs to be placed in the context of the list of places (Bolton, Bury, Burnley, Nelson, Colne, Todmorden, Halifax, Huddersfield, Harrogate, Wakefield, and Hull) where drivers were willing to continue after the siren, which was far longer than the places where they stopped.[58] In some cases, the public supported the unions. In Sheffield people were more dubious about trams than buses running after the siren, because of the fear that enemy bombers would see the flashes from trams.[59]

There is some limited evidence that the issue of working after the siren caused friction between management and employees, but the evidence is remarkably thin. The managing director of a firm manufacturing components parts for Hurricanes, Spitfires and bombers clearly expressed his lack of sympathy for, and distrust of, his workers when he wrote on 23 September 1940 that during the previous week their production from the night shift was down 30 per cent, because of workers staying in the shelters and receiving time and a fifth, and double time on Sundays. He ideally wanted any payment for workers in shelters to be stopped, but if that was politically unacceptable, he wanted them to be paid the equivalent unemployment rate. 'The activating motive for staying in the Shelter is not, in the general case fear: the men themselves have abandoned the pretence that this is so.'[60]

So far, interpretation of the significance of people working after the air-raid siren and the way in which the system operated, has relied on records from the period. There is some memory evidence (collected decades later) of discord, despite the almost universal belief, at the time of these recordings that the population all pulled together during the war. Issues such as working through the siren, and the appropriate payment, were not always easily resolved. These issues could create tensions between employers and employees, so that war, rather than dissolving tensions, created new war-related ones, revolving around safety and money.

One employee of an aircraft factory later recalled that although there had been a system worked out for payment during raids, nevertheless it created a range of problems. At a time of national emergency, relations between workers and employers at an aircraft factory could be amazingly petty. At the Chiswick works of the aircraft manufacturers Handley Page, there was an arrangement that if air raids took place in the works' time they would pay wages, but if raids took place at lunchtime, after or before work started, the firm would not pay the wages. On one occasion the warning went at one minute past 8 a.m. and everyone was in the shelter until 11 a.m. The starting time for work was 8 a.m., but workers were always allowed two minutes' grace. The doors were shut at one minute past 8 a.m. as the warning sounded; some workers had not quite clocked on and were shut out. They did not get paid for the three hours. When trade-union representatives went to the management and pointed out that some of the workers did not have a chance to clock on because the doors shut at one minute past 8 a.m. although they were always allowed two minutes' grace, the management threatened to stop everyone's wages for the three hours if the union insisted that two minutes past 8 a.m. was clock-on time, because the warning went at one minute past, which in the union's reckoning was before work started.[61]

One member of management in a dairy in south-west London, G. D. Simons, recalled his experiences of dealing with workers' pay during air raids, using the language of 'battle', not to refer to the struggle with Germany, but with the employees. He referred to a union leader as 'one of our deadly enemies', and concluded the account 'We won this battle'.

The issue of working through the siren highlighted tensions between management and men. Simons took exception to men diving for shelter and being paid, 'the honest ones who had seen the absurdity of sitting hours in the shelter were now called blacklegs.' Following negotiations, the firm refused to double government compensation payments if anyone was injured, but they did agree to the other demands for pay at double rate (what Simons called 'blood money'), a first-aid post, and roof spotters. 'Spotters were appointed and once more we settled down to more or less normal working . . . The men appeared more contented and it seemed as though the spotter system was the cure for the long hold ups we had been experiencing.' Working after the siren then became a bargaining chip in negotiations over men switching from night work to day work on which they earned less money.[62]

South Wales is the one area of the country where there was widespread unwillingness to work after the siren, but even here it did not apply to workers in all industries. There was a longstanding bitterness in relations between the two sides of the shipping and dock industries, which were soured even further by the war. At a time when the needs of productivity for the war effort were intense, poor industrial relations meant that productivity was not as great as in many other industries. Local circumstances therefore outweighed national ones, and the argument was conducted in public, as the animosity between the two sides of industry spilled out into the local press (see chapter 4).[63] As well as poor industrial relations making it more difficult to reach agreement, it was also the case that it was more difficult for men spread over a large area of docks to take cover as easily as office workers, who could go to a basement, or factory workers who were all concentrated in the same buildings and could go to shelters that were near their workplace. In addition, there were still areas of South Wales where men could not find work, so there were some civilians who were being asked to risk their lives in air raids at work, while others, cheek by jowl, were not even having to run the day-to-day risks of work.[64] By the time that the unemployed of South Wales had been incorporated into the war effort, the blitzes on dock and industrial areas had passed their worst.

War-weariness

In 1942 many non-industrial towns were bombed, in what were known as the Baedeker raids, and from then until the end of the war there were intermittent, but sometimes heavy, raids. From June 1944 south-east England had to endure pilot-less planes (V1s), popularly dubbed doodlebugs, and, from the autumn of 1944, V2s, for which it was not possible to give warnings. Even before June 1944, when the first V1s arrived, there is evidence that some Londoners were reaching the end of their tether. It was still the case that people reacted in a variety of ways to raids, but in the poorer areas of London there was resentment: 'We should not have to "take" them again . . . the Government should do something.' In heavily bombed parts of London, the remorselessness of raids was depressing. Reports suggested that after four and a half years of bombing, people's resistance was lower, but how far these comments and others, that claimed that people were not standing up to raids as well as during the blitz was the result of East Enders' experience of the blitz already having passed into legend is hard to know. We do not know if people were by now looking back on the early blitzes with idealised memories.[65] We do know, however, that the arrival of V1s led to the departure of thousands of Londoners, and for those left behind the strain was palpable. George Beardmore, who lived in Harrow, North London, wrote in his journal on 2 July 1944:

> Normal life is quite literally paralysed. Housewives run to the shops and run back to hang round their homes and duck at almost any noise overhead. Such children as go to school are said . . . to spend their time in the Shelters, in which lessons of a sort have been organised. At the office, which is representative of most, I imagine, an unspoken trepidation is always present. Our ears are forever cocked for *that* drone.[66]

When doodlebugs landed on British soil the Ministry of Information noted the initial 'shocked horror' that greeted them. The Ministry reported that the main reaction in London was one of incredible tiredness through lack of sleep and nervous anxiety over the 'weird and uncanny' nature of them, and the strain of listening for their approach. Fire-watchers complained bitterly that fire-watching was dangerous and pointless against the V1s, because although they did not cause fires they did kill people who were in exposed positions, and fire-watchers were losing more sleep than the rest of the population.[67]

Londoners were weary, strained and anxious. Although people did not believe that V1s would impinge on the outcome of the war (they arrived hot on the heels of the allied invasion of Normandy), there were wild rumours about the damage and casualties they were causing.[68]

By now many more women were in paid work than in 1940, and this in turn meant that more children were left on their own, not attending school and playing in the streets after the siren sounded. Indeed, with the arrival of V1s, many women stopped going to work in London in order to be with their children. In addition, those at work found it hard to concentrate, and more were taking to the shelters. People in London were divided over whether it was worse than the blitz. Some thought it worse because of the 'continuity and uncanniness' of the attacks, and they resented having to suffer attacks again. A minority thought that it would not be possible to stick it much longer and that there should be peace at any price. By late August 1944, reports had shifted their balance to emphasise that those who were 'fearful, strained and tired' were now in a minority. Likewise, when the V2s began arriving later in the year, people's reactions were divided, with some people preferring not to have warnings, as they did not have to worry about what might be coming. Again, there were rumours and accompanying anxiety about the devastation that V2s were causing, rather than actual experience. Women at home all day were reported as being nervous, which fits with other evidence from the earlier period of the war that people coped better when they were with others. As in the early years of the war, those in the provinces felt great sympathy for the plight of Londoners.[69] In early 1945, George Beardmore summed up what many Londoners must have been feeling, 'We are suffering, here at home, the worst period of the war. We are all – all of us, at the office, in the shops, and at home – weary of war and its effects.'[70] In the next chapter we will see that despite all the war-weariness and other constraints on people carrying on after the siren, there is overwhelming evidence that many people frequently ignored the siren.

Notes

1 Martin Ceadel, 'Popular fiction and the next war, 1918–39', in Frank Gloversmith (ed.), *Class, Culture and Social Change: A New View of the 1930s* (Harvester Press, 1980), pp. 161–84.
2 Anthony Aldgate, *Cinema and History: British Newsreels and the Spanish Civil War* (Scolar Press, 1979), pp. 150–81.
3 N. de P. MacRoberts, *ARP Lessons from Barcelona* (Eyre and Spottiswoode, 1938). Found at National Archives, Kew (formerly Public Record Office, hereafter PRO) Metropolitan Police file, MEPO 2/3632.
4 Rosemary Pritchard and Saul Rosenzweig, 'The effects of war stress upon childhood and youth', *Journal of Abnormal Social Psychology*, 37 (1942), p. 330.
5 University of Sussex Mass-Observation Archive, Air Raids, TC 23/9/T, Stepney.
6 P. E. Vernon, 'Psychological effects of air raids', *Journal of Abnormal Psychology*, 36 (1941), p. 459.
7 Helen D. Millgate (ed.), *Mr Brown's War: A Diary of the Second World War* (Sutton Publishing, 2003), p. 11.
8 P. E. Vernon, 'Psychological effects of air raids', p. 460.

9 Richard Broad and Suzie Fleming (eds), *Nella Last's War: A Mother's Diary 1939–45* (Falling Wall Press, 1981), p. 138.
10 Rev. S. Paul Shipley (compiler) *Bristol Siren Nights: Diaries and Stories of the Blitzes* (Rankin Bros, undated, but probably 1943), p. 9. W. A. Hanes, 24 November 1940.
11 Richard Broad and Suzie Fleming (eds) *Nella Last's War*, p. 141, 5 May 1941.
12 Alan Sillitoe, *Life Without Armour: An Autobiography* (HarperCollins, 1995), p. 51.
13 Art McCulloch, *The War and Uncle Walter: The Diary of an Eccentric* (Doubleday, 2003), p. 269; Colin Perry, *Boy in the Blitz: The 1940 Diary of Colin Perry* (Sutton Publishing, 2000), p. 120.
14 *Daily Herald* 8 August, 9 September 1940. Interviewees for this project still recall the horrors of an attack on Vickers' aircraft factory at Weybridge.
15 *Daily Herald* 6, 15 July 1940. Just over a week later, and despite pressure from the trade unions, the government announced that the Royal Commission on Workmen's Compensation was suspending its work without even producing an interim report. That trade unionists were willing to take risks and to work after the siren did not mean that they wanted plans for their long-term welfare put on the back burner. It had been the employers who had refused to continue sitting on the Commission. As in so many other aspects of life, working people wanted as much normality to continue as possible, and that included maintaining an active commitment to social policies.
16 Sian Nicholas, *The Echo of War: Home Front Propaganda and the Wartime BBC, 1939–45* (Manchester University Press, 1996).
17 *Western Evening Herald* (Plymouth) 7 January 1941.
18 PRO MH 76/508. Those running a risk at work were no more likely to die if they were casualties, than those who were casualties at home. An air-raid casualty was more likely to die at work or in the home, than if they were in the open, but less likely than if they were in a shelter. A higher proportion of shelter casualties died than casualties elsewhere.
19 University of Sussex, Mass-Observation Archive, Air Raids, 65/4/A, 2 September 1940.
20 Barbara Nixon, *Raiders Overhead: A Diary of the London Blitz* (Scolar Press, London, 1980), pp. 74–6; quoted in Peggy Scott, *They Made Invasion Possible* (Hutchinson, 1944), p. 142; League of Coloured People *Newsletter* 1940, 1941, 1942.
21 Barbara Nixon, *Raiders Overhead*, pp. 20, 31, 32.
22 Parliamentary Papers (PP), 1940–41, vol. iv, Annual Report of the Chief Inspector of Factories for 1939 and 1940.
23 PP, 1940–41, vol. iv, Annual Report of the Chief Inspector of Factories for 1939 and 1940.
24 R. C. Browne, 'A conception of industrial health', *British Medical Journal*, 1 (1947), p. 839.

25 PP, 1945–46, vol. xii, Annual Report of the Chief Inspector of Factories for 1944, and PP, 1946–47, vol. xi, Annual Report of the Chief Inspector of Factories for 1945.
26 PRO HO 186/1090.
27 PRO HO 186/2201.
28 *The Times* 3 January 1940.
29 PRO HO 186/2201.
30 PRO HO 186/2320.
31 PRO HO 186/2321 (casualty and mortuary services.)
32 Cornwall Record Office, Truro, CC/1/23/1, Cornwall County Council Emergency Committee Minutes, 27 October 1939; 26 January 1940.
33 PRO HO 186/1090.
34 PRO HO 186/2201.
35 PRO HO 186/2201.
36 Cornwall Record Office, Truro, CC/1/23/1, Cornwall County Council, Emergency Committee Minutes, 2 August 1940; DPP 62/24/2, St Ewe Parish Invasion Book.
37 PP, Annual Report of the Chief Inspector of Factories for 1939; 1940; and 1941.
38 *Hackney Gazette* 15 July 1940.
39 Note on sources: every Vickers' works submitted three-monthly reports to Head Office, reports on which this section is based. Management wrote all the quarterly reports, but they did not all follow exactly the same format. So, for instance, Weybridge, which built Wellington bombers and where Barnes Wallace developed his bouncing bombs for the dam raids, never included any information about ARP, the Home Guard, firewatching or roof spotters. All the papers cited are in Cambridge University Library.
40 J. D. Scott, *Vickers: A History* (Weidenfeld and Nicolson, 1962), pp. 281–91.
41 Cambridge University Library, M. S. Vickers' Document, Vickers' Quarterly Report (hereafter Vickers' Quarterly Report), Barrow, vol. 195, Naval Yard, vol. 195, Scotswood, vol. 195, Palmers-Hebburn, vol. 195.
42 Vickers' Quarterly Report, Barrow, vol. 196, Chester, vol. 196, Naval Yard, vol. 196.
43 Vickers' Quarterly Report, Manchester, vol. 197, Naval Yard, vol. 197.
44 Vickers' Quarterly Report, Barrow, vol. 198, vol. 206.
45 Vickers' Quarterly Report, Supermarine, Southampton, vol. 198.
46 Cambridge University Library, Vickers 1900, D. Le P. Webb, 'Never a Dull Moment: A Personal History of Vickers Supermarine 1926–60. Part II', Unpublished typescript, p. 117.
47 D. Le P. Webb 'Never a Dull Moment', p. 125.
48 D. Le P. Webb 'Never a Dull Moment', p. 124.
49 Vickers' Quarterly Report, Barrow, vol. 198.
50 Vickers' Quarterly Report, Elswick, vol. 200.
51 Vickers' Quarterly Report, Barrow, vol. 199.
52 Vickers' Quarterly Report, Palmers Hebburn, vol. 199.

53 Vickers' Quarterly Report, Palmers Hebburn, vol. 199, Barrow, vol. 199, and Naval Yard, vol. 199.
54 University of Warwick Library, Modern Records Centre (MRC) MSS TUC archive TUC 200/292.883.23; TUC 200/292.883.24; TUC, *The TUC in Wartime* (TUC, January 1941).
55 MRC, MSS TUC 883.23, 26 September 1940.
56 Trades Union Congress, *Annual Report* 1940.
57 Colin Croucher, *Engineers at War* (Merlin Press, 1982), p. 110.
58 *The Times* 31 October 1940.
59 University of Sussex, Mass-Observation Archive, Air Raids, TC, 23/10/P, Sheffield.
60 MRC, MSS 200/F/S1/22/31/174.
61 Imperial War Museum (IWM) Sound Archive, C. Jordan, 14415.
62 IWM Department of Documents. G. D. Simons 94/2/1.
63 *Western Mail* 3, 4, 5 October 1940.
64 *Western Mail* 11 December 1940.
65 PRO INF 1/292, Weekly Home Intelligence Reports (WHIR), 15–22 February, 22–29 February, 29 February–9 March 1944.
66 George Beardmore, *Civilians at War: Journals 1938–1946* (John Murray, 1984), p. 168, 2 July 1944.
67 PRO INF 1/292, WHIR, 13–20 June 1944.
68 PRO INF 1/292, WHIR, 20–27 June, 27 June–4 July 1944.
69 PRO INF 1/292, WHIR, 27 June–4 July, 11–18 July, 18–25 July, 25 July–1 August, 1–9 August, 15–22 August, 26 September–3 October, 10–17 October, 24–31 October, 7–14 November, 5–12 December 1944.
70 Beardmore, *Civilians at War*, p. 187, 28 January 1945.

4

Activities after the siren

Introduction

One of the most ubiquitous images that we have of the war is of people escaping, not experiencing, air raids. There are numerous studies of evacuees, some analytical and others anecdotal. Much oral history is based on people's memories of childhood evacuee experiences. This is somewhat inevitable as the biological clock ticks away. There are no longer people alive who remember what it was like to be old in the 1940s, and relatively few who were even middle-aged in the war. Novels set in the Second World War still take the experience of child evacuees as a central theme.[1]

Some of the most enduring images that we have of Londoners in the war are Henry Moore's shelter sketches. Moore produced roughly 400 such drawings, and some are on permanent display in art galleries, such as Tate Britain in London. In these haunting sketches, people are drawn as victims, as passive, depersonalised objects of horror and pity. They suggest entombment, death, decay and misery. They have endured and become universal symbols of civilians in war.[2] Yet, they represent only one aspect of civilians' experiences, and one period of the war. Moore drew them in 1940 and 1941, when the bombing of London was at its most intense, and when shelters were least adequate. Although it has been claimed that Londoners identified with Moore's drawings, a 1943 review of a National Gallery display of war art stated that Londoners felt baffled and insulted; this 'morbid and unreal' world was not their world.[3] For many, their experience was not one of passivity; they were not entombed, or even miserable. The years 1940 and 1941 were a period of intense activity for many civilians.

During the blitzes, everyone took cover, with the exception of civil-defence services, such as ambulance crews and the fire brigade. People were extremely frightened in the blitzes, and to be directly under the enemy bombers was a very different experience from watching dogfights, Ack-Ack and burning buildings in the distance. The after-effects of heavy air raids could also be very traumatic. On most occasions, however, the sound of the siren did not lead to a blitz or bombs in the immediate vicinity and, as we will see in this chapter, in these circumstances many people carried on with whatever they were doing and did not go to shelters.

Failure of sirens to sound before bombs were dropped, as happened in a number of places, always provoked protests, although once the policy of sounding a siren over a wide area and for every single enemy aircraft had been modified, it was inevitable that on occasions bombs would fall without warning. Sometimes lone planes broke away from the main formation and the radar did not pick them up in time. Occasionally, there were problems with the sirens themselves, as for instance in Bristol after a heavy raid when there was no electricity supply, or in north-east England when some sirens froze up during cold winters.[4] However, errors and failures in the system of warning did not, on the whole, lead to a loss of faith in the system.

'Carrying on' after the siren is normally taken here to indicate that people did not take cover, but there is also evidence that, whether or not people took cover, they might well continue with a 'normal' activity; so for instance, when there was an alert but no raid there was little or no decline in radio listening; when a raid was in progress about two-thirds continued to listen.[5]

There were a range of overlapping circumstances in which people carried on after the siren; what was a work situation for one person may not have been for another. Although certain industries were categorised as 'essential' to the war effort, many other forms of work were necessary for war industries and war workers to function. It would be artificial to separate workers in production from other workers. An aircraft worker may have used public transport, visited council offices, frequented shops, watched a football match, gone to the cinema or attended church. People's behaviour at work was not only affected by the nature of their work and by industrial relations, but by their wider lifestyle. Work cannot be analysed in a social and cultural vacuum. Work practices need to be placed in the context of wider experiences.

While a number of historians have referred to people carrying on after the siren, there has been no systematic collection of evidence. Unless there is an overall picture, the centrality of carrying on after the siren to the experience of war on the Home Front cannot be fully appreciated. The aim of this chapter is to demonstrate the extent to which people did not go to air-raid shelters or take cover on the sound of the siren; the reasons for this are analysed in subsequent chapters. In order to organise the evidence, this chapter will be divided between London and the rest of the country, although the boundaries were never clear cut, and while work, shopping, local authorities and leisure will be discussed in turn, here again there were overlaps. The behaviour of East Enders who remained throughout the blitz is included in the discussion of London as a whole, although it is important to remember that many left the East End, so the numbers involved were far less than would otherwise have been the case, and many clubs, shops, pubs and cinemas were not open for business, but were boarded up or destroyed.[6]

London

Work

The rescue services, firemen and ambulance crews were often at their busiest during raids. The local press highlighted their bravery, with headlines such as 'Battle While ARP Men Worked'.[7] From the outset, they did not take cover even when bombs were falling around them. Other workers gradually differentiated between an alert that planes were in the vicinity, and the alarm to take cover. Workers in the City of London responded in a mixed fashion to the first air-raid warnings. Some went to basements, while others sought out public shelters. While some sauntered off to the shelters, others, especially young people, perched on roofs and watched the sky. Lloyd's had its own large, deep, steel-and-concrete shelter; underwriters would leave their usual room and work below ground with their names marked above stands so that the brokers could still find them. The shelter became a microcosm of life above ground, with snacks and cigarettes on sale, and a barber's shop.[8]

In her wartime fictional diary Inez Holden wrote of the London blitz, 'The night-shift workers in their factories, Civil Defence men, nurses, roof-spotters, and so on take up their positions automatically'.[9] Working after the siren became normal practice in many factories, council offices, shops and hospitals.[10] Hospitals kept going after spotters had given warning to take cover, although some work in hospitals could not carry on as normal when the siren had sounded or an air raid was in progress. Patients at Westminster Hospital in London had to wait for radium, which was put in a 50-foot well during air raids, and X-ray treatment was also on hold during raids, because the generator was switched off.[11] Elsewhere it was not so much the type of activity as the location of work that determined how quickly employees took cover. In Whitehall the practice developed of evacuating the top two floors of a building when the siren sounded, and those on other floors continued to work until roof spotters gave the signal to take cover.[12] While central government offices worked to this principle, each local authority developed its own scheme.

Local councils

Councils next door to each other decided to work after the siren with roof spotters at rates that seem to have borne no relationship to the intensity of bombing in their area. In early September 1940, for example, Woolwich Council was uneasy about carrying on after the siren sounded – hardly surprising in a prime target area – and yet by the end of September, despite heavy raids, doubts had faded.[13]

On 18 September 1940, Bethnal Green's General Emergency and Finance Committee urged the heads of all council departments to arrange their work so that there was minimum disruption when the siren sounded: staff who wanted to go to the shelters in the basement were allowed to do so, but they had to take their work with them. The committee did not want members of the public who had come to the Town Hall turned away or kept waiting until after the 'all clear' sounded. Trying to ensure that council matters continued to function during air-raid warnings was a clear switch in policy from that adopted a year earlier.[14] Likewise, in Stoke Newington the council wanted staff to continue working after the siren, and to continue dealing with the public until they heard heavy gunfire.[15]

Many council services took place outside town halls, and policy decisions were needed to cover a range of day-to-day activities. In the autumn of 1940 Richmond-upon-Thames council issued its workers with steel helmets, and told them to carry on working after the siren sounded – until they heard gunfire.[16] Barnes Borough Council decided that funeral services at East Sheen cemetery should continue after the siren, so long as the relatives did not object, but the council wanted all organised games on its grounds to cease, whether the players wished to continue or not.[17] Work at infant welfare centres in Kensington continued after the siren at the doctor's discretion, although there were adjoining shelters for mothers and children who wanted to use them.[18]

The image of East Enders all congregating in shelters is a one-dimensional and therefore inaccurate picture. At the public baths in Bethnal Green, it was so difficult to persuade people to take shelter – even after the East End had been heavily bombed – that the Emergency Committee considered, but then rejected, installing klaxon warning hooters inside the buildings themselves, presumably because people washing themselves would not be able to stand the noise and would have to leave.[19] In nearby Shoreditch, the public baths had their own roof spotter.[20] In Stoke Newington, people using the baths were informed when the siren sounded, but it was up to them whether they carried on washing or went to the shelter.[21] Singing alone in the bath was perhaps as much a part of the East Enders' war experience as community singing in the shelter. While there was an element of choice in visiting the baths, and those who were anxious about raids could avoid it, shopping was a chore that women in particular needed to do whatever the circumstances.

Shops

Air-raid warnings initially disrupted women's shopping. Women lost time and money and were unable to perform one of their key domestic tasks. Before long, shops prided themselves – and even seem to have competed – in remaining open after the air-raid siren sounded. Once one shop remained open in an area, others followed; there was no point in needless loss of takings if roof spotters could provide a degree of safety.[22]

In September 1940 there was a good deal of variation in shops around London when the siren sounded. Some closed immediately, others stayed open until 'things got too bad', while a few stayed open to attract the trade of those shops that had closed (so some people obviously carried on shopping). All small tobacconists remained open, while some large ones shut; newsagents varied; food shops usually shut; and central London shops tended to stay open more than ones in the East End.[23]

Most people in the London area quickly ignored air-raid warnings, whether they were outside or at home.[24] Even after areas had been badly bombed, people did not all rush to the shelters. On 15 September 1940, when the siren sounded in Lewisham, an area that had already been heavily bombed, 'People moved to the shelters slowly, nobody ran'.[25]

When a siren sounded in London one morning in March 1942, after a lull of nine months, one Mass-Observer, who was standing outside Camden Town Station noticed that the streets were very crowded with women shoppers, but very few took any notice.

> One or two women instinctively looked up at the sky, one or two were hurrying along the street obviously with the purpose of getting home, here and there a shopkeeper popped his head out to see what was going on, but generally it can be said that things carried on just the same as usual . . . No hub-bub, no commotion.[26]

Another Mass-Observer in the Holloway Road described a scene of people looking up and talking, of continuing to walk down the road or going about their business, and of shelter doors opening, while a postman continued to deliver letters 'without any noticeable change in his countenance'.[27] People were inside and outside not only when shopping, but also for leisure.

Leisure

Not only town halls, but also dance halls, cinemas and youth clubs, continued to operate after sirens had sounded.[28] During the heavy raids on the East End of London in September 1940, music halls shut down; social clubs, dance halls and billiard saloons were empty fairly; and cinema attendances dropped, but those which were open tended to continue in a raid.[29]

Most cinema-goers stayed in their seats when the siren sounded.[30] In August 1940, cinemas in Balham and Tooting, SW London, continued to show films after the siren went and until the all clear sounded many hours later, and those who stayed in their seats had hours of entertainment well into the night. One happy woman commented, 'I never in my life had such a long and cheap show before – seven hours and seven big pictures, all for a bob!' [a shilling][31]

While cinema-goers were predominantly working class and young, there is evidence that more middle-class audiences also ignored air-raid warnings when they were enjoying themselves. Promenade concerts at the Queen's Hall continued regardless of the air-raid warnings. On 28 August 1940, Sir Henry Wood was conducting Brahms, Symphony no. 1, when at about 9 p.m.

> Suddenly a man in evening dress hurried through the orchestra and Sir Henry Wood stopped conducting. Immediately there came from the audience a sound like mingled laughs and groans, with a few claps. The man announced that the siren had gone (Here loud applause) and asked anyone who wished to leave to do so at once. There was more applause and general conversation. After about two minutes the concert continued. Observer did not hear the siren. Nobody in any part of the house left, as far as observer could see – he was standing in the Prom part.[32]

Restaurants and pubs stayed open during air raids, with the larger ones sometimes offering their customers an air-raid shelter on the premises. When customers were not allowed to stay, the usual reason was that there was too much glass around for it to be safe. In general, it was thought that restaurant business actually picked up during air raids, except in the East End where there was no gas. Pubs were little affected by raids, and tended to stay open.[33] George Orwell recorded in his diary on 17 September 1940, 'Yesterday, when having my hair cut in the City, asked the barber if he carried on during raids. He said he did. And even if he was shaving someone? I said. Oh, yes, he carried on just the same. And one day a bomb will drop near enough to make him jump, and he will slice half somebody's face off.'[34]

There is some evidence that the Ministry of Home Security (MHS) was more cautious and unwilling for people to carry on after the siren than the public themselves. At the beginning of the 1940 season, some football clubs adopted the practice of continuing to play after the siren, but were told by the FA that they had to stop doing this, as the MHS did not feel that it was justified in risking a bomb falling on a crowd of spectators in the open. The FA went along with the MHS's advice, but fans were disgruntled when matches had to be abandoned, and the

FA lobbied the government to change its policy. Early in December 1940, the MHS announced that football clubs could play on after the siren, provided that they had roof spotters and co-operated with the police.[35] Not only football stadiums but also dog racing stadiums eventually organised roof spotters, so as to continue after the siren.[36]

Most churches continued during air raids, but there was no fixed policy.[37] Protestant vicars publicly debated whether services should continue after the air-raid siren sounded; most did so. One Balham vicar's solution bore no relationship to the actual risk, but rather to the type of service in progress: if sirens sounded during Mattins (morning service) or Evensong, then the service ended immediately with a prayer or a blessing, but if the siren sounded during Holy Communion, the service continued.[38] Basing a policy on the type of service in progress, rather than on the actual danger, was not always a safe one. It was reported that a London church was damaged during Holy Communion, several of the congregation and the minister were injured and the minister's wife was killed.[39] A church in Tooting continued the service after the siren, but one of the church officials went on the roof as a spotter.[40] Methodist churches in South London decided to shorten services to one hour by ministers cutting the length of their sermons.[41] The response of churches towards the siren varied even within the same area. When the siren sounded across Richmond-upon-Thames one Sunday morning in early September 1940, some services continued but with ARP personnel and children leaving; some congregations broke off to go to a shelter and resumed the services later; and some worshippers did not hear the siren because the organ and singing blotted out the sound.[42] The Roman Catholic Cardinal Hinsley advised priests in his archdiocese that they should celebrate Low Mass rather than High Mass, in order that people could take cover in time when the siren sounded; in some cases services continued after the siren.[43] While many would have walked to church, to the shops, to cinemas or to work, others in London were dependent on public transport.

Transport

Over the summer of 1940 air-raid sirens disrupted public transport across the capital. Some underground, train, bus and tram drivers stopped when the siren sounded, while others carried on driving. Sometimes tube passengers reached train stations, only to find that the last main-line and suburban services had left. Heavy raids on London meant difficulties for transport workers and disruption to passengers.[44] In late October 1940, London Transport, with the agreement of bus drivers and conductors, introduced road spotters on duty at 123 key traffic points; the spotters were to advise drivers whether or not to continue in a raid.[45] Transport linked activities in the capital with numerous activities not only in the suburbs of London but also further afield.

The provinces

Disruption to transport during air raids caused more chaos than any other area of activity. In Wales, for instance, a Welsh transport firm's decision that services would continue after the siren, led to 'confusion and dislocation', especially on the trams. Some tram drivers stopped, while others tried to continue but were held up by those who had stopped.[46] It was then agreed that buses and trams would run in Cardiff during air raids, but this was voluntary and a small number of drivers decided that they would not drive on in raids. Inspectors stood at key points after the siren sounded, and buses continued under their direction, so long as there were no enemy aircraft overhead or bombs dropping.[47]

The air-raid siren did not unduly disturb people outside London. There were similar stories from many parts of the country: in Newcastle people stood around talking excitedly;[48] and in Swansea there was no panic, even after a heavy raid.[49] Citizens Advice Bureaux reported that in Darlington most people were very calm and regarded the raids as something 'to be put up with'; in Hull only 5 per cent were really nervous and inclined to panic; in Aberdare, Glamorgan, there was indignation at the time, followed by interest after the raid; in Newport, raids were regarded as a nuisance; and, in Aberdeen, raids were taken 'coolly'.[50] A middle-aged woman in Worthing recorded in her diary on 16 August 1940 that when she, her mother and another older woman were having tea, the siren sounded, but they did not interrupt the tea until there were planes overhead and the sound of gunfire – at which they adjourned under the stairs.[51]

In Bristol it was noticed that people went on walking at a normal pace when the siren sounded; by August 1940 they were so used to nightly air-raid warnings that they took no notice. One air-raid warden wrote to the *Bristol Evening Post* that the air-raid warning was a 'farce', as adults and children on the streets took no notice of it and the traffic continued. He thought that people should be made to take cover or some would be killed. In early September a warning flashed on the screen at the cinema that an air-raid warning had sounded, and the overwhelming majority of the packed cinema stayed in their seats. For those not in a cinema, watching searchlights was a favourite occupation of both men and women.[52]

By mid-September 1940 the Chief Constable of Liverpool was deeply worried about the public's lack of concern when the siren sounded,[53] but people were allowed to take responsibility for their own behaviour. So, for instance, the central market in Cardiff remained open during air raids, but there were notices warning people that they remained in the market at their own risk.[54]

Many councils adopted the practice of working after the siren. In early September 1940 Birmingham City Council's Lord Mayor was wary of the practice, but by the end of September 1940, when the city engineer and surveyor recommended that council employees should continue with their work or take shelter at their own discretion (with roof spotters to give warning), the Emergency Committee agreed to adopt the practice. The council initially warned its employees that roof spotters, posted in the council clock tower, were not yet trained, but people from the various council departments attended roof spotting courses, and by mid-November all corporation departments remained open after the alert.[55] From the end of September, Redcar council employees remained at their work until a roof spotter on the drill tower of the fire station gave warning; in early October 1940 Stockton Council employees were asked to continue their work after the siren sounded, while Middlesbrough Council installed a buzzer on the municipal buildings, as well as a roof spotter.[56] Portsmouth City Council had roof spotters not only on council buildings, but also on local hospitals and schools.[57] Cardiff employed roof spotters around the city, including the central library, which kept open during an alert with a spotter on the roof. During an alarm, both public and staff took shelter.[58] Even so, firms in cities such as Birmingham and Manchester often wanted to move faster than the local councils.[59]

On 25 September 1940, a Liverpool man wrote in his diary, 'With the "Alert" now operating throughout the country, the siren interrupts the working life very little. In fact people treat the warning note with complete indifference and wait until the more imminent sound of gun fire before taking refuge.' The system endured around the country for the rest of the war. Richard Brown noted in his diary on 9 April 1944 that most of the large shops in Ipswich had a spotter, who went on the roof at the alert and gave a warning when enemy aircraft were in the vicinity, at which point the shop assistants and shoppers went to the basement.[60]

A complex picture

Practices varied, and rumours abounded of people stopping work and either sheltering or wasting time by, for instance, going to the pub.[61] Not all employees in the same firm behaved in the same way, as is clear from an account written at the end of 1940 by Richard Brown, a works' ARP warden at Reavell and Co. in Ipswich,

> we get six pips when the town siren goes and all who wish then go to the shelters where one of us wardens takes care of them and notes their names and checks numbers. When the raiders are within 15-mile radius we get the tip from RAF observers and the hooter hoots for 1 minute when all who are left drop everything and run to the shelters. When the Jerry goes over the 15-mile line we come out and the remainder come out at the town all-clear.[62]

A snapshot of practices in the early months of air raids in a small sample of a dozen firms in the Birmingham area revealed the variation between and within firms; these practices may well have changed over the course of the war:

- only the handicapped went to the shelter from the 'alert' to the 'all clear'.
- those under the age of sixteen and a few elderly workers were instructed to take shelter on the 'alert', but few did so.
- all stopped work on the spotters' signal, but not all took cover.
- 1 per cent went to the shelters on the 'alert', and the rest on the spotters' signal.
- 10 per cent carried on during imminent danger, after the spotters' signal.
- all production staff waited for spotters' signals, while a small proportion of office staff waited for the 'all clear'.
- half of elderly workers went to shelter from 'alert' to 'all clear'.
- women took shelter on 'alert', men on the spotters' signal.
- young people took cover on public signals.
- 15 per cent of the workforce took shelter on the alert.
- a few workers took shelter on 'alert' and waited for the 'all clear'.
- 350 out of 575 workers not on urgent work went to the shelter from 'alert' to 'all clear'.[63]

While there is a range of evidence that shows how carrying on after the siren and not taking cover was the norm, except when bombs were immediately overhead, it is clear (from this and the previous chapter) that not everyone behaved in the same way, and that there were variations in practices. In contrast, the media presented a far more homogeneous reaction to air raids.

Reconstructions of activities after the siren

Throughout the war there were reconstructions in the press, on the BBC, and at the cinema and theatre, of people continuing with their activities after the siren sounded. The way in which we interpret this material is fraught with difficulty because of its ambiguity. Just because there were statements in the media that people were continuing after the siren does not mean that this was the case. The claims may have been made to encourage such behaviour. Distinguishing easy platitudes from actual performance is not always simple. Our interpretation is partly dependent on where and when the reconstructions occurred. Reconstructions in 1940 and 1941 were more likely to have contained at least an element of exhortation; representations later in the war, particularly in plays and feature films, are more likely to have been used to create an authentic atmosphere in a scene: the audience saw what they knew to be happening in real life.

The production and arrival of the newspaper through the letterbox, on the newspaper stand or in the shop, was proof in itself of the message that the country was carrying on. Even when there was no written message, it was present in the physical existence of the paper. This was in stark contrast to what many had expected. Nevil Shute's novel, *What Happened to the Corbetts*, published in April 1939, portrayed the feared effects of war: as soon as air raids started many people did not go to work, no newspapers were printed and information was hard to come by. In fact, throughout the war there were high, and rising, newspaper sales. In 1939 ten and a half million national daily newspapers were sold. The *Daily Express* had a circulation of two million, and the *Daily Mail* and *Daily Mirror* both sold one and a half million copies a day. In 1939 the circulation of *The Times* was 213,000. During the war four out of five men and two out of three women read at least one newspaper every day.[64] One can assume that those who bought a paper read at least part of it, while other family members may also have looked at it. It is impossible to know which sections of a newspaper people actually read, how many believed what they read, and whether this had any effect on their behaviour.[65]

The press seamlessly merged facts and opinion. As early as 1 July 1940 the *Daily Herald* claimed that the 'main effect of these raids is this. We are getting used to them'.[66] When it reported that the government had 'bidden us to rejoice in the privilege' of sharing in the dangers of the Forces, it announced that the public (entirely undifferentiated) 'gladly accepts' this definition of its responsibility (with no evidence to support its claim).[67] During the 1940 blitzes on London it repeatedly announced that sirens did not stop work.[68] Along with claims of work continuing after the siren, the national press reported the bombing of Britain, although it was prevented by censorship from immediately naming cities, or, in the case of London, actual areas or targets; the whole nation, nevertheless, read reports of the regions under attack.[69] The press gave accounts not only of work continuing after the siren, but also of work after air raids. After the November 1940 blitzes on Coventry, the *Daily Mirror* published pictures of the burnt-out cathedral, destroyed shops and people trading in a makeshift fashion with the headline, 'A City Keeps its Faith – Goes on Working'.[70]

Local newspapers remorselessly reported on the whole gamut of daily activities that continued after the siren sounded, including petty crimes.[71] Often the reports were multi-functional, combining information, propaganda, entertainment and local interest. The traditional page filler of local weddings, and the new topic of carrying on after the siren, were linked perfectly in headlines such as 'Married During Raid'.[72] In mid-September 1940, when footballers at Selhurst Park continued playing for a minute or two after the siren sounded in order to finish a game and then sauntered off the pitch while supporters filed out chatting, apparently unperturbed, a local newspaper hailed their behaviour as proof of the 'calm spirit of the British people'.[73] Local newspapers carried headlines such as 'Daylight Raid Has Many Thrills', and 'Looking for Souvenirs Before All Clear', as well as graphic descriptions of dogfights, which the censor never banned.[74]

The local press provided accounts of people in the area who worked after the siren sounded, and presented it as normal and laudable behaviour. One editorial claimed that workers in practically every industry continued to work after the siren sounded, so that the Nazi tactic of paralysing production in essential industries was doomed to failure. The paper went on to assert that many wasted hours had been eliminated and 'another of the dictator's projects for helping in the defeat of this country has been nullified by the loyalty and pluck of the British workers'.[75]

Accompanying the accounts of people continuing activities after the siren, newspaper reports tended to downplay the risks of air raids. One local paper put the dangers of working after the siren and the risk involved in the context of the risks and dangers of ordinary work and accidents which occurred on a daily basis, unrelated to war risks.[76] In 1942 the editor of the *Kent Messenger* rationalised the risk of not taking cover with a comment, which may or may not have been made to him,

> First Jerry has got to get to England, then he has to find Kent, and of all the towns in Kent he's got to pick just the one I live in, then he's got to find my street, and having found it to pick out my particular house, and if he can do all that and drop a bomb on me, well it's just too bad.[77]

Nothing could surpass the drama of actual raids, and the message was how well people were coping, and how little they were affected by the raids.

Newspaper text was complemented by visual material, either photographs or cartoons. One of the most popular cartoons was Giles in the

4.1 'Never mind about it not being 'arf wot we're giving them – let's git 'ome.'

Daily Express and *Sunday Express*. Giles had started his career as an animator, and his cartoons had the quality of a moving image. He drew them in a rectangular panel shaped like a cinema screen; his backgrounds were precise, rather like stage settings, and he always identified with ordinary, unpretentious people.[78]

On 27 February 1944 a *Sunday Express* cartoon by Giles captured an older (although not elderly) working-class woman's cheerful unwillingness to be disturbed by Hitler when she is in the street one evening with an air raid in progress, and her husband pleads: 'Never mind about it not being 'arf wot we're giving them – let's git 'ome' (see figure 4.1). In this cartoon, traditionally heroic and abstract values: patriotism and bravery, are personified and made concrete in an unheroic character: these are no longer the qualities of a remote, male, youthful, military elite, but of an older, working-class woman. The challenge to gender stereotypes is strengthened by the husband, not the wife, holding the two children. The message about the qualities of the working class would have been understood by lovers of Giles' cartoons: they would have known that in contrast he drew the upper-class as buffoons; as conservative, elderly and out of date; or as unpleasant characters. This cartoon presents, in an amusing and memorable way, an image that it would take

4.2 'I said the air-raid warning's sounded: pass it on ...'

a string of words to convey: feisty, determined, brave, tough, spirited, indomitable, intrepid, doughty and standing ground in danger. In this one cartoon, we see reconstructed and interpreted what politicians, journalists and film-makers spent the entire war attempting to convey.

That cartoons could appear of people in air raids also suggests that it was not a subject beyond the pale of decency to comment upon (see figure 4.2).

There were never, in contrast, cartoons of people killed and maimed in air raids. It is worth pointing out that the cartoon of the old men, presumably deaf and certainly blithely ignoring the siren, contrasts with the evidence of older people being more edgy about air raids than younger people. None of these are subversive cartoons; they are part of the dominant media presentation of people coping in air raids.

As with the production of newspapers, the BBC as messenger came to embody and symbolise the message. Like newspapers, the BBC demonstrated a commitment to carrying on during raids. Its example and message reached most of the population. (Ninety per cent of households had a radio.) The BBC set an example by adopting the policy of continuing to broadcast during air raids, at some expense to its employees' life and limb.[79] Although on occasions broadcasting was interrupted during a raid, for technical reasons, there were also live commentaries from the roof of Broadcasting House, describing air raids over London. On 8 September 1940 Thomas Chalmers and Raymond Glendinning provided panoramic, graphic, awesome, exciting and dramatic, but not frightening, commentaries on the bombing over Woolwich and the docks. That they could broadcast their commentaries live from central London (Broadcasting House is close to Oxford Circus) demonstrated that the bombing was geographically contained, and did not prevent the rest of London from working.[80]

Talks and sketches spoke of people continuing with their work and other activities during and after raids. When Virginia Cowles spoke on the BBC Home Service of carrying on during an air raid, she pointed to women who carried on, and asserted 'Bravery is not a quality that people are born with. Bravery is determination'. She gave the example of her maid and her secretary, who both carried on with their work the day the heavy raids began on London. At first her secretary's hands were trembling, but she got used to the noise and within ten minutes she was calm and composed, 'as though the noise outside were nothing more than the celebrations on Empire Day'.[81] The BBC also broadcast interviews with people coping well with the after-effects of heavy raids, interviews that were down to earth, reassuring, forward looking but riddled with clichés.[82] When listeners switched off the BBC and went out to the cinema, the sounds of people carrying on in air raids were enhanced by visual images.

Trawling the narratives, *mis-en-scène*, characterisations and composition of British wartime films does not reveal 'deep psychological dispositions' of the British, as Kracauer argued was the case in 1920s German films.[83] There is no 'secret history' of the period revealed in these films. Neither is there oblique symbolism, as Monaco detected in films, or psychological dimensions, as Bergman argued, that help us to understand people's behaviour at the time.[84]

When we move from the implicit to the explicit, however, we see people behaving on screen in air raids as they did in real life. In this sense, we see art reconstructing life. The idealised British characteristics of many of those on screen, however, are a fiction of the film-makers. Whether these characterisations are a reconstruction of what the British wished or believed themselves to be like, we do not know. Many in the audience would have recognised elements of their own behaviour in air raids, but there was no confusing the fictional and real worlds, and this must have contributed to the enormous popularity of the films, for, as Allen and Gomery have argued, the distance between the film and the real world is an important part of people's enjoyment of film.[85]

Wartime films rarely portrayed civilians at work, although there were cinema images of people carrying on at work after the siren sounded until roof spotters gave the warning. *In Which We Serve* (1942), *The Demi-Paradise* (1943) and *Waterloo Road* (1944) have shots of people who are not at work and who do not take cover when the siren sounds. In all these feature films, such images were incidental to the main themes of the films, and film critics did not comment on them in their reviews. It would be a mistake, however, to assume that critics reflected the reactions of anyone but themselves, and so we have no idea what these images meant to audiences. Although all these films were popular, this gives no indication of what impact, if any, they had on cinema-goers.

In the film *In Which We Serve*, none of the three women at home in an air raid on Plymouth take cover in a shelter, although the one who goes under the stairs (a common practice in the blitzes on Plymouth) is the only one of the three to survive. In *Waterloo Road* there is a brief scene where people are going to the shelter one evening at Waterloo Station after the siren has sounded. One couple, with a light-hearted (rather than heroic) air, comment that they're going to the cinema, not the shelter. The soldier husband and the wide boy (a flashy civilian, making money by dubious, normally black-market, means) – who is trying to steal the soldier's wife – ignore air-raid shelter signs and the heavy air raid in progress as they fight over the wife. They both survive the fight and the air raid. In *The Demi-Paradise*, which discussed the British character in an explicit, and perhaps rather heavy-handed fashion, there is a scene that depicts men and women civilians of all ages calmly ignoring the siren. At the start of the film, a Russian, played by Laurence Olivier, dislikes the British but, following a series of experiences in England, he changes his mind. Angus Calder claimed that it was as a result of the Russian observing the behaviour of the British in air raids that he changed his mind, but my reading of the film is that the air raid was only one of a number of factors, including an ability to laugh at oneself; an understated sense of duty; a warmth that is not immediately apparent; and continuity in local rituals, which altered the Russian's view of the British.[86] Film-makers' non-sensational treatment, as Chapman has noted, was typical, certainly from the middle years of the war, of all the 'great' British films set during the war,[87] and, as we have seen, of the way in which newspapers reported civilians in air raids. Documentaries and newsreels treated air raids in a similar fashion.

Humphrey Jennings's *Fires Were Started* (1943) is a riveting reconstruction of behaviour in a heavy raid during one night of the 1940–41 London blitzes. It depicts people, all with their own individual characteristics, continuing with their normal routine and duties in a collective effort in the most extraordinary of circumstances. Jennings did not film in real time, but he did use real firemen, real locations and real incidents. William Sansom, a journalist who worked as a fireman during the blitzes, was certain that 'the film was true to life in every respect', but as Aldgate and Richards have argued, the film transcends reality, as it celebrates the heroism of ordinary people, their individuality and their culture.[88]

Newsreels were both visual and aural (there was always a commentary, typically spoken with great urgency in an upper-class accent) and comprised a series of short items, so they did not require much concentration. Items in newsreels tell us what the five newsreel companies deemed newsworthy, topical and important to show the nation. Some were explicitly educational, for instance, *What to Do in an Air Raid*, but, far more often, newsreels presented news items in tones that sounded as if they wanted to uplift and encourage the nation, although the effect may well have been merely to irritate. Newsreels frequently referred to people 'carrying on', although this usually meant after, rather than during, air raids, for example in August 1940 at Bristol docks and in Croydon, and in September 1940 in London. In November 1940, one newsreel showed factories carrying on after bombing. The slogan 'Business as Usual' conveyed the same message in language revived from the First World War. One newsreel commentary, which followed shots of bomb damage to Canterbury Cathedral, proceeded to run 'carrying on' during an air raid into 'carrying on' after air raids at factories: 'Britain carries on during the raids . . . and this is one of many factories that are carrying on after the bombing.' In September 1940 a newsreel showed that the filming of the feature film *Kipps* continued after an air-raid warning, and the newsreel then went on to 'all types of work' continuing after the siren with roof spotters. Over the course of 1940 and 1941 newsreel commentaries became more propagandist and unpopular, although their growing unpopularity may have been more to do with the fact that the news on the war front went from bad to worse. Features on working through the siren and roof spotters came at a time when most people still approved of newsreels.[89]

Events that featured on a newsreel gained a far wider audience than those who actually experienced them first hand; they had an immediacy with which newspapers, but not feature films, could compete; and they showed people around the country what those in other areas were experiencing (except when images were censored, as for instance after the March 1941 blitzes on Plymouth). Whether people were only interested when their own city or area was mentioned; whether they chatted through the newsreel until the feature film came on; or whether they watched them avidly, we do not know; presumably, people did all these things. Just as most people stayed in their seats at the cinema during air raids, so too did the far smaller proportion of the population who attended those theatres that remained open.

Theatres initially closed on the outbreak of war, but quickly reopened. Some performances continued during raids on London, so actors and actresses worked through air raids; the Windmill Theatre and the Unity Theatre kept their doors open during the blitzes on London, while some theatres cut down performances to matinées only, during periods of heavy raids. During the flying bombs in 1944, eight theatres remained open for the entire period. Theatres were as likely as any other building in London to be hit: The Little, Queen's, and Shaftesbury were all destroyed, and the Duke of York's, Old Vic and Royal Court were badly damaged.[90]

In Terence Rattigan's *Flare Path*, which opened in London in August 1942 (after all the major ports, industrial centres and historic cities had experienced air raids), there is a passing comment about people getting used to air raids and ignoring them; it is not integral to the story line or character development, but, by slipping in a comment which would have resonated with many in the audience, it contributes to the authentic wartime atmosphere of the play, which is exploring the impact of war on relationships:

> Doris: The sirens have just gone in Skillingworth . . .
> Peter: Purely as a matter of idle interest – is there a shelter here?
> Patricia: I don't know. If there is I don't suppose anyone would bother to use it.
> Peter: I suppose if I'd been in England longer than a mere three months, I might become as blasé about raids as you are.[91]

Much of the contemporary material about people's reactions in air raids comes from 1940–42, but the evidence relates to the period before and after heavy raids, and there does not seem to have been any greater fear or unwillingness to carry on after the siren sounded after people had experienced blitzes. Contemporary material from 1944–45 during the period of V1s and V2s lays greater emphasis on fear and panic. In part, this evidence reflects the fact that initially there was a widespread assumption that people would panic and would find it very hard to cope with raids; when most people stood up to raids this was something to be commented upon, as it was something of a surprise. By the later stages of the war it was assumed that people would not panic in raids, and therefore where there was evidence of stress and panic it tended to be remarked upon, as this was now more surprising. People did find V1s and V2s terrifying, because of their unpredictability and of the helplessness people felt in the face of them.[92] Even so, evidence still points to most people wanting to carry on as far as possible in raids. When the doodlebug campaign started, there was a noticeable fall-off in production, but it soon picked up. Absenteeism due to workers' anxiety about their homes (repairing homes when hit, as well as evacuation) was the main reason why production fell – not people leaving their work stations following the air-raid siren. Alarm periods for taking cover in factories were actually less than during piloted aircraft raids. In the later stages of the war, many factories used roof spotters and a final 'crash dive' signal. Some firms tried to maintain production by organising a system for informing workers when their homes were damaged, and by helping them undertake urgent repairs.[93]

Most people did not go to the shelter on the sound of the public air-raid warning. Behaviour was never as homogeneous, however, as the media reconstructions, for not everyone reacted in the same way or at the same pace (as this chapter and chapter 3 have demonstrated). In the chapters 5 and 6 we will analyse in detail the factors that enabled most people to continue after the siren. In chapter 5 we will focus on the industrial experience and see in detail how the system of roof spotters facilitated working after the siren.

Notes

1 For example, Mick Jackson, *Five Boys* (Faber and Faber, 2001).
2 A useful study is Julian Andrews, *London's War: The Shelter Drawings of Henry Moore* (Lund Humphries, 2002).
3 Quoted in Adrian Lewis, 'Henry Moore's "Shelter Drawings": memory and myth', in Pat Kirkham and David Thoms (eds), *War Culture: Social Change and Changing Experience in World War Two* (Lawrence and Wishart, 1995), pp. 120–1.

4 Bristol Record Office, Bristol City Council Minutes Emergency Committee, 7 December 1940; Teeside Record Office, DC/ST/2/69, Stockton Borough Council Emergency Committee, 20 January 1942.
5 National Archives, Kew, formerly Public Record Office (hereafter PRO), PRO INF 1/292, Weekly Home Intelligence Reports (WHIR), 4–11 December 1940.
6 E. Doreen Idle, *War Over West Ham* (Faber and Faber, 1943), pp. 52–4.
7 *Croydon Times* 21 September 1940.
8 *City Press* 23 August 1940, 25 October 1940.
9 Inez Holden, *It Was Different at the Time* (Bodley Head, 1943), p. 85.
10 W. C. Berwick Sayers, *Croydon and the Second World War* (Croydon Corporation, 1949), pp. 42–3.
11 *Westminster and Pimlico News* 27 September 1940.
12 Manchester Central Library Archives and Local Studies, City of Manchester Emergency Committee, 26 September 1940, Harry Haig, Regional HQ to R. H. Adcock, Town Clerk, Manchester, 23 September 1940.
13 Greenwich Heritage Centre, Borough of Woolwich Emergency Committee, 9 September, 30 September and 7 October 1940.
14 Tower Hamlets, Local History and Archives (THLHA), Bethnal Green General Emergency and Finance Committee, BG 701, 18 September 1940.
15 THLHA, SN/EMER/2, Stoke Newington Emergency Committee, 13 September, 3 October, 7 October, 9 October 1940.
16 Richmond upon Thames Local Studies Library (RuTLSL). Borough of Richmond, Surrey Emergency Committee Report to Council, 8 October 1940.
17 RuTLSL, Borough of Barnes Town Council meeting, 9 October, and 11 October 1940, vol. 48.
18 Kensington Central Library, Kensington Emergency Committee, 6 February 1941.
19 THLHA, BG 701, Bethnal Green General Emergency and Finance Committee, 12 September 1940.
20 THLHA, Metropolitan Borough of Shoreditch, S/A/2 ARP (Civil Defence) Committee minutes, 15 October 1940.
21 THLHA, SN/EMER/2, Emergency Committee, 23 October 1940.
22 *Croydon Times*, 21 September 1940.
23 University of Sussex Mass-Observation Archive, FR 408, Human Adjustment in Air Raids, September 1940; *The Times* 7, 11 September 1940; *Croydon Times* 21 September 1940; *Mitcham and Tooting Advertiser* 24 October 1940; *Surrey Comet* 6 November 1940.
24 Mass-Observation Archive, 23/5/B, Public Reactions to Air Raids in London.
25 Mass-Observation Archive, 65/5/A, 15 September 1940, Report on Sydenham and Lewisham.
26 Mass-Observation Archive, TC, Air Raids 12/C.
27 Mass-Observation Archive, TC, Air Raids 12/C.
28 Greenwich Heritage Centre, Borough of Greenwich ARP Emergency Committee, 14 December 1943; *Wimbledon Borough News* 23 August 1940.

29 Mass-Observation Archive, FR 408, Human Adjustment in Air Raids, September 1940.
30 Mass-Observation Archive, Air Raids, TC 65/3/G, 30 August 1940, and TC 65/4/A, 3 September 1940, London Survey.
31 *Mitcham News and Mercury* 30 August 1940.
32 Mass-Observation Archive, 23/5/B, Public Reactions to Air Raids in London, Night of Wednesday–Thursday 28–29 August 1940.
33 Mass-Observation Archive, FR 408, Human Adjustment in Air Raids, September 1940.
34 Sonia Orwell and Ian Angus, *The Collected Essays, Journalism and Letters of George Orwell. vol. II. My Country Right or Left 1940–1943* (Secker and Warburg, 1968), p. 374, 17 September 1940.
35 *The Times* 30 October, 16 November, 6 December 1940; *Western Evening Herald* 14 October 1940.
36 Mass-Observation Archive, 23/5/B, August 1940, Public Reactions to Air Raids in London; *Lewisham Borough News* 10 December 1940.
37 Mass-Observation Archive, FR 408, Human Adjustment in Air Raids, September 1940.
38 *Tooting, Balham, Mitcham and Colliers Wood Gazette* 7 September 1940.
39 *Bristol Evening Post* 23 October 1940.
40 *Tooting, Balham, Mitcham and Colliers Wood Gazette* 12 October 1940.
41 *South London Press* 6 September 1940.
42 *Thames Valley Times* 4 September 1940.
43 *Catholic Herald* 6, 20 September 1940.
44 *The Times* 27, 28 August 1940.
45 *The Times* 26 October 1940.
46 *The Times* 7 September 1940.
47 *Western Mail* 5 September, 19 October 1940.
48 Mass-Observation Archive, Air Raids, 23/10/C, Newcastle.
49 Mass-Observation Archive, Air Raids, 23/10/S, Swansea.
50 Mass-Observation Archive, Air Raids, TC 23/8/A, Reactions to Air Raids as Observed by Citizens Advice Bureaux.
51 Chris McCooey (ed.), *Despatches from the Home Front. The War Diaries of Joan Strange 1939–1945* (Monarch Publications, 1989), p. 45.
52 Mass-Observation Archive, TC, Air Raids, 23/8/1, Bristol, 28 August 1940, 2, 4, 8 September 1940; *Bristol Evening Post* 9 August 1940.
53 Liverpool Record Office, Civil Defence Emergency Committee Minute Book, 352/MIN/DEF/1/6, 18 September 1940.
54 Glamorgan Record Office, City of Cardiff, vol. 12, BCC/C/6/79, Civic Buildings and Markets, Committee, 10 December 1940.
55 Birmingham Central Library, Birmingham Record Office, BCC Emergency Committee, 11 September 1940, 27 September 1940, 17 October 1940, 15 November 1940.
56 Teeside Record Office, Borough of Redcar, DC/RE/2/10/2, Emergency Committee Diaries, 30 September; Stockton Borough Council, DC/ST/2/69,

Emergency Committee, 4 October; Borough of Middlesbrough, CB/M/C/2/ 111, 4 October 1940.

57 Portsmouth City Record Office, CCM40A/3, War Emergency Committee, 6 November, 21 December 1940, 12 May 1941.

58 Glamorgan Record Office, City of Cardiff, vol. 12, BCC/C/6/79, Proceedings of the Libraries Committee, 10 October 1940.

59 Manchester Central Library Archives and Local Studies, Emergency Committee, 3 October 1940; Birmingham Central Library, Birmingham Record Office, BCC Emergency Committee, 15 November 1940, 17 January 1941.

60 Helen D. Millgate, *Mr Brown's War* (Sutton Publishing, 2003), p. 237.

61 *Picture Post* 7 December 1940, various letters.

62 Helen D. Millgate, *Mr Brown's War*, p. 81.

63 PRO HO 192/1200, Birmingham and District Local Production Defence Committee.

64 John Stevenson, *British Society 1914–1945* (Penguin, 1984), pp. 402–5; Dennis Griffiths, *The Standard* (Macmillan, 1996), p. 298.

65 James Curran and Jean Seaton, *Power Without Responsibility* (Routledge, 1997), p. 68. The readership of many newspapers divided along class lines. Sections of the middle class read *The Times*. The working class read the popular press, such as the *Daily Herald*, *Daily Express* and *Daily Mail*; a cross-section of society read the *Daily Mirror* at the start of the war, although by the late 1940s it had lost its middle-class readership.

66 *Daily Herald* 1 July 1940.

67 *Daily Herald* 3 July 1940, editorial.

68 *Daily Herald* 11, 18, 28 September 1940. While the same newspaper (along with many others) reported with satisfaction the RAF's successful bombing of German targets, such as the marshalling yards at Hamm, it claimed that the *Luftwaffe* missed its strategic targets. Indeed, on a number of occasions the press would balance reports of German bombings missing their targets over Britain with items in the same edition claiming successes for the RAF over Germany, successes that were impossible for the reader to verify. *Daily Herald* 1, 3 July 1940. Compare too the *Yorkshire Post* report that many German bombs fell in open country, with accounts of the RAF's precision bombing of Berlin: 8, 17 June 1940; *Daily Express* 5 June, 25 June, 14 August, 28 August; *Express and Echo* (Exeter) 24 September 1940.

69 *Daily Express* 7, 19, 26 June, 27 and 28 August 1940.

70 *Daily Mirror* 18 November 1940.

71 *Croydon Times* 19 October 1940.

72 *South London Press* 27 August 1940.

73 *Croydon Times* 14 September 1940.

74 *Wimbledon Borough News* 20 September 1940.

75 *Croydon Times* 28 September 1940.

76 *Wimbledon Borough News* 22 November 1940.

77 H. R. Pratt Boorman, *Hell's Corner: Kent Becomes the Battlefield of Britain* (Kent Messenger, 1942), p. 23.

78 Peter Tory, *Giles: A Life in Cartoons* (Headline, 1992), pp. 37, 43.
79 Bruce Belfrage, *One Man in His Time* (Hodder and Stoughton, 1951), p. 112; Asa Briggs, *The History of Broadcasting in the United Kingdom. vol. 3. The War of Words* (Oxford University Press, 1995), p. 268.
80 British Library National Sound Archive, 3381, LP 3381f2, 8 September 1940.
81 Virginia Cowles, 'The women of Britain home service, 10 September', *The Listener* (26 September 1940), p. 462.
82 British Library, National Sound Archive, 12607, LP 9200b3, 2 May 1941, Plymouth air raids.
83 Siegfried Kracauer, *From Caligari to Hitler: A Psychological History of the German Film* (Princeton University Press, 1947, republished 2004). pp. v, 5.
84 Paul Monaco, *Cinema and Society* (Elsevier, 1976); Andrew Bergman, *We're in the Money: Depression America and its Films* (New York University Press, 1971).
85 Robert C. Allen and Douglas Gomery, *Film History: Theory and Practice* (Knopf, 1985).
86 Angus Calder, *The Myth of the Blitz* (Pimlico, 1991).
87 James Chapman, 'Cinema, propaganda and national identity: British film and the Second World War', in Justine Ashby and Andrew Higson (eds), *British Cinema, Past and Present* (Routledge, 2000), p. 194. For more detailed discussion of wartime films, see James Chapman, *The British at War: Cinema, State and Propaganda, 1939–45* (I. B. Tauris, 1998); for more discussion of *Millions Like Us*, see Sue Harper, 'The representation of women in feature films, 1939–45', in Philip Taylor (ed.), *Britain and the Cinema in the Second World War* (Macmillan, 1988).
88 Anthony Aldgate and Jeffrey Richards, *Britain Can Take It: The British Cinema in the Second World War* (Edinburgh University Press, 1994), pp. 220–37.
89 Nicholas Reeves, *The Power of Film Propaganda: Myth or Reality?* (Cassell, 1999) p. 162.
90 Simon Trussler, *British Theatre: Cambridge Illustrated History* (Cambridge University Press, 2000), p. 301.
91 Terence Rattigan, *The Collected Plays of Terence Rattigan. vol. 1* (Hamish Hamilton, 1968) Flare Path, Act II, Scene 1. The play formed the basis of the film *The Way to the Stars*.
92 Art McCulloch (compiler), *The War and Uncle Walter: The Diary of an Eccentric* (Doubleday, 2003), p. 269, 24 February 1944; p. 279, 22 June 1944.
93 PRO HO 207/20.

5

Roof spotters

Introduction

A single photograph taken for the Ministry of Supply (responsible for equipping the army) shows an idealised roof spotter (see figure 5.1). This spotter, taken on the roof of a Ministry of Supply factory, is clearly posed: he is looking through binoculars into the sun. The photographer has taken the shot from below the man, which along with his open-neck shirt revealing his hairy chest, his rolled-up sleeves, and his powerful body with legs astride, emphasises that he is a tower of working-class masculinity and strength. This is a man exuding, and creating, confidence. The photograph is suggestive of what is happening outside the frame: it is a factory working productively, without fear. The photograph is making silent reference to politicians' and journalists' loud calls to carry on after the siren, and to the language of 'front-line' civilians. The style of the photograph is similar to the British documentary tradition, with a dignified image of a working-class man, but it is closer to the socialist realism of photographers working in the Soviet Union. Although we do not know the name of the photographer, it is not surprising that s/he may have been influenced by photographic techniques from Russia. One does not need to be able to read another language to appreciate styles emanating from other countries.[1] The sharp, clear-cut image of the roof spotter was in reality at odds with the diversity of roof spotters and the complexity of the system.

The national agreement for working after the siren was reached on the understanding that raid spotters would be used to give warning of approaching enemy aircraft. Roof spotters who were already in a firm's employment continued to receive the wages for their normal grade or job. Spotters who were in a reserved occupation did not lose their reserved status when they became full-time or part-time spotters. Spotters who were aged over thirty or who were not in a reserved occupation could have their call-up deferred if the employer made out a case for them that was supported by the government department concerned with the firm's work.[2]

5.1 Roof spotter on a Ministry of Supply factory

While the principle of using raid spotters was straightforward, the system was infinitely varied, and often complex. Spotting differed from area to area, firm to firm, and institution to institution. Firms, offices and shops, and even schools, adapted the system to meet their particular needs. At one firm of printers in London, spotters did not go on the roof until the public alarm was given; they warned workers of an approaching aircraft with whistles. At a factory near Guildford, making vehicles for the army, a roof spotter was on duty from dawn until dusk. The alert was given by three short rings on the works' bell; when spotters saw enemy aircraft approaching they sounded a siren. At night the gatekeeper gave the alert, and an officer of the factory's fire brigade gave the alarm.[3] In the centre of London, roof spotters could gain additional help by keeping an eye on what other spotters were doing; in addition, a red flag, hoisted on Bush House when danger was imminent, was seen by a number of spotters.[4] Some spotters gave information not only to their own firm but also to others in the vicinity. At the Royal Naval College at Greenwich, for example, as soon as V1 (doodlebug) attacks started in June 1944, roof spotters were placed on the chapel dome, from where the chapel bell was rung as a warning. Local people quickly made use of this warning, which was relayed further afield by a whistle, hooter or bell.[5]

There were variations in the type of look-out post (or crow's nest as it was called); whether sound detectors were used; whether spotters worked in pairs or singly; whether there was always a spotter on duty or only after the public warning had sounded; the type of signal given by spotters, and whether visible signals were given; and whether employees ducked at their work station or ran for shelter when the spotter gave the alarm.

In some areas, fire-watching and roof spotting duties were combined, although this was not recommended: spotters and watchers could not look up and down at the same time. On railway lines fire-watchers and spotters doubled up and fire-watchers' posts were used for both sets of duties.[6] In some places the Fire Brigade and Auxiliary Fire Service attended lectures on both fire-watching and roof spotting.[7] There were some similarities between roof spotters and fire-watchers: they did not wear a uniform; the work could be lonely, boring, dangerous and uncomfortable. Roof spotting was not, however, compulsory. From early 1941, fire-watching, for up to forty-eight hours a month, was compulsory for men between the ages of sixteen and sixty who worked under sixty hours a week, and from 1942 it was compulsory for women up to the age of forty-five who worked under fifty-five hours a week. While there were plenty of women fire-watchers, there were few women roof spotters. Roof spotting was carried out instead of normal work-time duties, not in addition; roof spotting had a positive image that was linked with a popular hobby and the excitement of flight; and for some spotters there were clubs and tests that provided a sense of belonging to a wider organisation – even if spotting was carried out alone. Fire-watching was, on the whole, unpopular, with no *esprit de corps*,[8] but there were exceptions: St Paul's Cathedral had a group of voluntary fire-watchers on duty throughout the war, and one of them wrote a book about their experiences. A small exhibition of their work is still on display in the cathedral, and there is a permanent memorial to them on the cathedral floor. In some cases fire-watching strengthened local community ties. On 31 December 1943, Walter Musto, who lived in a middle-class London suburb, noted in his diary, 'After four years of war friendships have been formed and now from our local fire-watchers comes the whispered beginnings of a neighbourhood social circle, born of the fire-watchers' rota'.[9] Not all fire-watching or roof spotting was lonely work. Some local firms linked up to provide information to each other, and in some cases the Royal Observer Corps (ROC) provided warnings to groups of firms, in what became known as industrial alarm schemes.

Industrial alarm schemes (IAS)[10]

Some industrial, commercial and government establishments jointly developed and funded alarm systems linked to the ROC, in order to gain detailed information about the direction and distance of enemy aircraft, which they then used in conjunction with roof spotters. They thereby gained warning independently of, and often in advance of, public air-raid warnings. Later in the war, many women with children were in paid work, and they did not like the fact that they received warnings at work before their children, who might be at home – in the street or at school – unaware of impending danger, but by now the system was firmly entrenched.[11]

The system started from scratch during the Battle of Britain, and was refined over the years. From the summer of 1940 to the summer of 1941 the scheme was negotiated and put in place; from then until early 1944 raids were sporadic, but on the whole there was less danger for those in industrial areas than during the early period. Towards the end of the war, from June 1944 until early 1945, danger and the intensity of the attacks reappeared in southern and south-east England with V1 and V2 flying bombs and rockets.[12]

Numerous firms joined industrial alarm schemes. In the London area, a number of well-known firms such as Plessey, the Ford Motor Co., Standard Telephones and Cables, the Bank of England, Bryant and May, the BBC, LMS Railway, McDougalls, Fraser and Chalmers Engineering Works, Woolwich Arsenal, Siemen Bros, Kodak, Metal Box, GEC, Hoover, and J. Lyons all joined schemes. Indeed, the London Civil Defence Region put pressure on firms to join an industrial alarm scheme. Firms who informed the Alarm Controller that they were not interested in joining a scheme received a stiffly worded letter, which included the warning, 'a spotting staff relying entirely on its own human powers is only half equipped, and it would seem that a certain moral responsibility attaches . . . to ensure that information from whatever source should be available to these men.'[13]

Those firms that supplemented roof spotters with an IAS were, on the whole, satisfied. In March 1941, at a meeting of firms in the London area, it was reported that the Sperry Gyroscope Co. found the scheme generally of the 'greatest assistance', but did not rely on it entirely, and still used roof spotters. D. Napier and Son relied on spotters and regarded the IAS as supplementary to spotters. Ford Motor Co. found that the system worked very well and never experienced any difficulty with it, and Plessey Co. reported that they were satisfied that it was a 100 per cent improvement on spotters. In contrast, Simmonds Aerocessories did not find the system of much use, except for giving the direction of aircraft. Frequently the public 'alert' was received two to three minutes before the call from the local Ack-Ack.[14] At one of Handley Page's aircraft factories, they had what management described as a 'very efficient spotter system' allied to six other key factories in the district, connected by a special telephone circuit; in addition, Handley Page provided sound locator equipment and were hooked up with the Ack-Ack, so as to receive the plotting of all enemy aircraft the moment that they reached the coast.[15]

From June 1944 onwards, when V1s started to terrorise southern and south-east England, many more firms in these regions adapted the IAS. As in the past, an alert was sounded for those who wished to take cover when enemy aircraft were thirty miles away. A second warning no longer gave people enough time to head for a shelter, and instead they 'crash-dived' under cover where they were working in order to protect themselves from blast, flying glass and debris.[16] The Ford Motor Co. at Dagenham had an extensive system of ARP and, from October 1940, a whole gang of roof spotters, with as many as nine pairs of spotters on duty at any one time. The fire brigade, fire-watchers and spotters all worked together under the supervision of thirty-five ARP wardens. By the time of the flying bombs, spotters could not only plot hostile aircraft, but also the height, colour and bearing of flares dropped by the enemy. It was common talk among the workers that they would rather be at work than at home, as they felt that they were much safer because of the ample warning they always received. When flying bombs were heard passing over the factory, the hitch-hiker's sign would often be given, accompanied by the remark, 'On your way'.[17] The industrial alarm and roof spotting systems were widespread throughout the war, but did they work?

Did roof spotting work?

The effectiveness of the system of spotters in maintaining production is impossible to assess accurately. Only anecdotal evidence, not nationwide statistics, is available. Once spotters, armed with binoculars, started to perch on factory roofs, it was claimed that there was a dramatic decline in some areas in the number of hours lost. On 8 October 1940 Clement Davies, a Liberal MP (1929–62), estimated that in one place he knew (possibly in his constituency, Montgomeryshire) there would had been a stoppage the previous week of twelve hours, but by having spotters on the roof, the actual stoppage time was under two hours. On 11 December 1940 Ralph Assheton, Parliamentary Secretary at the Ministry of Labour and National Service, claimed that many hours of work had been saved by spotters.[18] It was estimated that in Scotland over a two-year period, 1,341,884 working hours were saved.[19] At a Vickers' aircraft factory in Manchester, between September 1940 and September 1944, there were 287 alerts totalling 360 hours; during the same period the roof spotters' alarm was sounded only 41 times and the total time of stoppages was only 65 hours. The roof spotters therefore gained the factory 295 hours of work, mainly at night, which saved 600,000 working hours.[20] One MAP factory estimated that the IAS meant that it produced an additional 400 aero-engines. Working hours saved as a result of the industrial alarm scheme between 1940 and 1945 amounted to 1,000,000,000 – the equivalent, according to Herbert Morrison, of five infantry divisions. The scheme covered 15,000 factories, with a total warning staff of only 200. In London the scheme covered 2,500,000 workers, where there were 1,224 alerts averaging two hours each, but firms connected to the IAS were under warning for only a quarter of this time, so that 75 per cent of alert time was saved. During the flying bomb alerts, time saved reached 90 per cent of the alert time, and, for the whole country throughout the war, the saving was consistently 60 to 70 per cent.[21]

It is hard to unearth evidence of the system failing, but it did happen. A raid on Filton aerodrome in Bristol in early 1940 was thought to have 'seriously affected confidence' in the roof spotter system, because the spotter's warning did not allow enough time for workers to reach the shelters. As a result there were long stoppages during daytime alerts.[22] This was unusual, but it does underline the importance of workforces having faith in the system in order for it to be adopted and work effectively, and this is further illustrated by the case of London dock workers. Even when docks were hit, entailing the dangerous work of moving burning petrol and ammunition during raids, work continued, and dockers worked long hours of overtime. The Port of London Authority used ships' whistles to warn all dockers of approaching danger. When workers had a reliable system of warning, work continued. When there was uncertainty work would cease, and workers went to shelters for long periods. At Hay's Wharf, for example, work continued until a fault developed in the General Post Office (GPO) wires. The dockers refused to work until it had been repaired, which took seven hours.[23]

As with systems that relied solely on roof spotters, working after the public siren in a firm that was part of an industrial alarm scheme was meant to be voluntary, and the scheme was explained to workers in order to gain their co-operation. Firms displayed posters setting out what the different signals meant and the action workers should take.[24] Both images and written text were used in a variety of settings to explain the system and to gain the confidence of both the workforce as a whole and the team operating the system.

The industrial alarm scheme involved people working in different parts of a factory, on observation posts and in the control room. *Picture Post*, by presenting a series of photographs next to each other, graphically showed how people's work, despite being physically separate, was part of an integrated system (see figures 5.2–5.8).

A series of photographs conveys an action-packed sequence across a factory that an individual photograph of a roof spotter, such as appeared in other publications, could not achieve. The cinematic quality in the movement, sequence and narrative removes any sense of this being an isolated instant, as can be the case in single photographic images. The captions reinforce the pictures by providing concise commentary. The written text uses adjectives in its description of the system that reinforce the message: the system is 'foolproof', the observers are 'trained' and 'reliable', and the reports are 'accurate'. Labels superimposed on various members of the team contribute to the information in the pictures. While there is some accompanying text, it cannot compete with the arresting images. It is easier to understand the system once it is shown in pictures. Whereas most other photographs of roof spotters show clearly identifiable individuals, the roof spotter in *Picture Post* (Figure 5.2) is barely visible; yet instead of diminishing the interest of the picture, it is increased. We see the isolation of the spotter observing the sky from an ugly industrial steel ventilator on top of a building, which offers him the opportunity for doing his job and protects him, and the ordinary life of the city that needs preserving is hinted at in the background. *Picture Post* frequently criticised and harried the government (over training for the Home Guard, adequate shelter protection, and the privileges of the few that meant poverty and risk for the many). Yet, it carried a photographic

5.2 The eyes in the ventilator: a rooftop observer at his post

narrative of the IAS, which through its explanation, promoted the system. *Picture Post*'s carefully constructed explanatory pictorial narrative is rational and thoughtful, and relies far less on emotion and suggestion than the image of a roof spotter with which this chapter opened. The historian thus not only learns about how the system worked, but

5.3 Where the whole system is worked: inside central control

5.4 Keeping track of ARP

5.5 Keeping track of the bombs

also that it was supported by a wide range of opinion that included those who were frequently on opposite sides of the political divide. John Roberts interpreted the British and US documentary movements of the 1930s (which included *Picture Post*) as grounded in democratic paternalism.[25] This sequence is a case in point. Although *Picture Post*'s images of the working class in the 1930s tended to present them as passive and living in broken Northern communities, ravaged by unemployment, these wartime images tell the story of a people and system that are active and integrated. They are, nevertheless, quite conservative images: the working class are actively taking control of their destiny in the context of a firm, and by extension the nation, not of their class. The cinematic qualities of the *Picture Post* essay can be compared with moving-images' treatment of roof spotting and the industrial alarm system.

In *Millions Like Us* (1943) there is a five-minute sequence that depicts an industrial alarm scheme and roof spotters. These scenes were shot at an aircraft factory at Castle Bromwich, so it is reasonable to assume that the scenes were an accurate description of the way in which the system worked. The film had originally been conceived as a documentary propaganda film, but it was then enlarged and altered into a full-scale feature film. The industrial alarm scheme, raid spotters on the roof, and workforce taking cover in what appears to be a rather flimsy surface

5.6 A plane is coming: the rooftop observer phones

shelter, is one of the sequences that most closely resembles a documentary approach. It is an extremely clear depiction of the system. At the end of the sequence, the words ‘no hits, no damage, no casualties’ are heard, which suggests that part of the purpose of the sequence is to show the safety of the system. The film sends out a number of reassuring messages,

5.7 The men who take the call

about life in hostels, about the importance of the work, and the safety of the industrial alarm scheme.

Reviewers commented on the realism of the film, although it is impossible to know whether any of them had ever stepped inside a factory. Only one reviewer made any mention of the sequence, by including 'the ordeal of their first air raid' in a list of what the film showed.[26] Given that the sequence is vivid and detailed, and appears to be an accurate depiction of the actual system, it must have been familiar to many watching it, and this would have added to the films 'authenticity' for those already in industrial war work. By the time the film appeared, agreements had long been reached and practices established regarding working after the siren, so it is unlikely that this sequence could have influenced attitudes and practices. Air raids were already becoming identified with 1940–41, for when the warning to take cover is given, one of the women remarks, 'It's like old times'. By 1943 the risks to production and to workers from air raids were not as great as they had been earlier in the war, and other problems, such as labour shortages, unofficial strikes and absenteeism, had crowded on to the productivity graph. It is unlikely, therefore, that the sequence was intended as a key message of the film.

5.8 The siren is sounded

Reviewers commented on the film's more general themes, such as love, class relations and the role of women in the war, and on its realism, especially the way in which it portrayed the working class, not as cut-out clowns or cardboard patriotic heroes. Reviewers did not devote attention to the air-raid scene, which does not push the story along or develop the characters, although it is a convenient device for highlighting relationships.[27] The scene, so extraordinary to a later audience, was so embedded in wartime culture that it was not thought worth mentioning. To a later generation of historians watching the film, it is an interesting contemporary visual depiction of a quintessentially wartime experience that cannot be repeated in peacetime.

Individual firms also made efforts to ensure that workers understood and had faith in the system. At the Royal Arsenal at Woolwich, in order to correct an impression, widespread at the outset of V1 attacks, that almost every loud-sounding missile had passed directly overhead and that insufficient warnings were being given, works' committee representatives were invited to visit the roof spotters' cabin and control room, which was on the office roof. Soon after the group arrived, a raid began. They saw how bombs were plotted on the map, how many were brought down before reaching London, and how the warning was given for those that had not been shot down. They were asked to go outside the cabin and observe. They saw how evacuation to shelters was almost complete before they could pick up the distant hum of the doodlebug. Then, as the missile came nearer, the noise increased to a roar, the bomb was seen, its course watched breathlessly, until finally it dived to earth and exploded a good three-quarters of a mile away. After this incident, criticism of the warning system ceased.[28]

Although industrial alarm schemes were more sophisticated than lone spotters, the human factor – in terms of relationships and perceptions – was still important to the operation of the system, and this can best be illustrated by focusing on individual firms. The section below draws primarily on two sources, contrasting in their nature – one is a contemporary written source, and the other is a memory oral source – yet similar in their evidence. Both sources show the strict gender division of labour, not born of custom and practice but newly instituted, between male roof spotters and female teleplotters; the need for workers to have confidence in the system in order for it to operate effectively; the importance of local co-operation between firms; and the dangerous position in which a minority were placed in order to protect the majority.

Hawker's

In 1940 Hawker's, an aircraft factory in Kingston upon Thames that produced Hurricanes, the most numerous fighters in the Battle of Britain, engaged Edward Griffith to run their alarm system. Griffith in other circumstances was unlikely to have worked in a factory: he had been educated at Eton and Brasenose College, Oxford, from whence he had followed in his father's footsteps as a solicitor. He was unfit for military service, but, in 1940, at the age of thirty-six, Hawker's employed him to run its air-raid alarm system. At the end of the war, Griffith wrote a detailed account of the system. The scheme, which operated from 1940 to 1945, involved over 180 local firms as well as SHAEF HQ under General Eisenhower. Over the course of the war the alert sounded for 1,250 hours 59 minutes, but the 'take cover' warning lasted only 207 hours 41 minutes, so saving 1,043 hours 18 minutes of work time, not only at Hawker's, but also in all the other firms that were linked up to the scheme.

The IAS department consisted of controllers, roof spotters and teleplotters. Initially, there was a Chief Controller, a deputy and two assistant controllers, along with six teleplotters. In 1942, and again in early 1944, the number of staff was increased. At first the roof spotters were all Hawker's volunteers, but soon outsiders were appointed so that trained workers would not be diverted from production; in late 1940 the firm engaged full-time roof spotters who were always on the roof when the factory was working; from February 1942, the night shift continued on a full-time basis, but, during the day, volunteers from the drawing office were summoned by a signal, known as 'OWL', for observer's warning light, when enemy aircraft were plotted fifty miles away. (The OWL was also given to the ARP, AFS and Home Guard.)

All three roof spotters at Hawker's were ex-sailors, so they were used to working responsibly in a team at times of great danger, and they may also have gained knowledge of aircraft during their naval service. The controllers and teleplotters came from a wide range of backgrounds, but were overwhelmingly working class. The women had previously worked in shops and hotels, in the ATS, WAAF and NFS; one had been a mannequin, another a hairdresser, and one middle-class woman had worked at her husband's architectural practice. The previous occupation of only two of the controllers is known: one had been a solicitor (Griffith), and one had been a storekeeper on night shift. The range of previous occupations was not unusual in wartime, although the class mix was probably unlikely in other departments of the factory, where employees were distinctly management or workpeople. How well they got on together is impossible to tell, but Griffith rated most of them highly.

There was a wide age range, although the men tended to be older, and there was a clear distinction in the work that women and men undertook. Surviving information on the IAS staff shows that all the controllers were men, aged between thirty-three and forty-eight; the roof spotters were all men, aged between forty-eight and fifty-four; and the teleplotters were all women, aged between nineteen and thirty-seven. This gender division was a common feature of industrial alarm schemes.

Although the work was linked with the glamour of aviation and the RAF, working conditions were far from glamorous, and could be perilous. The controllers and teleplotters, engaged on highly responsible and potentially dangerous duties, worked in a concrete shelter, with artificial light and no direct access to fresh air. There was intense activity followed by long periods of waiting, during which there were practice drills, hourly tests of the telephone lines, and some office work for other departments. The spotters, meanwhile, were on the roof, protected only by sandbags and steel plates, in an exposed and uncomfortable position. Spotters were always the most exposed to danger. For them, there was no last-minute dash to the shelter. On 4 October 1940, when the Germans dropped a 500-lb bomb on the factory, the spotters did not budge from their post: here were men with more steel in their nerves than in their helmets.

How did the system work?

In October 1940, Hawker's opened a control room in an air-raid shelter adjoining an old police box at the works' entrance; a plotting board was installed and staff were taken on and trained in its use. By 11 November, private telephone lines from Bromley and Horsham were ready to supplement the line from the gun site. The Control staff started work, initially just in daytime, but from 8 December, when more had been trained, at night as well. From then until the 'stand down' in May 1945 the alarm control room was staffed day and night, without a moment's break.

For the system to work effectively, it was essential that everyone at Hawker's had faith in it: it was no good having a system with which some people would not comply, or one which caused industrial unrest when its whole *raison d'être* was to maintain production. One way of creating confidence in the system was for people to understand exactly how it worked. To this end, soon after communications with Bromley and Horsham had been established, members of both management and workpeople visited Bromley ROC Centre, where they were shown how the ROC picked up enemy aircraft over the Channel and over Europe by radar, a state-of-the-art system which the Germans did not at this point possess, and how the ROC then telephoned its information around the country. After the visit, both management and workpeople approved the industrial alarm system, and from then on everyone waited for the spotters to give the 'take cover' signal before they went to the shelters. Until then, it had been the rule rather than the exception to go to the shelters when the siren went off.

The ROC at Horsham and Bromley telephoned information to the teleplotters on the movements of enemy aircraft that the plotters then entered on a large-scale grid plan of south-east England. Aircraft were represented on the grid by counters that indicated the direction of each raid, the number of aircraft and their height. Circles drawn on the grid showed distances of six miles, fifteen miles, twenty miles and twenty-five miles from Kingston. The plotters set off a warning buzzer for the Factory Defence Services (FDS) – daytime roof spotters, Home Guard, NFS and ARP – when enemy aircraft approached within forty miles of Kingston.

At night, there were full-time roof spotters; during the day, part-time spotters went on the roof when they received the FDS warning. The roof spotters operated the take-cover warning. (When no roof spotter was on duty the alarm control room gave the take-cover signal.)

Hawker's organised a system whereby local firms were telephoned information on the plots of enemy aircraft, and in effect were given a running commentary on the progress of the raids. Each firm could decide when to take cover. Although it was quickly agreed that Hawker's would provide this service, it was not until May 1941 that the system was up and running, because of the difficulty of getting dedicated telephone lines installed when Post Office engineers were repairing bomb-damaged lines as well as installing extra ones. Gradually, more and more firms were added to this 'multiphone system'; firms that could not be linked direct to Hawker's (because of the limit on the number of telephone lines) were linked to another firm with an established link to Hawker's.

The system initially involved Hawker's, the Ministry of Aircraft Production and the Ministry of Home Security, along with thirty other firms, but, over the course of the war, it expanded considerably. Griffith commented on the goodwill that existed between firms over the operation of the system, evidenced by the fact that little was put in writing about the operation of the scheme. Even Griffith, a trained solicitor, did not see the need for the signed documentation normally associated with agreements between firms. For small firms to be part of a larger scheme was a great boon, as none of them could have run a scheme alone.

From 17 October 1940, whenever the take-cover warning was sounded in daylight, a chequered barrel was hoisted on top of the mast of the roof, to indicate that an attack was imminent. At the request of the Town Clerk and the Kingston Chamber of Commerce, Hawker's agreed that when their roof spotters sounded a 'take-cover' warning in the factory, a chequered board (later a drum) would be put up on the roof of the Guildhall, Bentall's departmental store, and Kingston County Hospital. So, the system combined state-of-the-art technical sophistication with very simple devices. This was a local system, adapted to local needs, between factories, shops and the council, which helped not only those with commercial and production needs but also the general public, bringing them together in a non-profit and non-commercial co-operative relationship.

Memories of a plotter

The memories of one plotter who worked for Fraser and Chalmers, an engineering firm in south-east London, which ran an industrial alarm system embracing seventeen firms by 1945, reinforces evidence from contemporary records. According to Eileen Rogers, before the IAS was introduced, everyone went to the shelters when the siren sounded, and stayed there, sometimes for hours, still receiving their pay. In 1941, Mrs Rogers became a plotter quite by accident; she was already working at Fraser and Chalmers when a friend decided to become a plotter and suggested that she join her; without any knowledge of what it entailed, she agreed. During the day the plotters were high up in an exposed part of the factory, just below the roof spotter, although at night they were at the gate. The plotters received information through their headphones that they plotted on grids; when 'hostiles' were within a certain distance they warned all the local firms by a bell and if the planes were plotted within a five-mile radius on the grid they rang the bell again and everyone took shelter.

There was a clear gender division of tasks. Eileen Rogers was one of four women plotters who worked in shifts, day and night, two plotters on and two plotters off; in addition, there was a male roof spotter during the day. She does not remember his job as being any more technical or responsible than that of the women plotters. Indeed, in comparison with what the plotters were doing she did not think that the roof spotter did an awful lot: he was interested in aircraft and would let them know what kinds of planes were passing overhead. She could not recall a single occasion when the plotters were not able to warn people in time. People 'relied on us to be exact. We never had no incidents'. In May 1945 the firm's ARP officer wrote to her, 'Your constant attention to your work has inspired confidence in all the employees to carry on in spite of Enemy Action', and the following month a letter on behalf of all the firms referred to the feeling of confidence which existed during periods of bombardment.[29] As with those who recall their time as roof spotters, Mrs Rogers does not dwell on the danger of the work. Although the plotters never took cover even when the signal was given that an attack was imminent she has no memory of fear, 'it was just a job . . . I never thought I could get bombed.'[30] One explanation for male roof spotters playing down any fear of danger is that the men did not want to admit to it to a woman, but in the case of Mrs Rogers there was no such gender-inspired factor. The above exploration of Hawkers and Mrs Rogers's experiences draw attention to two general aspects of the system: gender divisions and dangers, which are both worth further discussion.

Why the gender division?

Although men were taken away from their ordinary work for which they were trained, few women trained or worked as roof spotters. In contrast, while women rarely perched in crows' nests as roof spotters, they were used as teleplotters in firms that were linked to the ROC. Roof spotters and teleplotters could be equally at risk, for neither left their post when a raid was overhead, so the gender division of labour was not due to one activity being more dangerous than the other one. At one factory that was hit twice, one of the women control-room operators was blown off her seat and lost her headphones. The whole IAS was put out of action. Her first thought was to get in touch with the officer-in-charge, whom she eventually contacted by telephone. She was answered by a sleepy voice saying 'That was a near one – it shook us here'. She replied with heat 'It bloody well hit us'.[31] Teleplotting was very similar to work undertaken by WAAFs when they plotted the position of approaching enemy aircraft. Perhaps teleplotting was thought of as similar to women's work as telephonists, although the only connection between the two was that teleplotters received information by telephone. Even so, associating women with teleplotting does not explain why so few women were roof spotters. Teleplotting, and a host of other jobs on which women were employed during the war, required strong nerves, so it could not have been that women shied away from, or were protected from, dangers.

There is no evidence that on the rare occasions when women were roof spotters that they were less competent or more nervous then men spotters. Unusually, the Bank of England employed both men and women as spotters. On one occasion when a woman was on duty, a flying bomb, with engines still running, appeared out of a low cloud in a steep dive heading apparently straight for the spotters' post. Rushing into the post, the woman gave a 'crash dive' warning so that staff could get under their desks and lie flat. For some reason, the bomb swerved sharply at the last moment and crashed on to a building about fifty yards away. Although hundreds of windows were badly damaged in the Bank, and about 400 people were at work on the side of the building nearest to where the bomb landed, the only casualties were four people with slight cuts.[32]

Yet, there was definite antagonism to women spotters. There was such hostility to women as spotters that *The Aeroplane Spotter* carried an article supporting women spotters, and claiming that women had passed proficiency tests in aircraft recognition. It continued 'The fair sex is showing that it intends to tackle this new and unfamiliar job of aircraft recognition as thoroughly and with as much perseverance as it went about domestic duties in the past'.[33]

Women roof spotters and teleplotters were in a similar situation to that of numerous women who operated in a culture where gendered notions of people's appropriate contributions to the war remained strong.[34] As Philomena Goodman has argued, views about gender roles were stretched, not fractured, in wartime.[35] Sonya Rose has described the way in which gendered notions of patriotic involvement led some to argue that fire-watching should be an exclusively male preserve.[36] When women civilian pilots in the Air Transport Auxiliary first flew aircraft to RAF and Fleet Air Arm bases, there was hostility in the press, including *The Aeroplane*.[37] It may have been that gender stereotyping meant that workforces had more faith in male spotters, whom they assumed to be calmer and more knowledgeable than women, although we have no evidence that this was the case. There were, however, other reasons, which had nothing to do with stereotyping, that made spotting attractive to men. Roof spotting may have been more appealing than a tedious job on the shop floor, which is why some men would have wanted to keep it to themselves. Roof spotting, with its technical knowledge and potential danger, engendered an inward-looking male network. The ROC, which gave warning when enemy aircraft flew over the coast, was a men-only organisation until 1941, when the first women were admitted. These women faced hostility from groups of men who wanted to keep their close-knit posts to themselves but, as alternative demands for men's time and labour grew, it was impossible to hold out against women altogether and, in the latter stages of the war, women were essential to the ROC.[38] As we will see in more detail below, boys and men had an especial interest in aviation and aircraft recognition. Aeroplanes were associated with the glamour of the RAF, and this made roof spotting especially attractive to men and boys. The *frisson* of danger may have been attractive to younger men and boys in particular. As with the RAF, roof spotting had an unpleasant and dangerous downside.

Dangers of roof spotting

Roof spotting could be cold, lonely, boring, stressful and dangerous. While some doubted the efficacy of roof spotting or of training roof spotters, if a spotter was unable to make a correct judgement he or she would be the first to know it. Not for nothing did spotters discuss at a national conference whether they would hear a bomb before it hit them.[39]

Roof spotters were not only at risk from enemy attack, but also from far more mundane dangers, such as slipping off a ladder or roof. In the autumn of 1940, not long after roof spotters had been introduced, fifty-two-year-old Arthur Partner, a roof spotter for Allders, a departmental store in Croydon, died following injuries he sustained when he lost his footing on the roof in the dark and fell fifteen feet to the ground below. Part of the roof had been fenced to avoid such accidents occurring, but not the section from which Partner slipped. At the inquest the store claimed that Partner had been issued with a dim torch, but he did not have it with him, and a policeman pointed out that roof spotters – along with ARP personnel – were forbidden from using a torch after a siren had sounded at night. Allders subsequently finished fencing the roof, and the local press, alert to local civilian heroes, wrote in detail about Partner's bravery.[40] Younger roof spotters also died. In the autumn of 1944 Albert Okey, a twenty-three-year-old instrument maker, who had been a roof spotter for a year at an engineering firm in Southfields, south-west London, slipped and fell as he was climbing the steel ladder up to the crow's nest. He enjoyed roof spotting, he had climbed the ladder at least 100 times before, it was not wet or slippery, but he had been working at least fifty-three hours a week, so he must have been extremely tired.[41]

Looking back on the system, should the historian convey their own sense of the precariousness of the system? The language used to describe the system will affect the way the reader also perceives the system. A London firm of printers posted an official notice on 5 September 1940, in which they explained that spotters would 'take up positions' on the roof on receipt of the official air-raid warning. They would 'despatch messengers' over the building when immediate danger threatened, blowing their whistles while 'descending the buildings'.[42] As a historian, one would suspect that the official notice would be written in such a way as to convey calm and control, and indeed this one is written in the language of near-military order. The historian, in contrast, when describing the system, may wish to convey their own sense of the danger of the situation by replacing 'take up positions' with 'clambering', and replacing 'despatch messengers' with 'send people scuttling and scurrying'. Sixty years later, is the official, formal notice or the historian's wording more likely to convey the atmosphere of working through an air-raid warning?

There was little recognition at the time of roof spotters' risks. Despite the dangers, roof spotters did not gain extra wages, or danger money. The local branch of the National Union of General and Municipal Workers asked Liverpool Council to increase the wages of roof spotters because of the danger attached to the work; the council referred the question to the Regional Commissioner, who replied in the negative, and Liverpool Council's roof spotters failed to gain their hoped-for monetary recognition.[43] When Southampton Council proposed paying their roof spotters £6–£8 a week, ratepayers created such an outcry on the grounds that there were many people in danger who did not receive such generous payments (air-raid wardens earned £5 a week), that the council backed down.[44] The London borough of Chelsea paid its roof spotter £3 a week plus a five-shilling bonus, which it raised in 1941 to £3 5s plus a five-shilling bonus.[45] There was no financial compensation for the dangers of roof spotting, but training may have reduced the risks and offered a non-monetary compensation by making the work more interesting.

Training for roof spotters

At one end of the scale, training involved a carefully organised and graded syllabus, covering aircraft recognition, signals, communication, equipment and the duties of a spotter. It went beyond what was strictly necessary to include the theory of flight, aircraft construction and the weather.[46] Roof spotters took the same tests as the ROC. At Standard Telephones in London, the spotters knew individual distinctions between planes, and could recognise them from their general shape; they formed an opinion about the degree of danger enemy aircraft posed from the formations that they adopted and the way that they were approaching. The system relied not only on training, but also on having an older and a younger spotter working together, on the assumption that the young one would have a quick eye and the older one a steady influence.[47] At the other extreme, there were spotters with no training or knowledge of aircraft; all they could do was to look out for any plane approaching and give a warning. Roof spotting was not straightforward. Although the public was convinced that they could tell a British plane from an enemy one by its sound, expert opinion was divided, but tended to the view that this was not possible.[48]

The RAF undertook the first courses for roof spotters at Hendon, north London. Once trained, they returned home to train others as spotters. People who went to Hendon were figures of authority in their locality, and were already used to training others: they were either already involved in ARP at a senior local level, or in related work. Middlesbrough sent a police inspector, while nearby West Hartlepool sent an ARP instructor.[49] Coventry also sent an ARP instructor.[50] Not surprisingly, shortages of labour created tensions over the use of council staff. In Cardiff there was a tussle between the city engineer, struggling with repairs to bombed buildings, and the ARP Committee who wanted a member of the rescue and demolition squad to attend a roof spotting course in order to train others working in local businesses.[51]

Roof spotting courses were organised the length and breadth of the country. In Plymouth the courses attracted employees from a number of local firms, including the main departmental store, Dingles; two local newspapers, the *Western Evening Herald* and *Western Morning News*; City of Plymouth transport, the Post Office and the Co-op, which is an indication of the range of people working after the siren. The most concentrated period for courses was up to the end of 1940.[52]

The local press played a central role in providing information about the courses, which not only alerted potential spotters to the training available, but also indicated to local people that spotters would be thoroughly trained, and therefore trustworthy. By running articles on roof spotting, the *Western Evening Herald* advertised the courses and informed its readers about what the courses taught. One headline announced 'City Roof-Spotters Will Learn to Pick Out Nazi 'Planes'. The article went on to explain that roof spotting courses taught how to distinguish enemy planes and how to judge their height, speed and distance. The *Herald* underlined the importance of the system to the war effort: it quoted Captain Covernton, who was in charge of training in Plymouth, Torquay, Paignton, Brixham and Cornwall, 'In this way we can foil Nazi raiders in one of their chief objects – the interruption of vital national work – by carrying on, even though the sirens have sounded the "alert".'[53] The newspaper presented roof spotting as exciting and, because of the RAF's involvement, as glamorous, with headlines such as 'RAF Test City's Jim Crows'. It reported that the training included a visit to an aerodrome and seeing a Spitfire, Lysander, Blenheim, Gloster and Anson in flight, as well as models of German fighters, bombers and troop carriers. A pilot officer showed the trainee spotters around the aerodrome, where they saw aircraft workers preparing machines for flights, and watched planes taking off and landing.[54] At a time when RAF pilots were treated like gods and there was a great interest in aircraft, the excitement of the training must have whetted the appetites of potential spotters, and helped to create confidence in the system. Other local newspapers ran features similar to those in the *Herald*.[55] Photographs appeared that showed trainee spotters inspecting aircraft, and learning about aeroplanes – a sight that must have appealed to many a bored worker. The *Illustrated London News*, for example, carried a photograph of trainee spotters inspecting the undercarriage of a plane. Newspapers presented roof spotters not only as heroic but also as offering the opportunity for people to carry on in safety.[56]

Documentaries and newsreels also projected confidence in roof spotters. Roof spotters appeared in propaganda films. Humphrey Jennings's *The Heart of Britain* (1941) is a ten-minute documentary film, set in northern industrial areas. There are brief shots of two roof spotters, with helmets and binoculars, accompanied by a voice-over, 'On a hazy day Jerry comes droning over about three miles up. When the roof spotters think he means trouble they send the mill girls down to shelter for a few minutes'. A specific newsreel feature on roof spotters in October 1940 'Jim Crow Sees Planes At First Hand' aimed to endow the system with reliability (the spotters are trained) and a link is made with the RAF, as the spotters visit an RAF station.

The roof spotter's equipment was basic: it might include warm, waterproof clothing; a gas mask; a helmet (although most spotters could not get hold of a steel one) with 'RS' on it; binoculars, and a map of the area. One Bristol firm, with a quick eye for a commercial opening, marketed hard-wearing swivel chairs as 'The Jim Crow Spotter's Chair'. The Ministry of Home Security recommended that firms supply their spotters with booklets of silhouettes and photographs of German, Italian and British planes.[57] Some employers provided their spotters with additional aids. West Hartlepool Council supplied roof spotters with copies of the magazines *Aeroplane* and *Flight*.[58] Metal Box gave their spotters models of aeroplanes; Dunlop Rubber enlarged pictures of cloud formations from the *Encyclopaedia Britannica*, while films called 'Aircraft Identification' that showed aeroplanes in flight were made for firms to hire or buy.[59] Aircraft recognition was central to the system.

Spotters' clubs

Interest in aircraft recognition was stimulated by spotters' clubs, started at the instigation of spotters themselves, with government approval. The first one, formed at Southend, was mentioned in *The Aeroplane Spotter* and other clubs quickly followed. The ROC also started clubs. Some schools formed clubs, with links to aircraft modelling clubs. Peter Masefield, the editor of *The Aeroplane Spotter*, who helped start clubs, was keen for clubs to focus on aircraft recognition rather than roof spotters' duties. *The Aeroplane Spotter* started a section just for spotters' clubs. On 3 May 1941 the National Association of Spotters' Clubs was formed, with the aim of helping its members become more expert at raid spotting and aircraft recognition; in the summer it adopted its own official badge.[60] In early 1942 there were nearly 300 clubs with 1,811 members who had gained a third-class aircraft recognition certificate, and 377 with second-class certificates. By the autumn, over 6,000 certificates had been issued. By the end of 1942, there were roughly 500 clubs.[61] The growth of spotters' clubs fitted with the wartime popularity of associational life, encouraged by government. This was a period when the state was intervening in every nook and cranny of civil society, and often it was hard to draw a line between the two. State intervention did not undermine civil society, but encouraged it.

It was not just roof spotters who joined clubs, but also other people with an interest in aircraft recognition. Richard Brown wrote in his diary on 21 February 1941, 'Talking of planes I'm getting a bit interested in spotting. It's rather a fascinating hobby but will be difficult to get reliable silhouettes according to *Aeroplane Spotter*. It's a weekly which I've just started taking. I've wondered about trying Argyle Street to see if there's a class I can join.' He did join a club, as he explained in June 1941, 'It started last February with a letter in the *Star* from Buxton, who is now our secretary, suggesting forming a club in Ipswich. A dozen of us met and the club was duly launched. After a few weeks we advertised and had a bumper meeting of twenty-five.'[62]

Many spotters' clubs arranged proficiency tests, with qualifying certificates of various grades. The clubs aimed to disseminate information, keep interest in aircraft recognition alive, and promote efficiency among roof spotters.[63] ROC material was used, such as small cards with silhouettes of enemy and allied aircraft from three different angles. A number of books were produced during the war, in order to help the ROC, roof spotters and others who needed to be able to recognise enemy aircraft.[64] Spotters' clubs were more than evening classes in aircraft recognition. Club meetings discussed general news items relating to aircraft, showed films, and held quizzes and inter-club competitions. In the first fortnight of January 1942, twenty-seven meetings of clubs were held in different parts of the country.[65] Their activities went beyond the basics required, and actually turned a necessity of wartime productivity and safety into a wartime hobby. They reflected a desire for belonging to a group, independent of work or family. Spotters developed new skills, knowledge and interests, quite voluntarily at work, which were solely related to the war; these skills were not going to earn them extra pay or promotion. Interest in roof spotting and spotters' clubs ebbed and flowed according to enemy activity and the perceived risk from enemy aircraft.[66]

Although the number of roof spotters' clubs varied around the country – the south-west England, for instance, had relatively few clubs in 1942, despite a number of spotters having been trained in 1940 and

1941 – clubs gained considerable responsibility in the latter part of 1942, when the Ministry of Home Security agreed that clubs would take over training. The Ministry wrote to local authorities telling them to give assistance to clubs, for instance, by providing meeting places and somewhere for them to store their equipment (such as books, charts, models and films). In south-west England, the Regional Raid Spotter Instructor, J. D. Fry, was responsible for training club instructors and keeping training up-to-date. In areas where there were not any clubs Fry trained spotters in groups of a dozen over three days.[67]

Popular interest in aviation and aircraft recognition

While the idea of working after the siren and of using spotters to warn of approaching enemy aircraft was born out of wartime experience, the enthusiasm for roof spotting and the willingness of many to act as roof spotters, have their roots in pre-war developments that were then stimulated by the Battle of Britain. Wartime aircraft recognition was built on a well-established popular hobby, a pre-war popular enthusiasm for aviation, and the exploits of a national fictional hero. Aircraft recognition offered non-combatants of all ages the chance to participate in the thrills and excitement of war, while sidelining its horrors, stresses, tedium and drabness. Whence came its glamour?

In the years before enemy aircraft flew over Britain, there had been a groundswell of popular interest in flying. This interest really took off in 1927 when the American Charles Lindbergh flew alone across the Atlantic in a one-engine monoplane. An international competition of seaplanes between 1913 and 1931 for the Schneider Trophy, which Britain eventually won and kept, was followed avidly. Not even the ill-fated flight of the airship R101 quenched the public's thirst for the sight of airships and aeroplanes.

Boys of the 1930s – soon to be the nation's war workers – were especially interested in aviation. In 1928, the magazine *The Modern Boy* was launched with prominent coverage of aviation. W. E. Johns wrote an aircraft spotters' column 'What plane was that?' and by 1932 he was writing full-length articles for the magazine. In 1931, the magazine published its *Modern Boys' Book of Aircraft*. More importantly, in 1932 a monthly *Popular Flying* magazine aimed at adults took off. It carried articles of general, non-technical interest, such as the Paris Air Show and debated the question of whether fighters or bombers should be prioritised in the aircraft-building programme. It was much less technical than the well-established *The Aeroplane Spotter*. Johns was its editor, and author of a series of adventure stories about a Royal Flying Corps teenage pilot Squadron Leader James Bigglesworth, or Biggles, who was to become the hero of many a child, and indeed adult. Children and adults devoured Biggles' stories, not only in the magazine but also in books and annuals. The circulation of *Popular Flying* rose from 22,576 copies in 1933 to 24,543 in 1934, and before long to 32,067 copies. In 1938, another magazine, *Flying*, was launched to meet the huge demand for stories and features about flying. Authors other than Johns wrote air action novels. Reading stimulated a boys' hobby for aviation that was soon to become a national necessity. Reading was complemented by model aeroplane making and by air action films.[68]

During the war, popular interest in aviation continued apace and expanded to include girls. The *Girls' Own Paper* as well as *Boys' Own Paper* carried columns by Johns, and, at the instigation of the Air Ministry, he wrote a series of action-packed books, such as *Worrals Flies Again* (1942) and *Worrals on the Warpath* (1943) with a WAAF pilot, nicknamed Worrals, as the eponymous heroine.[69] Johns made his stories relevant to the current war not only with Worrals, but also with exciting and highly improbable stories such as *Biggles Defies the Swastika* (1941), *Spitfire Parade* (1941) and *Biggles Sweeps the Desert* (1942). His popularity was second only to that of Enid Blyton.[70] Many of Johns' stories were written or adapted for children, with their strongly drawn characters without much complexity and clear-cut 'good' British and 'bad' enemy characters. Both Biggles and Worrals always outwitted the enemy in the end. In addition, children's toys often had a military or aerial theme, and children's model aircraft were even used for training in aircraft recognition, so emphasising the link between a hobby and wartime necessity.

The greatest stimulus to the enthusiasm for aviation came with the Battle of Britain, when fighter pilots became overnight heroes. Churchill expressed the nation's heartfelt gratitude in what must be one of the most famous phrases ever uttered. While the war was still being fought, the film industry reflected and contributed to the interest in aviation and the RAF, with films such as *Target for Tonight* (1941), *Dangerous Moonlight* (1941), *The First of the Few* (1942), *One of Our Aircraft is Missing* (1942), *Journey Together* (1943) and *The Way to the Stars* (1945).

Images and information that were once confined largely to specialist journals now appeared in the national and local press. Local newspapers contributed to spreading images of aircraft with their, not always accurate, pictures of planes, such as enemy transporters – printed with the aim of helping the public identify invading paratroops. Newspapers carried outlines from different angles of various aircraft, including Focke–Wulf troop carriers and Junkers with the caption 'Cut this out and stick it up!'[71] One paper included a feature on 'How a Spitfire is Built', illustrated with a photograph of the finished article.[72] While critical of the inaccuracy of some of the pictures that appeared in newspapers, aircraft recognition specialists argued that it was important that the public could tell a friendly plane from an enemy one, so that they did not take unnecessary precautions, or indeed risks.[73] Decades later, the writer Alan Sillitoe remembered that as a boy he and his school friends memorised the silhouettes of German planes that appeared in the newspapers.[74]

Aeroplanes permeated all aspects of life: an advertisement for a shop's Christmas bazaar pictured Father Christmas flying with his toys in a plane (which looked remarkably like a British fighter in outline)![75] An advertisement for mackintoshes pictured an aeroplane with the caption 'On Top Whatever The Weather'.[76]

Poems were adapted:

Rock a bye Messerschmitt near the tree top,
When the guns fire the pilot will rock,
Up go our fighters – now watch the plane fall,
Down will come Messerschmitt, pilot and all.

Spitfire funds

The central importance of aircraft to wartime culture is well illustrated by the extraordinary wartime phenomenon of people voluntarily giving money to the government to 'buy' aircraft, usually Spitfires. Spitfire funds show one of the ways in which people created a practical and emotional link with aircraft and the RAF; they help us to understand the importance of aircraft in wartime culture and why roof spotting was such as popular activity. These funds did not originate with government, but grew up spontaneously, and in competition with each other.

The Ministry of Aircraft Production came up with a notional sum of £5,000 as the cost of building a Spitfire, but it is not strictly correct to claim, as Addison and Crang have done, that the fund was one of Lord Beaverbrook's publicity campaigns.[77] Beaverbrook did not make appeals for the fund or lend his name to the appeals of others; he did, however, write 'thank you' letters that many of the recipients and newspapers (not only the *Daily Express*) chose to publicise. Beaverbrook and MAP did not campaign for, or get involved with, any of the fund-raising activities.[78] This was a masterstroke of simplicity and understanding, for it maintained the sense of the funds being people-driven and not a response to yet more wartime cajoling by government. They were not, moreover, the result of an artificially created 'spontaneity' by the press. Money had already started to flow into MAP when the *Daily Express* encouraged people in different towns to club together to 'buy' an aeroplane and printed a letter from a reader in Brighton, who pointed out that the USA made a speciality of playing on the *esprit de corps* of different US cities.[79] Britain did not need lessons from the USA in city culture; its competitive funds were already under way. The press certainly reported contributions, the naming of aeroplanes, and Beaverbrook's thanks. It thus offered the opportunity for people to imitate what others were doing and to compete with them. Like the press, the BBC also announced the sums that different towns had collected. Both the press and the BBC thus publicised to a national audience the contributions of towns, which may have fuelled the competitive aspects of the collections and ensured that people knew that their efforts and sacrifices were known about, and, by implication, appreciated. (The importance to people of national knowledge of their city's sufferings is returned to in chapter 6.)

Visualising roof spotters

While Spitfire funds were a quintessential part of early wartime culture, particularly between 1940 and 1941, roof spotters remained central to wartime Home Front culture until the last months of war. One way of demonstrating the way in which they became embedded in wartime culture is by analysing the media's treatment of them, particularly in visual texts. We have already discussed two striking photographic images of roof spotters, but there were many other ones. Roof spotters leant themselves to photographic images, especially when they were surreal ones.

Many unusual pictures appeared during the war, so it is not surprising that roof spotters appeared among them. In September 1940 a picture of two priests roof spotting for Westminster Cathedral was published. An image of priests as roof spotters shows men, regardless of their civilian calling, playing a part in protecting people in wartime and defending their country. The vulnerability of the cathedral, and the need for unarmed priests to defend it, underlines the wickedness of the enemy and hints at God being on Britain's side.[80]

The press used photographs as an integral part of their features on working after the siren and of roof spotters. The *Daily Express* carried a front-page photograph of a roof spotter who had been at his post when bombs fell on the John Lewis department store in Oxford Street. The report claimed that the spotter, aged sixteen, was unusually young, and it made great play of his youth (the headline announced 'Boy Keeps Watch as Bombs Hit Store'); his enthusiasm for roof spotting; and his steadfastness and bravery when the bombs were dropping. The report fleshed out the roof spotter by giving his name, his job at the store, the area of London where he lived, and a description of his family, with a comment from the boy's father. The following day, as if to balance the story about the boy spotter, a photograph appeared of a nurse staring into the sky, with a caption explaining that this girl was a nurse at Great Ormond Street hospital. The paper informed readers that student nurses were helping to build a sandbagged post for permanent spotters. This 'girl' spotter had not performed any special act of bravery, although the picture of a nurse acting as a spotter was more arresting than that of the boy, which just showed his face, and female spotters were a rarity. The paper provided no information about the nurse, and, although she was referred to as a girl, she may have been older than the boy. The reference to her as a girl may simply have been the current practice of referring to young women as girls, or it may have been because the paper had tried to find a comparable female story, and this was the closest that it could get to one. The day before, the story had been all-important, the next day the photograph was more so.[81] As well as featuring in reports, pictures of roof spotters were even used in advertisements.[82]

Not only the sight, but also the sound of roof spotters, was reconstructed in British culture. On 11 September 1940, a roof spotter gave a talk on the BBC home service, describing how his knowledge and interest in aeroplanes led him into roof spotting. He conveyed the danger, but in an upbeat fashion, 'We've got to be out in the open, under fire all the time with only a steel helmet and a pair of field glasses for protection, but still it's good fun and we've got to enjoy it.'[83]

Roof spotters were an integral part of people's experience of air raids; they were as much a part of the sight of war as were sandbags and signs for shelters. John Taylor pointed to the way in which official publications and the illustrated press used photographs of people looking up towards the sky, searching for signs of threat or defence; the upward gaze was symbolic of optimism and hope, of vigilance, of calm and confidence, and of looking to the future.[84] The roof spotter was an icon of all these messages. When Ritchie Calder published his account of the London blitz in 1941, he not only referred to roof spotters in his text, but also included a photograph of roof spotters (see figure 5.9). Their inclusion is instructive, not only because an extraordinary activity is made to look quite ordinary and unexceptional, but also because of the way that the photograph is composed. Calder's book is presenting an account of Londoners standing up to the Blitz with bravery and collective support. These spotters, a far cry from the heroic image that opened this chapter, reinforce the points that Calder is making. In a book where all the people are heroes, the reader is presented with a group of spotters, not a single one; as a group they are part of a collective effort. Their poses are unheroic; they perch on sandbags. They are suggestive of cross-class

5.9 Spotters scanning the sky from a city roof during an air-raid alarm

endeavour, for one wears an open-neck shirt, while the other wears a collar and tie (the former is probably more typical). There is, however, one message in common with the spotter at the beginning: they are looking in different directions, their eyes and ears see and hear all around, so they present a picture of a safe system. This could be a roof anywhere; there is no famous London landmark to attract our attention; the people not the place remain centre stage.

The cartoon in figure 5.10 appeared in the *Daily Herald*, a popular left-wing newspaper, at the start of the London blitzes, and was surrounded by text about the heavy raids on London. It contained an easily recognisable national figure and London landmark. It was heavily referential. Roof spotters are now national heroes; Nelson was renowned for his front-line stance in battle – a role that roof spotters have now adopted. The cartoon encapsulates two historic moments of danger to the country, and readers know the victorious outcome of the first one. Nelson, although dressed in archaic uniform and holding a telescope, has turned to address not only sailors, but also civilians, through the modern device of a microphone. This is a reference to the changed nature of war. The background suggests a lighter, optimistic note, with birds, not enemy aircraft, hovering in view. The written text and visual image

5.10 London's roof spotter and his message

are interdependent. The caption gives it an up-to-date immediacy; the play on words is less of a command than the original words of Nelson, and offers a definite and thus reassuring message. It is an arresting cartoon of a celebrated person and a famous place, and of the historical and contemporary; it also includes a comic element, all of which may have helped to lodge it in the readers' minds.[85] While the *Daily Herald* linked roof spotting with an admiral, there was no suggestion that spotters were the stooges of the rich, famous and powerful. Another cartoon explicitly presents roof spotters on the side of the workers. The interests of roof spotters and workers are distanced from the management.

The press used cartoons to communicate the normality of working after the siren. Roof spotters were never the butt of jokes, as were ARP wardens or the Home Guard, perhaps because they were not in place before they were required, but played an active role with responsibilities that were immediately useful; they acted for the workforce from which they themselves were drawn, and they did not possess powers to order people around[86] (see figures 5.11 and 5.12).

Appearing in cartoons showed that roof spotters and working after the siren was worthy of comment; cartoons encapsulated in 'shorthand' a quintessentially wartime activity that needed no explanation at the time, and only made sense at this particular moment: before the summer of 1940 they were inconceivable, and after the war irrelevant.

We have already seen the way in which one feature film, *Millions Like Us*, integrated a sequence about the industrial alarm scheme, and the use of roof spotters in documentary and newsreel footage. Another wartime film to portray roof spotters, *The Foreman Went To France*, original narrative by J. B. Priestley, uses the sequence as a device for setting up the story that is to follow. The opening shots show roof spotters watching a raid from the roof, and then one spotter beginning to tell the other spotter about the foreman's visit to France in 1940. The sequence is light on propaganda, but there are interesting similarities and contrasts between it and the rest of the film. In the opening sequence with the roof spotters, we see the collective bravery of Britons in Britain, work practices that are essential to the war effort, working-class heroism and the daily contribution of civilians. In the rest of the film we see the individual bravery of Britons in France, who are thereby making a major contribution to the war, and working-class heroism in a one-off situation. Like *Millions Like Us*, the film was highly praised by reviewers, who made no comment about the extraordinary behaviour of the workforce during an air raid.[87]

Roof spotters were central to wartime narratives of the ongoing experience. Yet, they have been almost entirely ignored by historians, and

5.11 'OK! Full speed ahead! . . .'

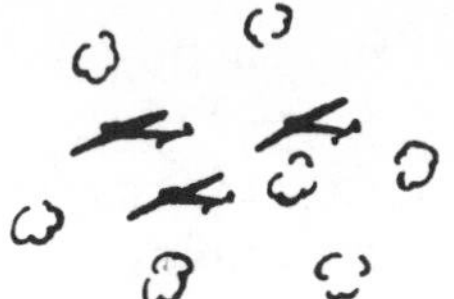

5.12 'Yah, windy!'

mistaken for fire-watchers. Why then has roof spotting failed to register in public histories of the war?

Roof spotters' invisibility is part of the absence of analysis of people carrying on after the siren; roof spotters were fewer in number and less visible than fire-watchers; they were not a part of ARP services and therefore have not received attention when ARP wardens, rescue services, ambulance crews and firefighters have been remembered; they did not wear a uniform, which automatically downgraded their status in wartime when a uniform signalled a contribution to the war effort, and was especially important in denoting the masculinity of the male civilian; despite the potential dangers of roof spotting, few were killed, so roof spotters do not form part of the public commemoration of the war dead. Images of civilians without uniforms focus on passive evacuees, shoppers in queues for rationed goods, and air-raid shelterers. Images of factory workers tend to depict women but not men. Much of the public ritual of remembering the war in Britain focuses on those in uniform, and this links with past wars, when only the military were commemorated; the mass of civilians who resisted sieges or were affected by them were bypassed in the process of the creation of heroes and heroines. In reality, there was no clear-cut divide between the role of those in and those out of uniform, or between the Armed Forces and civilians: the RAF initially trained roof spotters, who then trained others, so, like the apostolic succession, a link between the RAF and all trained roof spotters existed. Roof spotters also used the same training materials as the RAF, ROC and naval observers. Some roof spotters had previously served in the Armed Forces, while others joined up later: wartime roles and identities were not fixed but changed over a six-year period. The multifarious roles that one person might have played during the war as an evacuee, a worker, or a member of the Forces, are often overlooked, as public histories present group histories of, for instance, women in the factories or in the auxiliary forces, evacuees, the ARP services, or men in the Forces, rather than the changing individual histories over the course of a developing war. It is not too late, however, to capture the memories of some of those who were young spotters during the war.

Roof spotters remember[88]

Why they did it

Those who explained how they became roof spotters gave one of two explanations: either they were aircraft enthusiasts who chose to do it as an extension of their hobby, or they had no choice. A roof spotter for Brighton Council was enthusiastic and knowledgeable. He, like many boys, was interested in aeroplane spotting and making model aircraft even before the war broke out. At school he joined the ATC, subscribed to the *Aeroplane Spotter*, and helped form a school club affiliated to the National Association of Spotters' Clubs. When he left school and moved to Brighton Technical College, he volunteered to supplement the town's roof spotters. He recalled that the council wanted young people with knowledge of aircraft recognition, because the older men had problems with it and failed the tests.[89] One described himself as an 'avid aero-spotter'. He had volunteered for the RAF at school, but been rejected on health grounds.[90] Roof spotting was the closest that he was going to get to the RAF. Another man had also wanted to join the RAF, and had been interested in aeroplanes since he was a small boy. He volunteered for roof spotting, because it was 'exciting' to see everything, rather than to be huddled in the smelly shelter with earth floors at the brewery where he worked.[91] Yet another explained that he had been interested in aircraft from a young age.[92]

In contrast, one roof spotter had worked for Kingston Council, where it was 'difficult not to volunteer'. He wrote that it was 'a duty I was required to undertake'.[93] One man who had been a spotter on his school roof, doubted whether the boys had any choice, while two fourteen-year-olds in work, one of whom had made model wooden aeroplanes when a boy, thought that they were chosen because they were young.[94] One of them said 'I was the youngest there. Somebody in their wisdom decided to send young John onto the roof when the siren sounded. I didn't have any say in the matter. I think it was basically because I was the only non-productive person there. It was easier for them. You didn't argue.'

Children and young people roof spotting

'Youth' was a recurrent theme among roof spotters' reminiscences. Children were look-outs for enemy aircraft from the Battle of Britain in 1940 to the era of doodlebugs in 1944–45. A woman recalled that in the summer of 1940, as a fifteen-year-old schoolgirl, she took her turn in sitting on top of step-ladders in a garden on a hilltop in East Sussex, armed with a pair of field-glasses, watching for invading enemy paratroopers. If she saw any invaders she was instructed to telephone the local soldiers.[95] A man recalled that, at the age of fifteen, he and other prefects sat on the roof of the school chapel when the air-raid siren sounded, while the rest of the school carried on working. He remembered the boys' role but it was not until he recently read a copy of the school's history that he discovered (or learnt what he had once known) that the masters used to go on the roof at night. A roof spotter at Cheapside, east London, remembered all the spotters being young people.[96] Another man had been a spotter at the age of sixteen for Fuller, Smith and Turner, a brewery at Chiswick, west London, while another was aged sixteen or seventeen when he undertook combined roof spotting and fire-watching.[97] One respondent described himself as a 'young lad' when he roof spotted for a small electrical engineering factory in Clapham.[98] One man was fourteen years old in 1944, when he roof spotted for a firm in Kingston upon Thames that built ambulances; another was aged fourteen and a half when he worked for G. F. Amory in Ballards Lane, Finchley, north London. He remembered being the only boy working there: the others were all old men. He was chosen for roof spotting – which involved climbing up on the roof with a tin hat and whistle, and listening for V1s – because he was the youngest and 'most fleet of foot'. One man had volunteered for roof spotting at a firm in Northwood Hills, Middlesex. He recalled it as 'more adventure than worry' and 'a bit of a lark for younger ones', although older roof spotters probably took it more seriously. He thought the younger ones were more agile at getting up on the roof.[99] Another was a fourteen-year-old at a colliery near Sheffield when he, and another boy the same age, combined roof spotting with fire-watching at the head of the mine shaft where they had a good view of approaching enemy aircraft.[100] One man was a roof spotter in Hackney, east London, from 1943 to 1945, when he was aged twenty-six to twenty-eight, but he had four younger lads in his team.

The youth of many spotters calls into question the dominant emphasis in much wartime literature on steps to protect children, particularly through evacuation schemes. While the *Daily Express* emphasised that a sixteen-year-old spotter was unusually young, memory evidence suggest that in fact there were many young spotters. As well as children on school roofs, firms chose children and young people for a dangerously exposed job, precisely because they were young: they were less productive as they did not have the experience of older, trained workers, and they were supposedly nimble at climbing up on roofs. Their youth did not protect them, but actually placed them at greater risk. While the pool of roof spotters to be interviewed is obviously skewed by age, this does not alter the fact that young people were purposely put in positions of risk.

Training

Although there is evidence in the records of training schemes and of an association of roof spotters, no-one remembered receiving training for roof spotting (although people did remember training for fire-watching), and no one remembered any club or group of roof spotters unless, after the war, they had continued to be involved in organisations relating to aircraft recognition. Most people have forgotten or never knew about, the formal, institutional, and national aspects of the scheme.

Most roof spotters said that they had never received any training, although one had learnt aircraft recognition in the Home Guard. One man remembered the training in detail. He was able to describe the aircraft recognition cards (still in his possession) that were used for instruction and testing and the test requirements.

Roof spotters do not recall women spotters. As with others who worked after the public siren, the role of trade unions is remembered as irrelevant, either because interviewees were not in a trade-union 'shop', or because it was not a subject on which they remember unions expressing a view. Instead, they remember the scheme as being widely adopted, but as a result of informal agreement, decisions made at their own place of work, or personal choice.

The role of the roof spotter emerges as a highly responsible one, in which many people put a great deal of faith. Roof spotters themselves tend not to dwell on the dangers and stresses of the situation. Indeed, many talk of the excitement, and some of the fact that they got out of their usual work. It may be that older men do not want to talk about feelings of fear to a younger woman; it may be that they have filtered out the stressful memories; or it may be as many of them said, that they were young and genuinely liked the thrill of spotting. Two roof spotters did, however, refer to the danger. One wrote 'When the Siren sounded I left my lathe and raced up the steel runged ladder to the "spotters nest" on the roof . . . We lost one Spotter who fell off the steel ladder on to concrete below'. He recalled the danger of getting on to the roof and the danger of being hit.[101] Another spotter remembered it as something which he could get a lot of fun out of, but also as being dangerous, but he had been with the BEF in France, and did not think that he would get killed.[102]

The use of memory material has contributed to our knowledge of roof spotting in a number of key ways. It reveals the lack of choice that some people now feel that they had in undertaking roof spotting duties, as well as the lack of training and organisational support for many, which is not apparent from the contemporary evidence that, in contrast, documents the training and organisation of roof spotters. Roof spotting was, for the most part, remembered as exciting, which in part reflects the modesty of roof spotters; no one boasted about their heroism. It also brought to light the way in which children and young people were singled out for a risky and responsible duty, which is in direct contrast to the picture of adults protecting children from the risks of war through evacuation schemes.

For a number of the men interviewed for this project, roof spotting was a minor event in the period before they were called up, and often they were keen to go on to talk about their experiences in the Forces. This suggests that it was not a significant wartime experience for them, so that their memory of it has not been kept fresh by periodic reminiscing. Likewise, for those who worked as civilians for all or most of the war, roof spotting and working in air raids is not a subject that they have been encouraged or helped to remember by popular interest in the subject. Some interviewees recognised that the passage of time limited their recall. For almost everyone, it was the first time that they had been asked about their experiences of working after the siren or of roof spotting. This meant that many people were keen to talk about it. It also meant that their memories had not been distorted by subsequent portrayals on the screen, in novels or other oft-repeated wartime images. A number of those interviewed were pleased to be able to paint an alternative picture to the dominant post-war one of civilians passively hiding in shelters or moving to safer areas of the country. One of the most striking aspects of representations and media treatment of non-uniformed civilians contributing to war production in air raids and of roof spotters is the difference between the war and post-war periods.

Conclusions

Although the IASs were originally conceived as a means of maintaining industrial production, a number of local authorities joined schemes.[103] The willingness of local firms to co-operate for self-preservation and production was a peculiarly wartime phenomenon with no peacetime implications. The war created common interests among people in the same area, whether it was the East End of London, which was heavily bombed or in other areas which were potential strategic targets. It was part of a strong sense of local community responsibility and identity felt during these years which, although referred to by historians and reflected in popular local histories of the war, has not been adequately analysed by historians. (This is not to suggest that there were not tensions and often a lack of communication between local authorities and local firms, or that differences within firms evaporated, but rather that these divisions need to be set alongside an enhanced local/city identity which operated at the same time.)

Roof spotting and working after the siren emerged during the Battle of Britain, but they continued until the latter stages of the war, and were especially important when Germany sent V1s over to London. A practice begun during the Battle of Britain took on a life of its own, so that by the end of the war many had forgotten or never knew about the initial struggles and conflicts over the system, but instead took it as part and parcel of wartime life. This quintessentially wartime activity became a normal part of many people's lives, an activity that they barely questioned, and which has until now eluded the analysis of historians.[104] Roof spotting and industrial alarm schemes were systems that were put in place in order to enable people to carry on at work after the siren sounded. People's willingness to carry on after the siren involved not only putting these systems in place, but changes in hearts and minds. In chapter 6 we will see how this came about.

Notes

1 Humphrey Spender, for instance, who worked briefly for Mass-Observation before the war and for *Picture Post* during the war, subscribed to the German magazine *Querschnitt* (Cross Section) and a film magazine *Close-Up*, that carried stills from Russian films. British Library, National Sound Archive, C459/43/5.
2 PRO HO 207/20, Local Production Defence Committee: London. Meeting, 30 January 1941; British Library, National Sound Archive, C459/43/5.
3 Surrey Record Office, Woking, Dennis Specialist vehicles 1463/WN 1. Safety in Air Raids notices, 22 November 1940 and 2 December 1940.
4 Gordon Robbins, *Fleet Street Blitzkrieg Diary* (Ernest Benn, January 1944), pp. 13–14.
5 PRO HO 207/20.
6 Bernard Darwin, *War on the Line: The Story of the Southern Railway in Wartime* (The Southern Railway Co., 1946), p. 192.
7 Teeside Record Office, Borough of Redcar Emergency Committee Diaries, DC/RE 2/10/2, 6 November 1940.
8 Angus Calder, *The People's War: Britain 1939–1945* (Panther, 1971), pp. 239–40, 371, 392.
9 Art McCulloch (compiler), *The War and Uncle Walter: The Diary of an Eccentric* (Doubleday, 2003), p. 258.
10 This whole section draws heavily, often verbatim, from the account of Hawker's alarm system written by Edward Griffith, now in the hands of his son, Michael Griffith, who kindly gave me full access to his father's papers. I am extremely grateful to him and to his sister for their help.
11 PRO INF 1/292, Weekly Home Intelligence Reports, 8–15 September 1942.
12 Leeds Central Library, City of Leeds, Air Raids Precautions and Civil Defence Committee Reports to the Council, 25 November 1940.
13 PRO HO 207/20, not dated.
14 PRO HO 207/20, Report of the first meeting of alarm controllers for the London area, held at London Regional Headquarters on Wednesday 12 March 1941.
15 RAF Museum, Hendon, Aviation Records Department, AC 70/10/80 box. 1, R. E. Nicholl, Handley Page to Commander King–Hall, Director, Factory Defence Section, MAP, 8 November 1940.
16 PRO HO 207/20, Changes with flying bombs.
17 PRO HO 207/20; Hilary St George Saunders, *Ford at War* (Ford, 1946), pp. 23–4.
18 *Hansard*, vol. 365, col. 8, October 1940, Clement Davies; vol. 367, cols 923–4, 11 December 1940, Assheton.
19 PRO HO 186/915, Industrial Alarm Scheme. Reviewed after two years.
20 Frank Rowlinson, *Contribution to Victory: An Account of Some of the Special Work of the Metropolitan-Vickers Electrical Co. Ltd. in the Second World War* (Vickers, 1947), p. 173.

21 *Western Mail* 14 May 1945. 'Works Alert Saved Millions of Man Hours'.
22 PRO INF 1/292, WHIR, 4–11 November 1940.
23 PRO HO 207/20.
24 PRO HO 207/20, poster. In the film *Millions Like Us*, a poster explaining the system is pointed out to a group of visiting RAF personnel.
25 John Roberts, *The Art of Interruption: Realism, Photography and the Everyday* (Manchester University Press, 1998), pp. 58–64.
26 Reviews in: *Observer* 3 October 1943, C. A. Lejeune; *Guardian* 28 December 1943, D. S.; *Evening Standard* 2 October 1943, Mary Hunt; *New Statesman* 16 October 1943, William Whitebaite; *Sunday Times* 10 October 1943; *Monthly Film Bulletin* 10, p. 133; *Today's Cinema*, 4934: 61 (24 September 1943), 1, 8 and 10.
27 *Ibid.*
28 PRO HO 207/20.
29 Correspondence in the possession of Mrs Eileen Rogers, plotter at Fraser and Chalmers, Erith.
30 Interview with Mrs Eileen Rogers.
31 PRO HO 207/20.
32 PRO HO 207/20.
33 *The Aeroplane Spotter* 7 May 1942. This and other aircraft recognition material was consulted at the Royal Aeronautical Society Library, London.
34 Women in the Home Guard are one example: Penny Summerfield and Corinna Peniston-Bird, 'Women in the firing line: the Home Guard and the defence of gender boundaries in Britain in the Second World War', *Women's History Review*, 9 (2000), 231–55.
35 Philomena Goodman, *Women, Sexuality and War* (Palgrave, 2000), p. 73.
36 Sonya Rose, *Which People's War? National Identity and Citizenship in Britain 1939–1945* (Oxford University Press, 2003), pp. 111–12.
37 Philomena Goodman, *Women, Sexuality and War*, pp. 79–80.
38 Derek Wood, *Attack Warning Red: The Royal Observer Corps and the Defence of Britain, 1925 to 1975* (Macdonald and Jane's, 1976), pp. 123–4. Until 1941 it was the Observer Corps, and then the Royal Observer Corps.
39 University of Warwick Library, Modern Records Centre (MRC). MSS 200/F/3/S1/22/32/67–82 Meetings of ARP officers and spotters 18 and 19 February 1941 to discuss spotters' technique and working through the siren.
40 *Croydon Times* 2 November 1940.
41 *Wandsworth Borough News* 15 September 1944.
42 Imperial War Museum, Misc. 60, Item 929.
43 Liverpool Record Office, 352/MIN/DEF/1/6. Liverpool Civil Defence Emergency Committee Minute book no. 6, 28 October 1940, 6 November 1940.
44 *Southern Daily Echo* 24 October 1940.
45 Chelsea Library, Borough of Chelsea, War Emergency Committee Minute Book, 1 January 1941.
46 PRO HO 207/148. Skeleton syllabus of the instruction for the Training of Raid Spotter Members of Clubs of LRC and NASC.

47 PRO HO 186/499, 10 December 1940, Bertram Matheson's visit to Standard Telephones, 9 December 1940.
48 *The Aeroplane Spotter* 1 January 1942.
49 Teeside Record Office, County Borough of Middlesbrough, CB/M/C/2/111, Civil Defence Control Administration, 4 October 1940; County Borough of West Hartlepool, Minutes of the Emergency Committee, 25 September 1940.
50 Coventry City Record Office, CCA/1/4/48/1, National Emergency Committee, 26 September 1940.
51 Glamorgan Record Office, City of Cardiff, vol. 11, BC/C/6/78, Proceedings of ARP Committee, 27 September 1940.
52 Teeside Record Office, County Borough of West Hartlepool, 2 January 1941.
53 *Western Evening Herald* 1 October 1940.
54 *Western Evening Herald* 9 October 1940.
55 *Southern Daily Echo* 23 October 1940, *Hackney Gazette* 7 October 1940; *Bristol Evening Post* 11 October 1940.
56 *Wimbledon Borough News* 1 November 1940 had a picture of Ely's roof spotter, Mr Longdon, and another spotter appeared in *Mitcham News and Mercury* 22 November 1940.
57 University of Warwick Library, Modern Records Centre (hereafter MRC), TUC archive, MSS TUC 292/883.212/5, Ministry of Home Security leaflet, Notes on Raid Spotting; 'The Jim crow spotters chair', *Labour Management*, March 1941, p. 37.
58 Teeside Record Office, County Borough of West Hartlepool, Minutes of the Emergency Committee, 30 October 1940.
59 MRC, MSS 200/F/3/S1/22/32/67–82, Meetings of ARP officers and spotters held on 18 and 19 February 1941 to discuss spotters' technique and working through air raids.
60 Tim Hamilton, *Identification Friend or Foe: Being the Story of Aircraft Recognition* (HMSO, 1994), p. 102.
61 *The Aeroplane Spotter* 26 February 1942 and 24 September 1942; PRO HO 186/1784, not dated, unsigned.
62 Helen D. Millgate, *Mr Brown's War: A Diary of the Second World War* (Sutton Publishing, 2003), pp. 92, 109–10.
63 PRO HO 186/805, unsigned note, 22 April 1941.
64 Examples from the many produced include: Air Training Corps Gazette, *Aircraft Recognition Test* (1942); *Anon., Aircraft Recognition Tests: What is It?* (The Aeroplane, 1940), C. Griffith (compiler), *Raid Spotters Note Book* (Charles Petts, not dated).
65 For example, *The Aeroplane Spotter* 1 January 1942 and other wartime issues.
66 PRO HO 207/148, Club Training Officers, National Association of Spotters' Clubs, Policy and Training.
67 Plymouth and West Devon Record Office, Plymouth, 1561/CD/IU/1, Factories' correspondence relating to civil defence precautions, March 1941–May 1944. Office of Regional Commissioner Circular to all ARP controllers, 30 September 1942.

68 Peter Beresford Ellis and Jennifer Schofield, *Biggles! The Life Story of Capt. W. E. Johns* (Veloce Publishing, 1993), pp. 122, 124, 126, 130, 133, 142, 151 and 163. Much more could be written about 'the cult of the air' but unfortunately it would be too much of a diversion here.
69 Peter Beresford Ellis and Jennifer Schofield, *Biggles!*, pp. 177 and 187.
70 Peter Hunt, *An Introduction to Children's Literature* (Oxford University Press, 1994), p. 130; Brian Doyle (compiler/ed.) *The Who's Who of Children's Literature* (Hugh Evelyn, 1968), pp. 158–9.
71 *Westminster and Pimlico News* 21 June 1940; *Oxford Mail* 20 June, 22 June, 24 June 1940; *Yorkshire Post* 20 June 1940.
72 *Western Evening Herald* (Plymouth), 26 November 1940.
73 C. Griffith, *Raid Spotters Notebook*, not dated.
74 Alan Sillitoe, *Life Without Armour: An Autobiography* (HarperCollins, 1995), p. 49.
75 *Southern Daily Echo* 20 November 1940.
76 *Southern Daily Echo* 24 October 1940.
77 Paul Addison and Jeremy Crang, 'A battle of many nations', in Paul Addison and Jeremy Crang (eds), *The Burning Blue: A New History of the Battle of Britain* (Pimlico, 2000), p. 248.
78 David Farrer, *The Sky's the Limit: The Story of Beaverbrook at MAP* (Hutchinson, 1943), p. 78.
79 *Daily Express* 3 July 1940.
80 *Express and Echo* 24 September 1940.
81 *Daily Express* 19, 20 September 1940.
82 *Daily Express* 23 November 1940. In this case, a picture of a roof spotter is used to advertise a relief for rheumatism with the words 'You can't hear the approach of this enemy.'
83 'Roof spotting', *The Listener* (19 September 1940), p. 406.
84 John Taylor, *A Dream of England: Landscape, Photography and the Tourist's Imagination* (Manchester University Press, 1994), pp. 205–9.
85 *Daily Herald* 9 September 1940. On 23 September 1940, another cartoon of roof spotters appeared that was less heavy with symbolism and more devoted to the comic.
86 David Langdon, *Home Front Lines* (Methuen, 1942, first published 1941). Drawings first appeared in *Punch* and *Lilliput*, pp. 30, 45, 59 and 66 include roof spotters and people ignoring the siren.
87 *Monthly Film Bulletin*, 9, 100, p. 41; *Today's Cinema*, 4708:58 (10 April 1942).
88 People who undertook roof spotting duties were contacted via local newspapers. Of the 15 roof spotters who shared their memories, some gave written accounts; some were interviewed on the telephone; and some gave additional interviews in person. They are referred to below by initials and date of correspondence and/or interview.
89 A. B. 13 December 2000, 15 January 2001.
90 D. H. 2 November 2000.

91 G. H. J. 28 October 2000.
92 W. H. P. 20 November 2000.
93 C. G. D. 15 November 2000, 17 November 2000.
94 D. F. 1 December 2000; J. Ke. 19 December 2000, J. Kn. 12 October 2000.
95 M. J. 20 November 2000.
96 D. H. 2 November 2000.
97 R. R. 1 November 2000.
98 E. P. 8 October 2000.
99 R. T. 1 November 2000.
100 E. G. 9 November 2000.
100 R. T. 1 November 2000.
101 C. F. E. P. 20 October 2000.
102 P. T. 13 October 2000, 1 November 2000.
103 Teeside Record Office, CB/M/C/2/111, Middlesbrough Civil Defence Control Administration, 6 December 1940; Redcar Emergency Committee Diaries, December 1940, 21 February 1941.
104 Knowledge of roof spotters is now so hazy that some historians mistake them for fire-watchers. In Neil Rattigan's analysis of class in wartime films: *This is England: British Film and the People's War, 1939–1945* (Associated University Presses, 2001), pp. 147–8, he devotes attention to *The Foreman Went to France* in which the opening shots are of roof spotters on a factory roof. Rattigan repeatedly refers to them as fire-watchers.

6

Reasons

Introduction

In 1945 a journalist, who had closely observed and reported on Plymouth during the war, argued that Plymothians' ability to 'carry on' despite air raids and blitzes had been due to 'the spirit of the people' and the 'true British spirit'. He approvingly quoted a rejoinder to a Canadian who remarked on the bravery of Plymouth, 'not brave, just British'. A few years later a German – writing about the bombing of Germany – claimed that the national character of Britons and Germans had enabled them to cope with the presence of terrible dangers.[1]

We do not wish to sprinkle the blazing fire of a roaring good story with the cold water of realism, so much as to offer an alternative interpretation of the story. The explanations offered above for British people's willingness to carry on at work, in factories, in offices, in shops, in theatres and cinemas, in churches, and on buses, trains and trams is inadequate not only because it is too one-dimensional, but also because it is misleading. This chapter shows that most people learnt to control their fear in air raids, and the language that they used to express this process was 'getting used to' air raids. We have already seen in previous chapters that people gained confidence from roof spotters and industrial alarm systems at work, and that the media presented visual, sound and written images of people continuing work in raids. This chapter explores additional reasons that, taken together, explain people's behaviour in air raids. Workers' attitudes towards air raids were not only formed when they were at work; there were a host of influences on them when they were away from work. We need to put workers' behaviour in a wide cultural and social context.

Getting used to raids

We saw in chapter 3 how people had feared the prospect of war and were terrified in early air raids and in the blitzes. One should not underestimate the horror of the blitzes, but once people had experienced and survived air raids, they managed better in subsequent ones.[2] The gap between expectation and reality helped people to cope with air raids. In August 1940 Tom Harrisson wrote an article on civilians in air raids for *Picture Post*:

> For many months before air-raids came, people were expecting them. Deep down inside many of us were suppressing anxieties, and consequently building up rather exaggerated pictures of what air-raids might mean. Now air-raids have come to Britain . . . certain amount of relief. One is relieved to find how little bombs can do as compared with the mental picture one had. One is impressed to find that the effect on one's mind is very slight after the first shock.'[3]

Londoners found raids 'not so terrible once you have got used to them'.[4] As early as August 1940 (so before the heavy raids on London), there is evidence from various areas of London – Croydon, Kilburn and Streatham – that people were not perturbed when they heard air-raid sirens.[5] By early August 1940 Cardiff had experienced warnings practically every night and day, and raids on the docks and surrounding area had gradually increased in severity. According to the Chief Constable, the public had 'become accustomed' to the raids, although he worried over 'a certain amount of recklessness, people exposing themselves to danger unnecessarily'.[6] A civil servant who observed behaviour in Cardiff and Bristol in August 1940 wrote that the frequent air-raid warnings had 'acclimatised' people to the sound, and, as no serious attacks had occurred, most people continued about their business.[7]

Although letter-writers may have wished to allay the anxieties of friends, they were, nevertheless, in accord with more private material. In early October 1940, one letter-writer wrote 'one gets used to everything, and we are no longer frightened; we turn over and go to sleep'. A woman working at the BBC wrote a long letter to the USA explaining the change:

> At first, I think all of us were pretty scared although we didn't like to say so. But quite honestly, now, it's sort of part of life and it's taken for granted. I mean, every evening the sirens go off and you think there the bastards are again, and that is that. Most people just tacitly agree not to mention any loud bangs they hear, and pretend that they haven't heard them. Actually, it isn't that one gets callous, but one knows one's got to lump it, and human nature is an extraordinary thing. At first, of course, you are firmly convinced that every bomb is going to hit you in particular . . . Then they may come pretty near you and not hit you, and you gradually realize that the whole thing's a matter of luck anyway, so what the hell? . . . You can't forever go on saying 'that might have been me, or my house'.[8]

Walter Musto, who lived in the suburbs of south-west London, wrote on 11 September 1940:

> The night-long raids in London continue with increasing fury and devastating effect. Daylight raids are now so frequent that I have lost count of them. The nights are nightmares, the days we spend scurrying into shelters. . . . It is pitiful to observe the complete destruction of homes where not a vestige of treasured belongings remain, and the casualties and loss of life are appalling. The City itself is becoming a shambles. The sound near and far of exploding bombs and gunfire make a mockery of sleep. The drone of wandering night planes keeps nerves on the rack. Yet, in spite of all this, one slowly becomes accustomed to the changing conditions.[9]

Harrisson claimed 'Soon raids become a part of the routine of life'.[10] As early as mid-October 1940, it was reported that many accepted raids as part of an unpleasant routine.[11] People came to regard raids as just 'part of wartime conditions'.[12] It was reported that the general reaction to bombings, *especially when heavy*, was a stoical acceptance of their terrors and a determination to carry on as usual.[13] On 17 October 1940 a woman teacher in Kent wrote that she scarcely noticed 'the nightly droning of hordes of Nazi planes', and by the end of the year, 'whether through becoming accustomed or through blunted susceptibilities I don't know, but I don't feel any emotion now when the siren goes'.[14] Nella Last, who lived in Barrow, wrote in her diary on 27 October 1940:

> If anyone had told me I *could* [author's italics] have felt so unconcerned when an alert – or guns – sounded, I would not have believed it possible. The first bomb dropped made me choke with palpitation, and for a few days I jumped at the least bump or slam of a door. I can tell my feeling is shared by many women I speak to, and those very nervy people who liked to have a fuss made over them are beginning to get used to things.[15]

Bombing raids on Coventry in late October 1940 were said to have upset newer and younger factory workers, but elsewhere in the Midlands people took heavy bombing with increasing calm.[16] In early November a Liverpool man wrote in his diary that he no longer either immediately sought shelter or felt uneasy until the 'all clear'.[17] By late November 1940 the Ministry of Information detected a 'toughness of spirit' and 'indifference' to air raids that seemed to be taken for granted.[18] By Christmas 1940 it was reported, 'During the past few weeks acclimatisation to the dangers and difficulties of the blitz has steadily continued'.[19]

Blitzes, it was reported, were 'faced best' by those who had been expecting them, or who had already experienced a series of minor raids. Thus, secret home intelligence reports described the reaction of people on Clydebank as 'beyond praise', while people in Plymouth faced heavy raids in January 1941 with 'courage and cheerfulness'. When Plymouth was blitzed on 20 and 21 March 1941, the people stood up to the blitzes 'exceptionally well'.[20] Plymouth was 'physically exhausted',[21] but the weekly home intelligence compilers praised the people, especially those with air-raid duties to perform, who had shown 'great courage'.[22] In May 1941 Plymothians showed 'a high degree of courage and individual adaptability'.[23]

It was not automatic, but Londoners learnt to live with the sounds and sights of air raids. When a siren was heard in London in 1942 after a lull of many months, most people took no notice of it and carried on with whatever they were doing.[24]

Many experienced raids but did not actually come face to face with their worst aspects. They did not see or smell dead, badly burnt or mutilated bodies. Although people saw damaged buildings and bomb craters, most only heard about people being killed or injured. No one sitting in a cinema watching a newsreel or sitting at home reading a newspaper saw images of corpses or body parts. The press did not publish complete casualty figures of those killed and injured in raids.

Modification of standards of danger and security

Contemporary research suggested that while the sound of the siren, because of its loudness, unpleasant noise and terrifying associations, initially created fear, when the unpleasant associations did not always materialise, the sound of the siren no longer automatically led to feelings of fear. In addition, it was suggested that a series of false alarms and light raids led to a gradual development of psychological defences for overcoming terrifying expectations of danger. Such reactions fit with other anthropological and psychological studies that show that the more familiar a situation or event, the greater people's ability to minimise their perceptions of its risks.[25] It was pointed out that people adapted to 'raid reality' and modified their ideas about danger and security. As an example of this phenomenon, it was related how a doctor had expressed sympathy to a patient whose flat had been damaged and who had had a very narrow escape. The patient replied sensibly and unemotionally, 'You ought rather to congratulate me on my *good* luck'[26] [author's italics].

Familiarity on occasions bred a false sense of security, and the public's perception of the risk was not always accurate. On one occasion in Liverpool, bombs killed a number of shoppers who had not taken cover after the siren sounded.[27] In Southampton, a woman recalled many years later, 'people got that they didn't go to shelters: we'd had a few raids that were false alarms, but a bomb caught people'.[28] In Aberdeen there had been frequent warnings without bombs, when in April 1943, people were killed walking along the path, cycling down the road or simply watching the raid.[29] Some people developed a fatalistic attitude.[30]

It should be emphasised, however, that people did not take a passive and inert attitude to air raids. Experience and specific circumstances affected people's judgement. Apprehension was noted in Bristol among those living in badly built houses near Temple Meads station, where bombs had already fallen, and which was known to be a target. People living in the area were more inclined to sleep in public shelters at night than in Cardiff (about thirty miles from Bristol), where even the poorest homes were built of stone or stone and brick and were fairly solid, and where people felt less uneasy.[31] As will be seen below, there were loud calls for more effective ARP, in particular, safer shelters. Despite numerous infringements of the regulations, there was widespread concern that people should adhere to the blackout so as not to attract the enemy; and that Ack-Ack batteries and British fighters should always be engaged against enemy bombers. The demands for Ack-Ack merged practical and psychological protection. In September 1940 one woman wrote in a letter that she found the sound of gunfire 'really a rather comforting sound', another woman wrote in a letter 'guns are a perfectly heavenly sound', while yet another woman who had watched the first of the blitzes on the East End from the West End of London wrote in a letter that 'There didn't seem to be any gunfire at all, that was the horrible part about it'.[32] In Liverpool, John Davies recorded in his diary on 12 September 1940, 'The sound of the guns has a psychological effect on people – someone has said their noise is like music. The louder they bang the safer they feel.'[33] The following day an article in the *Daily Herald* on Ack-Ack was headlined 'Londoners Hear the Music of Guns and Rejoice'.[34] A report from Luton, north of London, explained in early October 1940, 'It is the dropping of bombs without any retaliation by gunfire which is getting on people's nerves; one woman down from London told me she felt far safer in London with the guns going off than she does here hearing German planes come and go as they please'.[35]

Two British academics who both published in the field of psychology – Philip Vernon, who was Head of the Psychology Department at the University of Glasgow, and Robert Thouless, who lectured at the University of Cambridge – pinpointed two important lessons that people learnt from experiencing air raids. First, there was a high chance of survival, which made people more optimistic and less apprehensive than before the bombing started. Second, being with others, having shelter officials present, and keeping active, helped to reduce anxiety. The body heat of others helped to thaw cold fear. The most common activities during a raid included talking, making tea or meals, playing games such as cards or darts, community singing, knitting or sewing in company.[36] Some people liked to carry on with their work, read or play the piano. Women and men, the working class and middle class, and all ages, could find something to do.

Responsibilities

People engaged in civil defence, air-raid wardens, police officers, fire-fighters, and ambulance crews, as well as paratroopers, submariners and pilots, all displayed conspicuous courage during the war. Civil-defence workers were in the open and active during air raids and blitzes. Objectively, they had most to fear, as they were most at risk, but actually having work to do was a palliative.[37]

Civil-defence workers' expectations and initial experiences were the hardest to bear. Barbara Nixon, an air-raid warden in Finsbury, London, who had previously been an actress, wrote in 1943 that in 1940 she had been very unsure about how she would respond to the sight of casualties; she had never seen a dead body, and was afraid that she might be sick at the sight of entrails. At her first incident, she was very unsure of herself, she was acutely self-conscious and as a protection she adopted a detached attitude. 'I had to watch myself, as well as the objective situation'. In later incidents 'one forgot oneself entirely in the job on hand.'[38] Towards the latter stages of the war, Peggy Scott gathered information about women at work. She quoted Dorothy Thackerah, a senior fire guard in Kensington, saying that she was frightened when raids began, but once outside in a raid she felt better; and a woman ambulance driver said that she felt strange when she first went out in a raid in March 1944 but she was all right once on the job. All the women ambulance drivers said that as soon as they had a job to do they were not afraid.[39]

Many years later, S. J. Rachman analysed studies of people feeling fear and displaying courage. He cited Dr Henry Wilson, who worked in a London hospital in 1942, who found that almost no one employed in essential services required help for psychological reactions to their work in air raids. In addition, Sir Aubrey Lewis, a psychiatrist at the Maudsley Hospital, remarked on the comparative invulnerability of firefighters and others in essential services, which he suggested was due to the fact that engaging in a socially useful occupation might have provided a form of 'inoculation' against stress. Indeed, some people who were previously in poor mental health were said to have considerably improved after taking up socially necessary work. Rachman suggested that this may have been due either to people feeling that they had more control over the situation, or because it distracted them from their feelings of fear.

Those in civil defence also received training and practice, which again is thought to help people prepare for dangerous work. Successful practice or experience increased people's sense of self-efficacy: courageous behaviour grew from a combination of competence and confidence. Activities that involved responsibility for others were especially useful in reducing people's fear; those with responsible tasks experienced increased courage: this was the opposite of learned helplessness; it was required usefulness.[40]

It was suggested at the time that responsibility had a stabilising effect. Many people said that when they had to look after someone else, their fears diminished, for which three reasons were suggested. First, the distress most people felt during raids was mainly due to a feeling of helplessness; by helping and comforting others, they stopped feeling like a helpless child and assumed an adult role. Second, they managed to 'project' the frightened part of themselves on to others, and so to keep it at a distance from themselves. Third, looking after others strengthened emotional ties, on which, more than anything else, mental resistance to the dangerous situation depended.[41] People formed a double attachment, to other people and to places: the people with whom they shared the experience of air raids, and the place where the raids happened.

The local dimension

In heavily bombed areas feelings tended to become localised: in August 1940 a raid on London upset the whole of the capital, but by early October people in Streatham or Stepney scarcely worried if Shoreditch or Lewisham were heavily raided.[42] Bombing and gunfire were taken as a matter of course, except where bombs actually fell.[43]

The experience of aerial attack enhanced a sense of local identity with, and pride in, London, which had the effect of making some young people want to share in the city's experience, not escape from it. On 13 September 1940, Colin Perry expressed pride and a sense of history; his language slides easily from London: the city, to Londoner: the citizen. His language reflected that of the media, and may have been written with an eye to publication.

> I would not quit London, my beloved City, the greatest in the world, in her hour of darkness for life itself. I am proud, glad to have the privilege of sharing her suffering in this, her most glorious, most bloody hour. The Epic of London will ring down through the ages, and people will marvel at the tenacity of the Londoner. I had thought him degenerate – but now I know that he is more resilient, resolute, tough and fierce than any other of mankind. Thank God I am a Londoner, and thank God that the freedom

> of the world rests on such able shoulders as those of my fellow man . . . It is a London hitherto unknown in history, a City in which every citizen represents the spirit to endure, the symbol of freedom, the castle of fortitude.

Just over a month later, on 16 October, his feelings were confirmed and he recorded, 'I should hate to leave my City in this her hour'.[44]

In his fictionalised account of life as a London ARP warden, John Strachey wrote in 1941, 'Ford [the ARP warden], who had never had much feeling for London – she had seemed too shapeless and unending – loved her for being the home of a steady, stubborn people.' Later in the novel he returns to the theme of Londoners' identity when describing reactions to the return of raids after the bombing of the provinces:

> Several Londoners next day said things like this, 'Well, we're glad they're back. Better come here than go after Coventry and Southampton and Bristol. We're used to it. We know what its like.' And, with a shake of the head they would add, 'I'm not so sure how they'll take it down there. It'll come very hard at first'.
>
> That was London's pride. That was her people's expression of their self-satisfaction. It was even partly true. No-one enjoyed the return of the raiders but it was genuinely a relief to know that they were here rather than over some port or northern industrial centre.[45]

After London's heavy raids in early September 1940, people in other cities put their experience of bombing in the context of Londoners' far worse trials, and many in the provinces expressed concern for London; in Leeds and Bristol people worried about how Londoners would stand up to the cumulative effects of raids throughout the winter.[46] A Liverpool man wrote in his diary, 'We feel that we are shirking the issue and not pulling our weight when we hear and read what London is going through.'[47] In Dundee the view was expressed that 'if only they would give us a turn, they might give London a night's rest', although the meaning here is ambiguous: was it a desire for a slice of the action or to spare Londoners?[48] By early October 1940, people in Aberdeen, the worst-bombed Scottish city at that point, thought it wrong to complain when they had suffered little compared with London.[49] In Bristol, accounts of raids circulating in the city tended to downplay the damage in Bristol compared with other cities.[50] After a heavy raid on Cardiff, in which people were killed, local talk tended to belittle rather than exaggerate it, and much of the talk about air raids continued to be about other towns, especially London.[51] Nella Last, writing in Barrow before it had received raids could not, however, identify with Londoners: 'I feel as if between me and the poor London people there is a thick fog, and it's only at intervals that I *can* believe it is our own people – not Spaniards or French or Dutch.'[52]

Accounts of London bombings helped people prepare themselves, and this seemed to contribute to people's ability to cope with raids. Once people's own area had been bombed, it fostered pride in their city, and even a rivalry, with sentiments such as: 'if London can take it so can we'.[53] A Portsmouth woman recorded that after the bombing of Coventry and other cities, people in Portsmouth felt sure that their turn would come, 'So certain were we, that I think we would have almost felt insulted if time went on & we were left out – as if we weren't important enough for Hitler's special attention'.[54]

The way in which Londoners developed their responses shaped the way in which the rest of the country reacted. This is not to reduce people's reactions to crude imitation, but to recognise, as sociological and anthropological studies have shown, that perceptions and acceptance of risk are related to social and cultural influences.[55] They are not emotional responses that occur in a vacuum.

There was a sense of relief that people's own city was sharing in the experience of bombing, and that they were acquitting themselves well. When Glasgow was heavily bombed in the spring of 1941 it was reported that there was a new sense of partnership with English blitzed cities and 'The people are now satisfied that they are bearing their full share of Britain's difficulties and bearing it just as well.'[56] An observer recorded that people seemed to think that they had been brought into the war for the first time 'and were rather proud of the fact'. All Glasgow newspapers gave prominence to statements by Cabinet ministers to the effect that Clydebank raids were as severe as anywhere in Britain.[57] A man whose house in Sheffield had had the windows blown out, but whose family was safe, wrote, 'Although it may be easy to say so not having suffered much inconvenience one feels proud to have shared in the trouble meted out to other parts of the country. After seeing what other people have had to contend with my wife & I are firmly resolved not to grumble at our own petty worries.'[58] Nella Last noted in her diary when the Regional Commissioner looked around Barrow and concluded 'Barrow is blitzed as badly as any place in England – London or Bristol included.'[59]

People's identity with their city was not merely an abstract one, but could be rooted in practical economics. After Exeter had been blitzed, many people there were anxious for Exeter to be restored as a shopping centre as soon as possible, in order that Taunton (roughly twenty-five miles to the north-east) would not gain at Exeter's expense.[60] Physical damage to one's own city was especially hard to bear, even if it was not as badly affected as other cities. J. B. Priestley spoke of the horror of seeing his home city, Bradford, damaged:

> it was far more of a shock to see a few burnt-out buildings in this town than it had been to see all the damage in London . . . I think the sight made a far deeper impression upon me than all the bombing I had seen for weeks in London, because it somehow brought together two entirely different worlds; the safe and shining world of my childhood, and this insecure and lunatic world of to-day, so it caught and held my imagination.[61]

National acknowledgement of local suffering and 'attention' from Hitler was extremely important to people. There was indignation in Plymouth, Birmingham, Bristol and Southampton after heavy raids, when the cities were described anonymously in BBC announcements about raids. In Bristol there was acute disappointment at the way in which news of raids on the city were handled; that Bristol was not given the same publicity as Coventry; and that the King had not visited Bristol after heavy raids.[62] George Orwell commented that people were incensed when the number of casualties in their area was underestimated in reports.[63] The demand for the naming of places in reports of air raids was also part of the demand for more specific news of raids and casualties.[64] When the Germans raided provincial cities, some Londoners expressed mild chagrin at not being centre stage.[65] The desire for recognition did not die down. It was reported in 1942 that when a town suffered daylight raids, it wanted to get the 'credit' of a mention; criticisms continued to be expressed of some towns receiving a mention but not others. When the book *Front Line* was published in 1942, it was reported from Liverpool that people were pleased that the city was given its 'rightful place' next to London.[66]

As well as expecting public recognition for raids, people were livid if their town was publicly criticised, as happened when the BBC broadcast criticisms of Norwich's poor blackout.[67] Yet, many people expressed fears about infringement of blackout regulations in their city, and criticised the organisation of local post-raid services. The Exeter press took issue with three London papers when they claimed that there was chaos in Exeter following a heavy raid.[68]

The media reconstructed people's experiences at the local level, and may have thereby reinforced a link between air raids and local identity. The provincial press underlined the work local people were doing as a direct contribution to the war effort,[69] and gave a local spin to stories of working after the siren. So, for instance, the *Bristol Evening Post* insisted that Bristol had pioneered the system of working after the siren with roof spotters. 'Though some London papers may claim to have originated the idea, we were ahead of them here.'[70] (It was the *Daily Express*,

Beaverbrook's own paper, that claimed to have initiated the system, and indeed it adopted a slogan for the nation 'Look Out and Work On'![71]) The provincial press highlighted the bravery of local airmen and civil-defence workers, including roof spotters.[72]

Apart from reporting local events, provincial papers also devoted space to the experiences of London, in particular the East End. Local papers across the country reported the heavy bombing of London, which was seen as suffering on an unparalleled scale.[73] In early October 1940 when the *Luftwaffe* was remorselessly pounding the East End of London, the *Glasgow Herald* pointed out that in the First World War, troops spent limited periods of roughly two weeks in the front-line trenches, yet already East Enders had spent five weeks 'in the front line'.[74]

The press did not immediately report bombings of the BBC in London, but when accounts appeared, the message was clear. Those killed were all heroes: 'Women Among Heroic Victims of Raid on BBC'. The damage and deaths were not underplayed, so that the bravery of staff was thereby clear: 'Broadcasting House Bombed. Staff Die At Posts . . . it was seriously damaged'. The steadfastness of the newsreaders was not in any doubt, and the grim humour of the staff was underlined: 'The first danger warning came from a roof spotter, who shouted down the telephone to the control-room "Look out! There's a big one coming". A moment later came an ear-splitting crash. "Butter fingers", said the control room duty officer'. The tragedy of the second attack was conveyed by the details of the policeman who was killed. He had been engaged for two months, and a description of his fiancée was provided. That the BBC was broadcasting news in German when it was bombed drew a stark contrast between the British, who were sending information to the Germans, while they sent the British bombs.[75]

Colin Perry articulated his experiences in the language that he read in the local press. He had already recorded in his diary his pride in London and his desire to be part of London's war experience when, on 30 September 1940, he wrote, 'The *Standard* tonight says that after the war when people are asked what they were in, they will say they were airmen, soldiers, sailors or, with pride, will boast they were a citizen of London. So, without effort, I am bang in the middle of war'. Again, on 9 October he wrote 'The *Daily Express* says that all our citizens should wear a badge which says: "A Citizen of London – 1940". How proud I am to be one. I can see now that Destiny has trimmed my wings, shot us out of St Albans and Southampton so that I may be present in my City's most noble hour. Thank God.'[76]

Experience of the raids not only fostered pride in one's city, but also in oneself. In October 1940 the censor wrote, 'whereas in June people seemed to feel that only Churchill stood between them and disaster, now the ordinary people of England have shown that they too could play just as stubborn and important a part'.[77] That 'part' in the war effort involved continuing with the normal routines of life and work, which is what most people wanted to do.

The importance of routine

'Need for normal work and amusement is felt by many people.'[78] Once bombs began dropping, there was a quick shift in emphasis away from automatically taking cover. People were keen to maintain a routine and to avoid disruption, even if this carried a risk. People would rather run the risk of catching a bus during an air raid than of being marooned in the blackout, unable to get home.[79] There was a 'mental opposition' to any dislocation of 'normal habits, routine or whatever one is engaged upon'.[80] By early October young people were reverting to their normal entertainment, despite the continued night-time bombing, 'because it takes you out of yourself'.[81]

People at work were also wedded to their routine. A civil servant recorded the reaction of a maid serving the breakfast in a Bristol hotel five minutes after the siren sounded one morning in August 1940, 'She said that she was "too busy to be held up by them things" and that there was time enough to shelter when the noise began'.[82] Elsewhere a woman worker commented dismissively, 'You can waste a lot of time on this air raid lark if you want to'.[83]

The importance of maintaining a routine for poorer families may have been related to the need not to waste money or food. One Mass-Observer talked to his hairdresser in London, who told him that when the last air-raid warning sounded, he went home to turn off the gas, but his wife responded 'What, when I'm just going to put the Yorkshire pudding in the oven; what about the Sunday dinner'?[84] A woman from Shoreditch, in the East End of London, later recalled that during the buzz-bomb raids they would all go to the shelter during the week when the alert sounded, but not on Sundays, as the mothers were cooking the Sunday dinner. Instead, she and another girl would listen out for the bombs at two different spots in the block of flats, and if they heard a bomb coming they would alert the block.[85]

Enjoyment

Not only did it become common practice to ignore the siren and carry on with whatever activity one happened to be engaged upon, but many actually enjoyed watching planes in dogfights.[86] In Southampton, people not only failed to take cover when the siren sounded, but many civilians gathered in parks or roads to watch the aircraft overhead. One Home Guard platoon described bombs dropping, planes circling the town and gunfire, and 'People still seen watching aircraft in preference to taking cover'.[87] In Bristol, people enjoyed watching the searchlights. An observer there thought that more men than women watched them, and that the men liked to boast about what they had seen, with the faint implication of how brave it was of them not to take cover.[88]

Many felt a real sense of excitement.[89] A young Southampton librarian described the sight and sound of an air raid on the city, and wrote 'Everybody was excited, the firemen dashing around getting ready for anything that might drop, the wardens anxious to get a glimpse of a dog-fight . . . Everybody felt extremely keyed up – exhilarated. "Bring the buggers down" we yelled . . .' Although worried about his relatives and friends in other parts of the town:

> I enjoyed the raid. The loss of life going on at the moment didn't occur to me until afterwards. – The raid served as a kind of stimulus such that after it I felt keyed up and kind of happy like when you're pretty drunk. I met some pals after the raid and we went over to my place where, together with my girlfriend, we had a snack tea and played the rowdier jazz classics and made a party of it. It was a good party largely because that residue of exhilaration – we all felt it – left after the raid which is all very interesting because we don't like the war politically, intellectually or – we thought – emotionally. Not that we think anything else can be done now. But, if you understand me, we are by education anti-war.[90]

In Caterham in Surrey, an observer noted that watching a dogfight was treated as a new and interesting sport, and the feeling when a plane came down was the same as when a goal was scored.[91] A large-scale air battle over Bristol was thought to have a 'remarkably stimulating effect on the thousands who watched the enemy planes being routed by our fighters'.[92] Colin Perry wrote again and again in his diary of the excitement he felt when watching air raids and dogfights.[93] A London actor wrote 'I may be an exception to the rule, but I thoroughly enjoy the air-raids. They really are stimulating . . . If it were not for the deaths and destruction and the finish of the theatre in London I could say I thoroughly enjoy Adolph's [*sic.*] worst efforts.'[94]

The excitement of raids never flagged. In the autumn of 1943, for Londoners the danger of watching the 'magnificent sight' added 'zip and verve to the experience' and many people treated the raid as though it were a football match, with 'advice being shouted to both searchlight and gun crews', although such behaviour also prompted criticism.[95]

Psychological studies suggested that feelings of excitement did not mean that people had no fear, but rather that air raids caused emotional tensions such as fear, excitement, and irritability, that could not be separated.[96] The feeling of excitement was much more closely associated with children and young people's reactions than with those of older people.

Age variations

People's ages affected their reactions to air raids. There is contemporary evidence to suggest that children and young people stood up to the risks of air raids better than older people, but there was far more interest in children's than older people's reactions.[97] Children were seen as taking their cue from adults. If parents were cheerful and showed no obvious fear, as was usual, children caught their spirit, while anxious parents passed their anxiety on to their children.[98] The attitude of adults, and of mothers in particular, was generally agreed to be crucial: children's behaviour was largely determined by that of the adults around them.[99] As most children coped well with the experience of air raids, there is an implied praise of working-class mothers. Children were more likely to be with their mothers than both parents, as a result of the call-up and of fathers being at work. Calm and coping working-class children were a reflection of calm and coping working-class mothers. This was a virtuous circle: people coped best when they had others to look after. Mothers, concerned first and foremost for their children's safety,[100] thought about the children and, in doing so, paid less attention to anxieties about their own safety; their apparent calm was then communicated to their children. As young people were often making a direct contribution to the war effort at work, it is significant that they were among those most easily able to cope with air raids. This underlines the importance of avoiding generalisations based on one social division, such as class.

The influence of working-class culture on the behaviour of troops in the First World War has been discussed by J. M. Bourne, who suggests that the working class were well able to adapt to the challenges of war because similar factors were at work in their lives in both war and peace: a sense of community, social cohesiveness, a capacity for endurance, solidarity in adversity and physical hardship; their strategies for survival included sharing, comradeship, conformity to social norms and a self-deprecating humour.[101] While this may also have been the case for working-class civilians during the Second World War, it is hard to prove an exact link, and assuming a direct link between working-class culture and behaviour in air raids can easily fall into the trap of relying on stereotypes for explanation. The varied attitudes towards, and use of, air-raid shelters in particular, should act as a warning against stereotyping people's behaviour in wartime.

Shelters

Shelters, whether public or private, were enormously important to people. During the heavy raids on the East End of London, many thousands took cover in shelters and the Underground. In other places, such as Chislehurst and Dover in Kent, thousands sheltered in caves for months on end. For some, the nightly trek became part of their routine.[102] Fury erupted at the inadequacy of shelters and the tardy response of the authorities to the demand of East Enders in particular for a safe nightly refuge.

Even so, most people did not go to public shelters, or even to ones in their own homes or gardens; some took cover in a cupboard or under the stairs. Many people simply stayed on the ground floor, perhaps in the hallway. One cannot be sure of the exact figures, but Mass-Observation found that in the early days of the intensive bombing of London the numbers of people going to shelters increased. Already by 26 September, however, Mass-Observation reckoned that 71 per cent of people slept in their own homes, of whom the majority slept on the ground floor or in a basement; 25 per cent slept in their own shelters; and a mere 4 per cent slept in public shelters.[103] Even if these figures are not accurate, they are indicative of where people slept. As the weeks dragged on, people in London and elsewhere were found to be increasingly sheltering at home.[104] In provincial blitzes, many stayed at home rather than go to public shelters.

People used shelters for reasons other than escaping air raids. Some went to shelters because the damage to their homes was so great that they were in effect homeless, or certainly could not sleep in their homes.[105] During the heavy raids on London in September and October 1940, it was claimed that many went to the Tilbury shelter for a companionable evening and cheap Salvation Army canteen meal, and then went home to sleep.[106] When the blitzes on the East End temporarily abated and later when they ceased, many continued to frequent deep shelters, either because they enjoyed the communal life or at least because it was preferable to a solitary night at home.

Some young people appear to have visited certain shelters for the opportunities they offered of meeting the opposite sex. There were widespread fears about the sexual morals of young working-class women, both in the auxiliary services and in civilian life. One policewoman, who patrolled central Liverpool, clearly expressed her personal moral condemnation of the behaviour of adults in shelters, but her reports also referred to the young age of the girls involved (she does not state their ages), which suggests that she also saw the problem as a more serious, child protection one, although there was no suggestion that the girls were not willing participants. She alleged that shelters in central Liverpool were a place for servicemen and seamen to meet with women and girls; there was excessive drinking, gambling and prostitution. Girls were attracted to the shelters less to take cover and more for the excitement of various servicemen and foreign sailors. On 6 October the policewoman wrote:

> The condition of this shelter tonight was most revolting. It was packed, largely with very young girls, generally accompanied by foreign or British seamen, many under the influence of drink. Five drunked [*sic.*] Norwegians tried to force their way past me into a plainly labelled "Women's Lavatory". Inside the lavatory girls were sitting on the top of the dividing partitions and making vulgar suggestions to the seamen.[107]

Just as people went to shelters for reasons other than to escape the bombs, one cannot assume that people who did not take cover were not frightened, or that the air raids and bombing were not affecting them. Some old disabled people did not use shelters, because they could not get down to them. Those with relatives often felt compelled to stay with them and not go to the shelters themselves either.[108]

One should not assume, moreover, that feelings can be judged from behaviour. In 1942 Orwell wrote of hearing an air-raid alert for the first time in ten months: 'Inwardly rather frightened, and everyone else evidently the same, though studiously taking no notice and indeed not referring to the fact of there being a raid on until the All Clear had sounded.'[109] Indeed, psychologists suggested that as well as controlling overt signs of fear by their behaviour, it was also the case that when people claimed not to be frightened in air raids, what they meant was that they got over their fear within minutes, hours or at least by the next morning;[110] this also helps to explain why so much contemporary, let alone memory, material provides relatively little evidence of fear. There were also more conscious reasons for downplaying fear.

There was social pressure among some not to go to shelters in air raids. George Orwell again recorded in his diary on 25 June 1940 that he got up in the night when the siren sounded and stood around talking. 'This is what everyone did . . . in the absence of gunfire or other excitement one is ashamed to go to the shelter'. Two months later he uses the same language of 'shame' to explain the behaviour of others in inner London: 'For the first 15 seconds there is great alarm, blowing of whistles and shouts to children to go indoors, then people begin to congregate on the streets and gaze expectantly at the sky. In the daytime people are apparently ashamed to go into the shelters till they hear the bombs'.[111] This comment may have been Orwell projecting his feelings on to others. On the one hand, one can assume that it is unlikely that he was alone in his feelings, but, on the other hand, one cannot assume that what one person felt was felt by all. Orwell comments on the number of false alarms in the early weeks, which would have reinforced the feelings of embarrassment in over-reacting by taking shelter. His comments about feelings of shame were made before the heavy bombing of London, and it is likely that social inhibitions disappeared or were reduced once people experienced heavy bombing. One of the worst effects of heavy night-time bombing was the loss of sleep.

Many people did not want to get up and go to a shelter at night because of the disruption to sleep, and consequently to their daily routine.[112] Staying in bed was thought to disturb sleep less than getting out of bed and going down to the shelter when the siren sounded, or spending the whole night in a surface shelter.[113] Typical was a woman who commented, 'I stayed in bed. I'd just got into bed and I heard it [the siren] go off, but I thought to myself, Well, I want to get the house tidy tomorrow and you can't keep going properly can you with all this popping up and down'.[114] People frequently commented on the problem of loss of sleep during air raids. Most of those in heavily bombed areas did not get enough sleep. During the blitzes on Plymouth there were serious problems of physical fatigue because civil-defence workers who were on duty all night often had full days of work ahead of them.[115] There were strong reasons therefore for people not to disrupt their lives any more than was absolutely necessary.

Shelters were not necessarily safe, and indeed, a common reason for not going to a shelter was a feeling that one was not safe anywhere.[116] Terrible rumours circulated about what happened to people in shelters that received direct hits, as for instance in Sheffield, where rumours spread about people being drowned and gassed in shelters.[117] The local press made it abundantly clear in reports of direct hits on shelters, that taking cover in a shelter, whether an Anderson shelter in the back yard or a public one, was no sanctuary from a direct hit. Such stories must have led people to question how much use there was in going to a shelter.[118]

As well as reports of shelters receiving hits, newspaper reports also highlighted the randomness of hits and the element of luck in survival – again calling into question the point of sheltering.[119] When the press reported hits on cinemas and shelters on the same page, at least those in the cinema had ended their days enjoying themselves – while the advantage of going to the shelter was not apparent.[120] With people reading these accounts, it becomes less surprising that very soon after raids began, people were not all rushing to shelters the moment the siren sounded: experience began to suggest that shelters did not offer complete safety. Indeed, some brick and concrete street shelters were death traps, and government steps to improve them did not completely alter their reputation. If one was not safe in a shelter, the desire to avoid the inconvenience and unpleasantness of shelters began to outweigh any benefits they had to offer. Indeed, people were often more conscious of the dangers of shelters when they were in them.

People often felt more nervous in shelters, where they had nothing to do but wait for a bomb to drop on them. 'While we worked at our jobs nervousness and even the knowledge that a raid was on left us completely. But as soon as we dived into the shelters . . . a feeling of nervousness and danger quickly returned'.[121] Shelterers could feel hemmed in. An army officer in a shelter with his wife and brother during an air raid wrote a few months later: 'We had been in a shelter but after a time the feeling of being shut in was too much for us and we decided, in what appeared to be a lull, to attempt to get away from the noise and horror around us.'[122] Harold Nicolson, a parliamentary secretary at the Ministry of Information, recorded in his diary on 24 September 1940, 'I don't mind being blown up. What I dread is being buried under huge piles of masonry and hearing water drip slowly, smelling gas creeping towards me and hearing the faint cries of colleagues condemned to a slow and ungainly death'.[123]

Shelters also had a number of practical disadvantages. Shelters were often overcrowded: the Horder Committee that was set up to investigate the effects of public air-raid shelters on health found this to be their main problem. They were erected at an erratic pace, and many had not been finished when bombing began.[124] Well into 1941 councils were still completing shelters.[125]

Stepney, which suffered some of worst bombing in the East End, was woefully ill-prepared in all aspects of ARP. Shelters were erected far too slowly, especially for an area that required extensive public provision of shelters because people did not have the space to erect private shelters.[126] Other areas also had problems and were slow to build enough shelters, but these areas never suffered the ferocity of the bombardment on Stepney.[127]

Problems of overcrowding were aggravated when one group of the population used shelters intended for another group. In Woolwich, close to the heavily bombed London docks, certain shelters were meant for commuters caught in a raid, but often other people would install themselves in the shelter before the siren sounded, so leaving no room for the commuters.[128] In north-east England it was alleged that wardens and shelter captains kept a shelter for their own use and refused to let other people into it.[129] Shelters could very quickly fill up – not only with people but also with their possessions.[130]

The negative experience of shelters was closely associated with the wartime crime wave, and, in particular, crimes committed by young people. Youth crime during the war was a Europe-wide phenomenon.[131] In Britain, the number of crimes on the statute book rose during the war; the recorded number of crimes and the recorded number of criminals both shot up. As it had been expected that youth crime would rise in wartime, the police were especially vigilant about catching young criminals, and then charging them. Local newspapers were full of reports of petty crimes, many taking place during air raids and in shelters, but one should not exaggerate the problem. Reading local newspapers uncritically could leave the impression that almost the entire country was involved in criminal activity, whereas in fact local newspapers filled much of their copy in war and peace with reports from local police and magistrates' courts, so inevitably, petty crimes loomed large in local newspapers. Anti-social behaviour in air-raid shelters was especially likely to reach the press because air-raid wardens often patrolled shelters, so bad behaviour quickly came to 'official' attention. The police were more likely to be on the scene quickly when trouble took place in the vicinity of shelters, and this too could escalate the seriousness of rough behaviour. So, for instance, when a couple of Canadian soldiers, who had been drinking, caused a disturbance in a shelter and one hit a policeman (who then walloped him over the head with his truncheon), both soldiers ended up in court.[132] The same behaviour in pubs, or on the street when no policemen were present, would go unrecorded.

The opportunities for criminal behaviour were, nevertheless, certainly far greater in wartime. The blackout meant that it was easy to avoid detection; shortages and high wages stimulated the black market; and it was harder for parents to know what their children were doing, even when the children were not evacuees. Young people preferred to use different shelters from their parents, or not to take cover at all.[133]

While the black market attracted both systematically serious and opportunistic thieving at work – especially in the docks and on the railways, and from homes and shops damaged in raids – air-raid shelters also offered an opportunity for fairly minor pilfering.[134] The effect on law-abiding shelterers was not, however, minor. When shelters were vandalised, it made them extremely difficult to use.[135]

A number of cities experienced vandalism and looting during and after air raids.[136] In May 1941, problems of looting and 'wanton destruction' had reached such 'alarming proportions' that some people were too afraid to take shelter in an attack, for fear of being robbed of their remaining possessions.[137] Problems of vandalism were not confined to London shelters, but were a bugbear in towns as far apart as Newport, Liverpool and Stockton.[138]

Not everyone wanted to spend time with intimate strangers, and antisocial behaviour must have deterred some from frequenting shelters. As well as violence against property, interpersonal violence also rose during the war. The worst violence occurred in queues, including those outside air-raid shelters, and inside shelters.[139] It is hardly surprising that when people of different ages were crammed together, for a mixture of reasons, and, when anxiety levels were high, tensions boiled over. There were thefts and fights in shelters.[140] We have already quoted the Liverpool policewoman's graphic description of the 'most revolting' and 'vulgar' behaviour in a Liverpool shelter.[141] Complaints abounded of 'misuse' of public shelters.[142] John Davies, who lived in Liverpool, wrote in his diary on 24 September 1940 that there was far too much bad behaviour in shelters; there were complaints about rowdyism and drunkenness. Manchester ARP wardens exhibited 400 Good Behaviour Posters in shelters, appealing for better standards of conduct.[143] From early October 1940, when London was still being pounded nightly, Colin Perry's mother and younger brother abandoned the shelter because they could not stand the rows that took place in it, and from then on they stayed at home with Colin and his father, who never took cover.[144] Cooped up in a shelter with an irritating person got on people's nerves: 'I am getting horribly tired of sitting with Mrs C. and her moaning in the shelter'.[145]

Some people's behaviour was so appalling that councils introduced strict regulations, and early in 1941 central government laid down rules governing people's behaviour in shelters. Under an Order in Council, Regional Commissioners set out rules for admission to shelters by ticket, and for shelter wardens to enforce the rules – if necessary by throwing people out of the shelter – which were clearly set out, and reflected problems already encountered: they prohibited drunkenness; 'wilfully disturbing' others; improper use of the lavatories; spitting; littering; giving or receiving money for reserving places; taking loaded firearms into shelters; bill posting; interfering with notices, lighting, ventilation, gasproof and any other shutters; smoking; singing or playing instruments; begging; collecting money; selling goods; distributing printed or other material; taking offensive or dangerous items into a shelter, including: items for heating and cooking, prams, animals, birds, furniture or bedding except stools, cushions or coverings. There were also measures to deal with those who were infectious or 'offensively unclean or verminous'.[146] Recorded complaints and incidents declined, which may reflect more infrequent use of shelters, both as a result of less bombing or people avoiding notorious shelters; more effective patrolling of them; better behaviour; or people being more resigned to the nastier side of shelter life.

Shelters could damage your health. Most shelters initially leaked, and even after floors had been cemented (not an easy task when cement was in short supply), many continued to flood or at least to be damp.[147] Ventilation was often poor and made worse by people smoking in shelters.[148] Some shelters were infested with rats.[149] Dogs were an added nuisance and a potential health hazard which many councils tried to ban from shelters.[150] The bad effects of shelter life on children were thought to be disturbed sleep, unsuitable food, insufficient air and the generally unsanitary conditions.[151]

Many shelters, especially in London, had unsatisfactory sanitary arrangements and there was enormous anxiety expressed in the local, national and medical press about the possibility of serious epidemics breaking out in shelters.[152] As well as the fear of infectious diseases spreading in shelters, which did not in fact occur, there were health problems associated with shelter life.[153] Shelter problems were not confined to London. People complained about the poor state of shelters over the length and breadth of the country.[154]

The issue of unhealthy and unsafe shelters turned into a full-blown political row. The Communist Party was at the forefront of demands for deeper and safer shelters,[155] but the campaign was part of an attack on privilege that stretched beyond the Communist Party. *Picture Post*, for instance, carried pictures of buildings with safe basements that people could not enter.[156] Across the country, calls were made for deep shelters that could withstand bombing. The press took up the calls for deep shelters, and both central and local government received a steady stream of deputations demanding the construction of deep shelters. Tenants' Defence Leagues and Vigilance Committees demanded better ARP.[157] At the annual TUC conference in the autumn of 1940 trade unionists discussed the lack of safe shelters and lobbied various councils to provide them.[158]

By early November 1940 there were fewer complaints reported about shelters, but there were still thought to be too few at schools, too few deep shelters and too much damp in them.[159] While complaints about shelters died down, they had sown seeds of dissatisfaction with 'authority' that were expressed privately (but picked up by the weekly home intelligence reports) and publicly. By early 1941 there were demands heard that if people were enduring the war, then there should be no return to the 1930s, and that the future should be planned.[160]

Mixed motives and reactions

Any of the above explanations could have contributed to people not wanting to use the shelters, or a combination of these reasons. Mixed motives for not using a shelter were expressed by one London man, who wrote that he wanted to be on hand to save his books and papers in the event of fire; the people in the shelter were nervous, and the woman next door chattered 'incessantly', which wore him to a frazzle; the shelter was small and stuffy and it was impossible to do anything in it; and, finally, it was much more interesting to watch the searchlights, see gunfire and count the bombs.[161]

Some also expressed contradictory reactions to air raids. After heavy raids on Swansea, someone commented 'we don't take any notice of the warnings, they happen too often, you just take it as a matter of routine . . . I don't mind telling you, my stomach turns over when I hear the warnings now'.[162] A woman in Eastbourne wrote that people outside were less frightened because they had the excitement of seeing planes shot down, but then went on to comment that most people admitted to feeling frightened.[163]

There is some evidence that people reacted differently to daytime and night-time raids; they got used to daytime raids more quickly than those at night. At the beginning of September 1940, before the blitzes on the East End started, a woman aged roughly fifty commented, 'You can at least see what you're doing, and you know it's easier to shoot them down in day', a man aged about sixty said, 'In the night they just drop their bombs anywhere and run', a woman aged roughly seventy complained, 'The shelters are so awful to get to at night', and a woman aged about thirty thought that it was bad enough losing time at work, but 'it's a bloody sight worse losing sleep'.[164]

Edward Glover, a psychoanalyst, commented at the time that the safety factor in choosing to shelter or to not take cover was heavily overlaid by irrational reactions and rationalisations. Ordinarily sane and sensible people of every class made decisions based on 'superstitions, feelings of omnipotence and every possible illogicality'. Even when people changed their behaviour in the light of raid experience, Glover claimed, this seldom amounted to more than replacing one form of superstition with another one.[165] One person's 'superstition' may be another one's faith.

Christianity

Anthropologists have shown how religion can reduce fears, anxieties and insecurities, especially during war.[166] The role of Christianity in sustaining people during air raids needs, therefore, to be addressed. While historians argue over why Britain declared war on Germany and then pursued a policy of total victory, politicians at the time presented the war as a moral one, driven by more than imperial, trading or balance of power self-interest; it was a clear-cut case of good against evil. To what extent did the moral imperative translate into a war that was sustained and succoured by religious conviction, and which may help to explain people's behaviour in air raids? The question is almost impossible to answer, for even if we had reliable information on people's religious beliefs, we have no way of knowing how far their overall beliefs affected them in specific circumstances. All we can offer are some speculative comments.

The best-known religious experience during an air raid is a literary one. In Graham Greene's *The End of the Affair*, set during the war, Maurice Bendrix is having an affair with Sarah Miles, wife of Henry. During an air raid, Maurice goes downstairs; when Sarah finds him she thinks that he is dead. Although she does not believe in prayer, nevertheless she prays, 'I love him and I'll do anything if you'll make him alive . . . I'll give him up forever, only let him be alive with a chance.' Maurice does indeed survive, Sarah keeps her part of the bargain with God, and it is the end of the affair.[167] Is this experience typical? We know from anecdotal evidence that people do engage in crisis-praying of momentary duration, but hard evidence of it is hard to unearth. Did people turn to God during air raids, and did religious conviction really influence their behaviour during and after raids?

There is some evidence that war heightened people's interest in religion.[168] In 1941 Arthur Mee published *Nineteen-Forty: Our Finest Hour*, a highly romanticised version of English history, shot through with a nationalistic Christianity and written in overblown, flowery language that could not be further from the grim reality of bombing. Yet, according to Richard Weight, it was a best-seller and highly praised in the press.[169] The following year, William Temple, an immensely popular Archbishop of Canterbury, 1942–44, published a best-seller *Christianity and the Social Order*. He also launched a series of public meetings that thousands attended in different parts of the country. Indeed, the first one, held at the Albert Hall in London, sold out two months in advance. Temple, as a number of other church leaders during the war, applied Christian principles to burning social and political issues (such as health, education, housing and social equality), so that it was extremely difficult to separate Christian values from social ones, which may well have helped to increase interest in Christianity at a time when there was widespread interest in social reform. Temple and a number of other churchmen offered a credible message as they linked Christianity with the reality of people's daily lives.

One of the most enduring images of Britain during the Second World War is a religious one: St Paul's cathedral stands as a national icon of faith, hope, endurance and unity. This unambiguous, strong, national image is in sharp contrast to the nebulous role of personal Christian conviction in wartime. Information about religious beliefs is very unreliable and hard to interpret. There are two key sources for the war period, church attendance figures and responses from Mass-Observation informants, but, as Mass-Observation pointed out at the time, most people have definite views on what their answers *ought* to be in response to questions about their religious beliefs and practices, and responses to questions need therefore to be treated with care.

British Protestant church membership fell throughout the twentieth century, by 6 per cent between 1900 and 1967, but by 13 per cent during the Second World War. War therefore speeded up a well-established trend. The greatest fall in regular worship occurred in the early part of the war, when evacuation, the blackout and new demands on people's time made church attendance more difficult for many; after 1941, church attendance crept up. In contrast to falling Protestant numbers, the Roman Catholic Church succeeded in maintaining its growth. Not only was church attendance much higher at Christmas and Easter than at other times of year, it was also greater at moments of crisis, when the churches pulled in large congregations. Roughly 25 per cent of the population, a phenomenally high number, participated in National Days of Prayer, and 60 per cent of the population thought them a good idea.[170] On National Days of Prayer (there was one every year on the anniversary of the outbreak of war, plus a number of additional ones) churches were packed to overflowing, and outdoor ceremonies attracted many thousands.[171]

Attendance at national days of prayer ceremonies was not, however, always entirely voluntary,[172] and there was some hostility to them,[173] but pockets of scepticism and irritation were relatively insignificant set alongside the enthusiasm across the country for attending services (which caught many clergy by surprise) or listening to broadcasts on the BBC when a National Day of Prayer fell on a workday. Why people voluntarily attended National Days of Prayer, and what they felt that they gained from the experience we do no know: was it an expression of community, or of religious conviction? Our knowledge of religious conviction during the war is limited and shaky.

Roughly four million people regularly attended church, many millions more were involved with churches at some level, and still more held spiritual beliefs. By the middle of the war, between four-fifths and three-quarters of the population paid some sort of lip service to religion, and about half had some definite interest in a religious faith – deep enough for them to pray at least irregularly. Among 1,500 Mass-Observation informants, about half claimed to pray regularly or occasionally; they were not asked about praying in air raids.[174]

In some large industrial centres there were Church of England, Roman Catholic and Free Church chaplains attached to hostels and factories, but only a small proportion of workers showed any enthusiasm for them. Many did not see the relevance of churches to their lives, and they were sometimes suspicious of chaplains' motives, a feeling that was paralleled in the Forces. Many were too tired for religious services and wanted to relax and be entertained after a hard work shift.[175]

The war appeared to confirm and strengthen people's existing beliefs, but we do not know which aspects of the war influenced people. Those who were already religious tended to place even more faith in religion; agnostics and sceptics tended to think that the war had shown how right they were to be agnostic and sceptical. In 1941 among one Mass-Observation panel, about 16 per cent felt that their faith had been strengthened during the war, and, in 1942, this figure rose to 26 per cent. The increase in faith was mainly among women. In 1941 and 1942 about 9 per cent felt that their faith had weakened during the war. Mass-Observation concluded that the faith of 'thoughtful' Christians had strengthened, but there was little sign of new people turning to Christianity in wartime. There was a revival of inspiration among the already religious rather than the birth of stirrings of faith among the previously faithless: the religious revival was qualitative, not quantitative.[176] None of this evidence gives any indication of the precise impact of air raids.

There was, of course, crisis praying during the war, which may have helped people to control their fears. There were believers who only actually prayed in a crisis, such as an eighteen-year-old man, 'Yes, during the blitz, when things were bad, I prayed to relieve my feelings. Not help – just nerves more than anything else.' There were also those who doubted whether there was a God, but who prayed in times of crisis, such as raids. A forty-five-year-old man commented, 'People get weak-minded when they're scared stiff. I pray that we'll be spared. Then I think some other poor devil's getting it, and I add on a bit about him. You're not reasonable when the buzz bombs are cutting out overhead.' Another twenty-five-year-old man who was also sceptical, when asked if he prayed replied, 'Well perhaps I might have, once or twice when we had the doodle bugs around so much. You sort of say a little bit in spite of yourself, as it were. It's fetched out of you before you know.' The particular circumstances of air raids prompted prayers, and a hymn was even composed for singing in the blitzes. It began: 'God is our refuge, be not afraid, He will be with you all through the raid', and ended, 'When bombs are dropping and danger is near, He will be with you, until the all clear.[177]

It is impossible to know whether those engaged in war work were likely to have been influenced by religious faith to carry on during raids and to run risks, but it is possible to speculate that, on the whole, this is unlikely. Although we have no information on people's class, work or area in relationship to their beliefs, we do know that those aged under forty, and men, that is those most likely to be engaged on war work, were those most likely to claim to have no religious beliefs.[178] All we can conclude, therefore, is that there is no compelling evidence that most people felt that they were helped by their Christian faith to run risks and to continue with their work after the siren sounded.

At the workplace

Many of the reasons discussed for people not taking shelter on the sound of the siren applied as much to people at work as away from it: getting used to the raids; a modified perception of danger and security; keeping active, including work, as a way of reducing fear; local or group identity; the behaviour of others, either directly observed or heard about; a pride in surviving raids, and a need or desire to maintain a routine. Some of the reasons why people disliked using shelters in particular would also have been applicable to workplace shelters: nervousness at being hemmed in; a feeling that one was no safer in a shelter that received a direct hit than anywhere else; inadequate, damp, poorly ventilated or unhealthy shelters; and social or group pressure not to go to the shelter. In addition, there were workplace-specific reasons for not taking cover on the sound of the siren.

Media

The media and the public put indirect pressure on certain groups of workers to carry on after the siren sounded. Whether it had any effect is impossible to know, but people were making decisions in the cultural context of media images, pressures and suggestions. The media attempted to pressurise workers to keep going after the siren sounded, by reporting and supporting the pleas of politicians and by using military metaphors for civilians (as discussed in chapter 2), as well as by giving the impression that this was what everyone else was doing and the normal way to behave (as discussed in chapter 4).

The impact of the BBC is difficult to extrapolate from other influences, but most of the civilian population had access to a radio; the catchphrases of programmes such as ITMA passed into common speech, and in the summer of 1940 it was suggested that widespread civilian bravado in not taking cover was in imitation of BBC and press reports.[179]

At the cinema people saw idealised British characteristics, which may have unconsciously planted seeds that mingled with other, more obvious influences, to influence behaviour. Many British wartime feature films portray working-class heroes and heroines, some of whom are civilians. Civilians in wartime films are imbued with characteristics that politicians and the media thought necessary for those willing to ignore the air-raid siren. These characteristics were also the ones that were depicted as part of the national character and thus part of national identity. National identity was at the core of national propaganda.[180]

Key national characteristics that were presumed by other media to be required characteristics of those ignoring air-raid warnings and working up until the roof spotters' warnings, and which were portrayed in some of the most celebrated wartime films included:

- A willingness to run risks: *The Foreman Went to France* (1941); *San Demetrio, London* (1943); *Fires Were Started* (1943).
- A sense of duty: *The Foreman Went to France*; *San Demetrio, London*; *The First of the Few* (1942); *The Demi-Paradise* (1943).
- Standing one's ground in danger: *The Foreman Went to France* and *San Demetrio, London.*
- Behaving like the military: *The Foreman Went to France*; *Fires Were Started*; *In Which We Serve* (1942).
- Bravery: *The Foreman Went to France*; *San Demetrio, London*; *Fires Were Started.*
- Sacrifice: *Fires Were Started*, *The Foreman Went to France*, *San Demetrio, London.*
- Calm: *The Foreman Went to France*; *San Demetrio, London*; *The Demi-Paradise*; *Mrs Miniver* (1942) when she disarms a German parachutist and hides his gun; the film fits this category in its depiction of the British, although it was American.
- Willingness to share dangers with the military, and fellow feeling between the two: *The Foreman Went to France* and *Fires Were Started.* In *Waterloo Road* (1944), a doctor shows fellow feeling with a soldier, who is the enemy of a shady spiv (an unlikeable character who certainly does not embody ideal national characteristics).

Wartime films tended to portray abstract and innate British characteristics – not prosaic, humdrum or selfish ones, or learnt behaviour.

As Richards has also pointed out, films about the people's war, whether featuring the Armed Forces or civilians, men or women, *The Way Ahead* (1944) (army); *The Way to the Stars* (1945) (RAF); *In Which We Serve* (navy); *The Gentle Sex* (1943) (women ATS) and *Millions Like Us* (factory women) portray the same features: comradeship, cooperation, duty, self-sacrifice, good humour and modesty. The same national characteristics appear in documentary films, such as *Target for Tonight* (1941), *Coastal Command* (1942), *Western Approaches* (1944) and *Fires Were Started*.[181] In this way, films, like politicians and print journalists, blurred the distinction between the Forces and civilians.

The impact of messages contained within films is impossible to judge. Young adults in lower economic brackets and with only an elementary education – the very people likely to be working in factories, docks and mines whom the government wanted to carry on working after the siren – were the most frequent cinema-goers, and thus those most likely to be watching these films.[182] There is no evidence that the films ever changed attitudes or behaviour, or helped people to cope, as has been argued, for instance, of American films during the 1930s.[183] Indeed, Reeves has argued that mass audiences responded positively to those films that confirmed or reinforced their existing attitudes; films that challenged existing views were far less popular.[184] The fact that people watched films and newsreels during air raids meant that the message of carrying on after the siren was in accord with many people's behaviour during their leisure time and, for those working in the cinema, during their work time.

The press tried to put more direct and negative pressure on workers by endeavouring to whip up animosity against those who did not carry on after the siren. The *Hackney Gazette* sternly criticised the way in which individual bus and trolley conductors were given the discretion to stop once the siren had sounded.[185] The local press named and shamed civil-defence slackers, who were called up in front of magistrates. (Court reporting was the bread and butter of local newspapers.)[186]

The South Wales newspaper, the *Western Mail*, reported on the unwillingness of workers in certain key South Wales industries to carry on after the siren. It adopted a highly censorious tone, with almost no attempt to give voice to both sides of industry or to explain the situation, despite devoting a good deal of precious wartime paper to the problem. In carrying articles on the subject, it gave the impression of delving into the problem, so for instance it carried an article by someone it described as a 'special commissioner', but the whole thrust of its reporting was distinctly hostile to any worker or trade unionist whom it did not consider to be putting the national interest first. It provided a platform for critics of the workers, whose voice, in contrast, was only heard as a defensive one.

On 3 October 1940, The *Western Mail* reported that the Ministry of Labour had set up an enquiry into allegations that employees in South Wales shipyards were not working as hard as they might; strict insistence on pre-war trade-union rules was hindering productivity, which was less than in other parts of the country, and work ceased on the air-raid warning, unlike many other areas.[187]

The following day, the same newspaper carried the headline 'Exploiting Alarm periods in South Wales Industries' and 'Obstructions That Must Be Removed'. An article claimed that the desire of both sides of industry to 'remove the impediment to taking cover' was increasing, but there was industrial friction and sharp differences of opinion over whether it should be compulsory or voluntary. The paper claimed that calls from the Home Secretary had had little or no effect, and it was almost universal practice in South Wales to stop work on the sound of the siren. Employees in offices of industries were continuing until warned by roof spotters, and they then went to well-equipped temporary basement offices, but a practice which employers and management were willing to arrange was not to be imposed on workers. Rather, they hoped that, by precept and practice, employees would adopt the Ministry of Home Security's policy, but they did not think that so much discretion should be left to voluntary action. The writer of the article argued that a whole range of factors prevented a swift solution: it was difficult for workmen scattered across a wide dock area to take cover at the last minute; there was friction caused by disturbing established trade union practices; labour leaders did not hesitate to exploit the situation to gain a rise in wages; and competent roof spotters were in short supply. There were also problems over ship repairers in South Wales ports getting their weekly wages, irrespective of time lost during an alert. They got overtime wages if extra time was needed to finish a job on which they were working at the time of the raid. Dockers' wages were made up to the minimum day rate of fifteen shillings, however long the alert lasted. At Cardiff docks, tippers had been demanding a higher guaranteed weekly wage, as well as full overtime payment of three shillings an hour for all the time that they were unoccupied during air raids on the night and Sunday shifts, plus what they might have earned under their tariff. Iron and steel workers had also received their daily rates for lost time. Tippers and trimmers, the paper admitted, had suffered greatly from the big decrease in the quantity of coal shipped from South Wales ports over the previous three months but, in all the other basic industries in the area, earnings had increased in real and nominal value. Employers complained that workers were reluctant to agree a relaxation of customary restrictions on output capacity. Even so, all the most important industries were now considering a scheme of roof spotters. It was expected that the largest munitions factory in South Wales would introduce roof spotters within a week. The group of workers that this journalist held up as paragons of national virtue were the miners, who despite industrial friction had displayed a 'common determination to serve the national interest': the Conciliation Board had agreed a system for working during air raids. The article concluded, however, that not all local workers and their leaders were equally dedicated to national service.[188]

On 5 October the varied responses and attitudes of workers and employers were read across South Wales, as the *Western Mail* printed accusation and counteraccusation, but with more comments from employers than from workers. All were quoted anonymously, which would have made it more difficult to substantiate or rebut any of them directly. Someone described as a 'well-known authority' (so attempting to invest him with 'authority' by the use of this term) in the steel and tin-plate industry in Swansea said that a number of workers were out to capitalise on the position for all they were worth. Another 'leader' (again a term which dignifies the comments) said that men ran to the shelters, and wanted shelter money so that the lost production barely affected them at all. When men had volunteered to do work in air raids, it was alleged that others had put pressure on them to stop. It was claimed that there was a demand for risk money, and for men to be paid when they had been delayed in getting to work, due to an air-raid siren. Two people from management who did not make hostile comments were not described as either a 'leader' or an 'authority'. One, described as a tin-plate manufacturer in Llanelli, stated that in some departments work had to stop on the siren, but that in other departments the work continued. A 'manager' stated that men were using 'common sense' and that while some were willing to take advantage, there was no question as to their loyalty and desire to pull their weight. He also pointed out that 'natural nervousness' was a factor to be taken into account. The sole trade-union leader whose views were printed made clear that the employers' accusations to the press were out of date, and he denied the allegations, claiming that they were misrepresentations. He argued that men were paid shelter money when instructed to leave their jobs. It was hoped, he continued, that there would soon be an agreement for working during air raids, although, following the Prime Minister's appeal, a spotter had been appointed and, within days, other departments were asking for spotters. The position now was that everybody worked through the siren.[189]

On occasion, the press put the honey in the headlines and a sting in the detail. *The Times* trod a careful path when criticising its readers for not working after the siren. It clearly did not want to give succour to the enemy by suggesting that air raids were undermining the country and having the enemy's desired effect, but neither did it want to suggest anything other than a splendid response. So a leading article on 18 September 1940, when the *Luftwaffe* was hammering London, claimed that the damage had not crippled London or the contribution that London's industries could make to victory. The strain of attacks were being 'magnificently borne' by 'all classes', while there was an 'upward surge of our war production', but between this praise were specific criticisms of those who took cover, including those likely to read *The Times*. The leader argued that it was not right for government departments, which should set an example to business and industry, to be seriously interrupted by every warning, and yet 'grave complaints' were made that the Post Office was virtually suspended; that civilians in service departments were not allowed to remain at work; and that transport for night workers – and to some extent day workers – was not sufficient.[190] The following day, *The Times* complained that people still experienced a bank, a shop, a Post Office or some other business shutting from the moment that the siren sounded. The role of the civilian in winning the war was stated explicitly, drawing on a military metaphor. 'The soldier does not go to his dug-out at stand-to, but to the parapet; and the work-bench, the counter, the railway platform, the sorting-room, and the desk are our parapets at our civilian stand-to.'[191]

The press created the impression that there was little tolerance of those who did not work after the siren. Even in London, when heavy raids took place in September 1940, complaints quickly appeared in the press of any who were thought to be holding up the public or business. *The Times* apparently received numerous complaints in September 1940 that there were delays in the mail, telephone calls and in telegrams, although the GPO was developing a system of roof spotters, and postal staff were encouraged to remain at their posts until danger was imminent. There were complaints about postal delays due to frequent air-raid warnings in London, and of bags of mail left on platforms for days.[192] By late September, however, post offices and sorting offices were working after the siren.[193] Such had been the volume of complaints against the Post Office that the General Secretary of the Union of Post Office Workers, T. J. Hodgson, publicly defended his members, pointing out that the Post Office was understaffed, as many workers had been called up, and thousands were working twelve hours a day, including Sundays; they were not afraid to do their duty, but many sorting offices had glass roofs, and 'Telephonists, holding the vital communications of the country, could be fairly described as in the front line'.[194]

The Times received complaints that the Ministry of Supply and Air Ministry did not answer the telephone after the siren had sounded, which at the very least points to an impatience with those who were not thought to be carrying on after the siren.[195] Faceless bureaucrats were a popular source of annoyance, as reflected in this ditty:

> 'Keep up your morale', says Whitehall –
> While underground it delves,
> 'Work on', they cry, to one and all,
> Then run to earth themselves![196]

After the war, Churchill confirmed the suspicions of 1940 that civil servants readily took cover. At first, whenever the siren sounded, all the occupants of a score of ministries went to the basements. 'Pride, even, was being taken in the efficiency and thoroughness with which this evolution was performed.' In order to encourage ministries not to abandon their work immediately the siren sounded, Churchill asked for all ministries, including the Armed Service departments, to circulate to each other the amount of time lost due to air-raid warnings. Naming and shaming resulted in a dramatic change of practices: 'It was amusing to see that the fighting departments were for some time in the worst position. Offended and spurred by this implied reproach, they very quickly took their proper place. The loss of hours in all departments was reduced to a fraction.'[197]

The acting manager of a Welsh transport company, W. Dunning, made a complaint in the national press about his workforce. He wrote to *The Times* that the government should state that civilians had to take risks if the confusion was not to continue, 'The Government should say that transport was the bloodstream of the community, and transport workers should accept the risk which any ordinary person in the street was accepting'.[198] (Government ministers encouraged but never enforced such a practice.) That *The Times* was willing to publish this letter indicates where its sympathies lay.

An alderman in Southampton wrote to the local newspapers to complain that while local bus drivers and conductors carried on after the siren for the convenience of the public, he had visited a tram and bus workshop where some of the men had immediately gone to the shelter when the siren sounded.[199] Attempts to protect the public, for instance at railway stations with glass roofs, were not always appreciated. One man wrote crossly to his local London newspaper that at Victoria Station he had been told to take cover instead of studying the indicator board after the siren sounded. As there were no planes or gunfire, and outside the traffic continued to move as usual, the shops were open and roof spotters were on a nearby building searching the skies 'with a rather bored' air, the man could see no point in having his movements restricted.[200]

Personal pressures

As well as the unquantifiable media pressure, stopping work when the siren sounded led to pressures at work for some workers and inconveniences for others. Initially, labour exchanges stopped work on the siren, which caused backlogs for staff and for men waiting for their dole. From late September 1940 employment exchanges kept open after air-raid warnings by using roof spotters.[201] In 1940, the willingness of drivers and conductors to continue after raids varied enormously. Even in the same area, drivers and conductors did not initially all react in the same fashion.[202] When bus and tram drivers stopped on the sound of the siren, it did not mean that they were reducing their hours at work, for if they waited for the all clear it could mean many hours before they themselves reached home. Taking cover was not necessarily the most convenient option.[203]

Employers

Pressure from employers led to some workers continuing after the siren. Although national negotiations had led to an agreement that employers could not force their employees to work after the siren sounded, local branches of trade unions had actively to defend this voluntary principle. When Plymouth City Council attempted to impose a blanket policy of working after the siren by docking the wages of those who took cover, the Amalgamated Engineering Union (AEU) and the Transport and General Workers' Union (TGWU) immediately leapt to their members' defence and forced the council to back down. Not only did the unions ensure that no one was pressured into working through fear of losing their wages, but they also negotiated a refund for all those who had already lost wages.[204] As well as those who carried on with work after the siren, some council employees were actually called out to work when the siren sounded; their unions (AEU, TGWU and the National Union of General and Municipal Workers) negotiated a minimum of two hours' pay when this happened.[205] In Bristol there were rumours that some of the council's employees, such as road sweepers, stopped work on the sound of the siren, but then did not take cover; instead they stood around watching the sky. The Planning and Public Works Committee heard stories of men allegedly stopping work, lighting up cigarettes and watching a raid. The city engineer complained 'It is obvious that this is not fair play'. It was suggested that the men should fall in line with other workers around the country, and that, when the siren sounded, one of them should be appointed a spotter while the others carried on work.[206] In some cases the pressure was more direct. When the TGWU informed Leeds Council that its members would not carry on after the siren, the council responded that they had to, and that it would provide raid spotters.[207] A member of the Amalgamated Engineering Union, who worked in an aircraft factory in Hayes, Middlesex, claimed that local employers were underhand and stampeded workers into accepting the spotter system, which, he stated, the workers did not want.[208] Those who were members of trade unions, nevertheless, were in a stronger position than non-unionised workers. How many non-union workers carried on after the siren because they lost wages is impossible to know. Piece-rate workers would have been particularly vulnerable.

Recalling the raids

In this study, over fifty people recalled carrying on with whatever they were doing after the siren sounded rather than going to the shelter, and other projects have collected similar material. It was not hard to find information which countered the dominant image of civilians as passive victims; as one respondent stated: 'The concept of the population fleeing in terror to the shelters at the sound of a siren and cowering therein is not an accurate picture.[209] One woman thought that film footage and interviews on television presented a very one-sided view, and that some of the images of people in shelters were 'ridiculous'. She pointed out that there would not have been enough space in shelters if everyone in London had gone to them.[210]

Most people explained their motives with a single, straightforward answer, which fits with the nature of evidence collected by other oral history projects.[211] They did not, however, all give the same answer. For this and other projects, the reasons which interviewees gave for carrying on after the siren fall into a number of broad categories, which often overlapped even if respondents did not explicitly link them.

Some people said that they carried on at work because of the need to win the war. The role of the civilian was spoken of in military language. One aircraft worker at Hawker's commented that 'there was a war on . . . we had planes to build', and 'we were fighting for our lives'.[212] One woman explained that people carried on at work because 'We had to keep the war effort on the move'.[213]

Some referred to the demands of their work. A woman civil servant at the Board of Trade said that during daylight raids the staff took cover behind a cupboard door to get away from flying glass, but otherwise they carried on working after the siren sounded. They would not have got any work done if they had gone to the shelter.[214] One man said that initially they had gone to the shelter, but there had been a loss of production. The firm he worked for in 1940 as an engineering apprentice, and the firm he moved to in 1941, both had roof spotters; he could not recall anyone who did not carry on until the roof spotters gave the signal to take cover.[215] Another man said that he could not recall anyone going to the shelter before the roof spotter's signal, because it would have meant lost production.[216] One woman said that they could not leave their work because they were supplying nuts and bolts to aircraft firms.[217] A woman doctor in south-east England said that nurses and doctors all carried on after the siren because they had so much to do.[218]

One woman thought that those on piece rates had lost wages when they went to the shelter.[219] Some remembered that there had been no practical alternative when they were at work but to ignore the siren.[220] Some thought that there had been pressure from others at work to carry on.[221] A man who worked in a firm producing lorries, remembers that no one in his shop ever went to the shelter, but they dived under the lorries.[222] An employee at Hawker's aircraft factory, building Hurricanes, remembered the inconvenience of going to the shelters, 'We got fed up running up and down'.[223]

Some spoke of civilians 'duty' to carry on at work after the siren. They said that as the Forces were doing their duty, civilians also had to do their duty, which was to carry on at work.[224] Explicit links were made between the experience of the Forces and of civilians: 'Lots of civilians saw more action than the troops'.[225]

Civilians in civil defence, such as those with ARP or Home Guard duties, went to their posts when the siren sounded. One man, who worked at Hawker's aircraft factory, was a member of the Home Guard, so, when the public siren sounded, he left his work, but took up Home Guard duties, looking for descending enemy paratroops and incendiaries.[226]

Some remembered that there were the collective or individual perceptions of the risk involved, often mixed with a sense of fatalism.[227] One man thought that it was up to the individual at his workplace whether they took cover or not; it depended on people's personal preferences: whether they had a 'disdain' for going to the shelter and felt no sense of risk.[228] One woman in Southampton later recounted that, as the war wore on, she did not go to the shelter, 'We'd think if going to die, die comfortably'.[229] A Southampton man remembered: 'As no bombs dropped every time there was a siren people became complacent'.[230] A woman doctor working in a hospital in Kent where they were dealing with D-Day casualties commented that they all carried on working when the siren sounded, as they didn't think that they would be hit.[231] Some remembered that roof spotters made them feel safe.[232] A number of people in the London area said that they got used to the sound of the siren and with carrying on at work.[233]

People often felt less frightened if they were doing something, preferably with others. One woman who lived in Dover during the summer of 1940 recalled that she dreaded the siren at night, but it was 'not so bad during the day when one was doing one's chores and there were other people around'.[234] A number of people recalled continuing with group leisure activities, such as games at a youth club; watching a film at the cinema, or enjoying a ballet at Sadler's Wells Theatre.[235] Whereas expert opinion before the war recognised that people were influenced by the behaviour of others, they had assumed that a panicky minority would influence the majority.[236] In practice it was the other way around. It was not fear, but bravery, that was contagious.

Many recalled that they recognised that shelters could never offer total protection.[237] Some did not like the idea of being underground in a raid at all. Two domestic staff at 10 Downing Street slept in the top rooms throughout the war, and never went downstairs in air raids. In the late 1960s, one of them wrote to Mary Soames, one of the Churchills' daughters, that they 'decided very early in the War that we didn't so much mind being killed outright as being buried alive'.[238]

A Portsmouth man recalled that the local art college he was attending would not allow him into the shelter because he was a pacifist, and so he used to sit on a park bench during raids. Even at home, however, the shelter was only used on one occasion, because the family got so badly bitten by small insects during the night, and instead they used it to store potatoes.[239]

People remember themselves and others responding in a range of ways to the siren, from great fear to indifference.[240] Not all members of the same family responded in the same fashion to air-raid warnings. At home, some members of a family slept in an Anderson shelter, while others preferred the comfort of their own beds.[241] Some remember enjoying the excitement of raids.[242]

People remember that their attitudes to raids in London went through phases. At first there was widespread fear, then people got used to the siren; later in the war, when the Germans sent over V1 and V2s, the fear returned: V1s had a certain predictability about them, but V2s appeared as if from nowhere.[243]

Contemporary and memory evidence reinforce each other in explaining people's motives: getting used to raids; making judgements about the risk; the importance of routine and avoiding disruption; pressure from others; wanting to continue with pleasurable activities; negative experiences in shelters and the knowledge that shelters were not always safe; and an element of excitement. Contemporary evidence also pointed to the sense of pride in one's city and to the way in which local experiences were placed in the context of others, which did not come through in memory material, which emphasised the need to win the war, contributing to the war effort and doing one's duty in a national context. Does this not come through in the contemporary evidence because it was so self-evident that people didn't need to state it, or is it because, sixty years later, people are not actually remembering their motives at the time, so much as providing a rationale which draws on the context of the war? People now use the language of the wartime propaganda and media.

Once we have a better appreciation of the extent to which people carried on in air raids, and the reasons for them doing so, we can also have a better understanding of what the alternative – of taking cover – may have meant to people. It meant inconvenience and an even more disrupted daily routine in shops, on public transport and in the street, than already existed under war conditions; it meant missing out on the exciting aspects of war, and pleasures foregone; it meant putting up with the unpleasant side of shelter life; for those on piece rates or in non-unionised firms it could mean losing wages; it meant possible social humiliation or embarrassment if others around were not taking cover; it meant potential discrimination from those employers who ignored the spirit of the national agreement and forced their employees to carry on. All these factors had to be weighed against the uncertain safety afforded by shelters.

Conclusions

People's reactions to the dangers and risks of war were not determined by an inherent British courage, but rather attitudes that changed and reactions that developed as a result of the experience of war. 'Carrying on' was, in effect, behaviour that was 'learnt'. It is not surprising that reactions to air raids were not predetermined, and actually changed with experience, for we know from psychological studies that people's attitudes are formed by a series of complex factors, which include direct experience.[244] Once some people ignored the siren, there were social pressures to conform to this new behaviour.[245] People were conscious of routine, day-to-day concrete factors, rather than abstract concepts of bravery, patriotism or a sense of humour affecting their behaviour in raids, and other research suggests that these mundane factors were also important in helping people cope after air raids. Public utilities, recreational facilities, the state of city centres and community support have since been identified as helping people to deal with the after-effects of raids.[246] Research on morale has also pointed to the importance of day-to-day factors, such as ARP, food, the cost of living, working conditions and health.[247]

The requirements of the circumstances (known as 'situational demand' in the jargon), were important in determining courageous behaviour, and this included a person's sense of responsibility to her/him self and others, the influence of others' behaviour and judgement, having something important to the event to do, repeated practice, and modelling, which was especially relevant to children, who modelled themselves on their parents' behaviour.[248] People's relationships with others were important, and help to explain their behaviour, including an unwillingness to use shelters. People underwent changes as a result of their experiences of air raids: their perceptions of danger and risk changed; their personal self-worth was enhanced; and their identification with the locality was strengthened. What is not certain is whether Christian faith, or government propaganda and the media (some of which were discussed in previous chapters) made much difference to people's behaviour: their aims are clear, but their outcomes less so.

The public and the government both wanted to carry on after the siren sounded, but they came to this conclusion from different angles. The government's priority was with production, while the public were motivated by a range of factors. So, while there was agreement over the desirability of working after the siren, as this conclusion was reached from different points of view and priorities, there was no general consensus in society between different groups. The nature of contemporary records means that it is not possible to draw conclusions about similarities or differences between women and men, or between classes, but it is clear that many working-class and middle-class women and men did ignore the siren. Carrying on after the siren sounded, cut across class and gender lines, and while this did not change class relations or reduce class divisions, it may help to explain why so many believed that they were less significant in wartime: here, in a critical aspect of wartime behaviour, there were no obvious differences in attitudes and behaviour between the classes. Likewise, government and the public were largely in accord over this crucial aspect of wartime life, and this may have contributed to the belief in wartime solidarity and consensus. From these assumptions, it is easy to see how a national public history created a belief in a national wartime culture, although at the time wartime culture actually reinforced a sense of local identity within a national context.

The most direct effect of war on civilians was that of air raids, and it is clear from the above discussion that civilians played a part in determining the extent to which they would be affected by raids. Collectively and individually, they took decisions and made choices about the risks of war and their roles 'in the front line'.

Notes

1 H. P. Twyford, *It Came To Our Door: The Story of Plymouth Throughout the Second World War* (Underhill, first published 1945, revised 1949), pp. 1, 7, 9; Hans Rumpf, *The Bombing of Germany* (White Lion Publishers, 1975 edn), p. 185. First published 1961 by Gerhard Stalling Verlag under the title *Das war der Bombenkrieg.*
2 University of Sussex, Mass-Observation Archive, Air Raids, TC 65/3/B LE, 18 August 1940; 23/10/T, Trowbridge.
3 Mass-Observation Archive, FR 313, 'Civilians in Air Raids', August 1940, Tom Harrisson for *Picture Post* 1 August 1940.
4 PRO INF, 1/292, Weekly Home Intelligence Reports (WHIR), 30 September–9 October 1940.
5 Mass-Observation Archive, TC, London Survey, TC 65/2/F.
6 PRO HO, 199/147, Report of effect of air raids on Cardiff, 16 August 1940.
7 PRO HO, 199/276, Visit to Bristol and Cardiff, 2–6 August 1940.
8 Imperial War Museum, 85/45/1, Georgie at the BBC to Mrs W. C. Bowman, 31 October 1940.
9 Art McCulloch (compiler), *The War and Uncle Walter: The Diary of an Eccentric* (Doubleday, 2003), p. 146.
10 Mass-Observation Archive, FR 313, 'Civilians in Air Raids', August 1940.
11 PRO INF, 1/292, WHIR, 7–14 October 1940.
12 PRO INF, 1/292, WHIR, 4–11 November 1940.
13 PRO INF, 1/292, WHIR, 11–18 November 1940.
14 Imperial War Museum 88/50/1, Miss S. M. Andrews.
15 Richard Broad and Suzie Fleming (eds), *Nella Last's War: A Mother's Diary 1939–45* (Falling Wall Press, 1981), p. 81.
16 PRO INF, 1/292, WHIR, 21–28 October 1940.
17 Imperial War Museum, 81/2/1, John Davies, 2 November 1940.
18 PRO INF, 1/292, WHIR, 18–25 November 1940.
19 PRO INF, 1/292, WHIR, 18–24 December 1940.
20 PRO INF, 1/292, WHIR, 19–26 March 1941.
21 PRO INF, 1/292, WHIR, 23–30 April 1941.
22 PRO INF, 1/292, WHIR, 7–14 May 1941.

23 PRO INF, 1/292, WHIR, 19–26 March 1941, 15–22 January and 7–14 May 1941.
24 Mass-Observation Archive, 12/C, Air Raids, 16 March 1942.
25 Quoted by a professor in the Department of Psychology at Yale University, USA, Irving L. Janis, *Air War and Emotional Stress: Psychological Studies of Bombing and Civil Defense* (The Rand Corporation, 1951), p. 110; Mary Douglas, *Risk: Acceptability According to the Social Sciences* (RKP, 1986), pp. 29–30.
26 Melitta Schmideberg, 'Some observations on individual reactions to air raids', *International Journal of Psychoanalysis*, 23:3 and 4 (1942), p. 160. (Schmideberg was a psychiatrist.)
27 *Liverpool Post* 23 September 1940.
28 Southampton City Council Cultural Services, Oral History Archive, CO 104, female.
29 PRO INF, 1/292, WHIR, 20–27 April 1943.
30 Colin Perry, *Boy in the Blitz: The 1940 Diary of Colin Perry* (Sutton Publishing, 2000), p. 144.
31 PRO HO, 199/276, Visit to Bristol and Cardiff, 2 to 6 August 1940.
32 Imperial War Museum, 86/5/1, Mrs M. L. C. Griffiths, 12 September 1940; 85/45/1, Georgie at the BBC to Mrs W. C. Bowman, 31 October 1940; 'B' in Bristol to Mrs W. C. Bowman, 31 October 1940.
33 Imperial War Museum, 81/2/1, John Davies, 12 September 1940.
34 *Daily Herald* 13 September 1940.
35 PRO INF, 1/292, WHIR, 30 September–9 October; 7–14 October 1940; 4–11 November 1940; 11–18 November 1940.
36 P. E. Vernon, 'Psychological effects of air raids', *Journal of Abnormal Psychology*, 36 (1941), pp. 459–61; Dr Robert H. Thouless, 'Psychological effects of air raids', *Nature* 148:3746 (16 August 1941), pp. 183–5.
37 P. E. Vernon, 'Psychological effects', p. 461.
38 Barbara Nixon, *Raiders Overhead: A Diary of the London Blitz* (Scolar Press, 1980), p. 25, first published 1943.
39 Peggy Scott, *They Made Invasion Possible* (Hutchinson, 1944), pp. 139–40.
40 S. J. Rachman, *Fear and Courage* (W. H. Freeman, 1978), pp. 34–44, 237–43.
41 Melitta Schmideberg, 'Some observations on individual reactions to air raids', p. 151.
42 PRO INF, 1/292, WHIR, 30 September–9 October; 14–21 October 1940.
43 Mass-Observation Archive, TC 65/3/A, London Survey, 18 August 1940, South London.
44 Colin Perry, *Boy in the Blitz*, pp. 133–4, 198.
45 John Strachey, *Post D: Some Experiences of an Air Raid Warden* (Victor Gollancz, 1941), pp. 43, 134.
46 PRO INF, 1/292, WHIR, 14–21 October 1940; 21–28 October 1940.
47 Imperial War Museum, 81/2/1, John Davies, 10 September 1940.

48 PRO INF, 1/292, WHIR, 30 September–9 October 1940.
49 PRO INF, 1/292, WHIR, 30 September–9 October 1940.
50 Mass-Observation Archive, Air Raids, TC, 23/8/1, Bristol, 8 September 1940.
51 Mass-Observation Archive, Air Raids, TC, 23/8/L, Cardiff, 10 March 1941.
52 Richard Broad and Suzie Fleming, *Nella Last's War*, 21 September 1940, pp. 74–5.
53 PRO INF, 1/292, WHIR, 30 September–9 October 1940.
54 Mass-Observation Archive, Air Raids, TC, 23/10/J, Portsmouth, 6 December 1940, Mrs Gweneth Dean.
55 Paul Slovic, *The Perception of Risk* (EarthScan, 2000), p. 221.
56 PRO INF, 1/292, WHIR, 26 March–2 April 1941.
57 Mass-Observation Archive, Air Raids, TC, 23/8/R, Clydeside, 13 April 1941.
58 Mass-Observation Archive, Air Raids, TC, 23/10/P, Sheffield.
59 Richard Broad and Suzie Fleming, *Nella Last's War*, 8 May 1941 p. 147.
60 PRO INF, 1/292, WHIR, 18 June 1942.
61 J. B. Priestley, *Postscripts* (Heinemann, 1940), pp. 81–2, 29 September 1940.
62 PRO INF, 1/292, WHIR, 25 November–4 December, 4–11 December 1940.
63 Sonia Orwell and Ian Angus, *The Collected Essays, Journalism and letters of George Orwell. vol. II. My Country Right or Left 1940–1943*, (Secker and Warburg, 1968) 3 September 1940, p. 370.
64 PRO INF, 1/292, WHIR, 30 September–9 October.
65 PRO INF, 1/292, WHIR, 4–11 December 1940.
66 PRO INF, 1/292, WHIR, 25 August–1 September 1942, 8–15 December 1942.
67 PRO INF, 1/292, WHIR, 6–13 October 1942.
68 PRO HO, 199/456; The importance to people of their own city playing a part in national events was reflected in popular attitudes towards politicians. In the autumn of 1940 there was little interest expressed in politicians, except when they came from the area. So, people in Bristol were 'delighted' when Ernest Bevin, a local boy made good, was appointed to the War Cabinet, and, when Neville Chamberlain resigned, only people in Birmingham (and Trowbridge, for no apparent reason) were sorry to see him go.
69 *Yorkshire Post* 12, 27 and 29 June 1940.
70 *Bristol Evening Post* 11 September 1940.
71 *Daily Express* 11 September 1940.
72 *Yorkshire Post* 17 June 1940; *Southern Daily Echo* 23 October 1940.
73 *Yorkshire Post* 16 September 1940.
74 *Glasgow Herald* 11 October 1940.
75 *Western Evening Herald* 7 January 1941.
76 Colin Perry, *Boy in the Blitz*, pp. 167–8, 185.
77 PRO INF, 1/292, WHIR, 14–21 October 1940.
78 PRO INF, 1/292, WHIR, 7–14 October 1940.
79 *Express and Echo* (Exeter) 10 December 1940.

80 Mass-Observation Archive, TC, 65/2/H, London Survey, 15 August 1940, Air Raid Warning (West London).
81 PRO INF, 1/292, WHIR, 7–14 October 1940.
82 PRO HO, 199/276, Visit to Bristol and Cardiff, 2–6 August 1940.
83 Mass-Observation Archive, Air Raids, 12/C.
84 Mass-Observation Archive, Air Raids, TC, 65/3/B HP, 21 August 1940.
85 Imperial War Museum sound archive tape 9563/2, Joyce Barrett (b. 1929) interviewed 1985.
86 Mass-Observation Archive, FR 355, Policy about civilians sheltering, August 1940.
87 Southampton City Council, SC/T, Acc 3749, SC/T9/73, 13–15 August 1940.
88 Mass-Observation Archive, Air Raids, TC, 23/8/1, Bristol, 8 September 1940.
89 Mass-Observation Archive, Air Raids, TC, 23/9/D, Harrow, 23 August 1940 DH.
90 Mass-Observation Archive, Air Raids, TC, 23/10/R, Southampton, 14 August 1940.
91 Mass-Observation Archive, Air Raids, TC, 23/8/M, Caterham, 7 September 1940.
92 PRO INF, 1/292, WHIR, 30 September–9 October 1940.
93 Colin Perry, *Boy in the Blitz*, pp. 112 and *passim*.
94 Imperial War Museum, 85/45/1, Dunstan to Mrs W. C. Bowman, 20 October 1940.
95 PRO INF, 1/292, WHIR, 5–12 October 1943.
96 Cited in Irving L. Janis, *Air War and Emotional Stress* (McGraw-Hill, 1951), p. 111.
97 The *BMJ*, for instance, carried a number of articles on children's health, but not older people's health, after raids. *British Medical Journal*, 18 April 1942; *BMJ* 25 January 1941, 1 November 1941, 8 November 1941; *Western Mail* 28 September 1940; Mass-Observation Archive, Air Raids, TC 23/10/T, 11 November 1940, first air raid; TC 65/3/G LE, 25 August 1940; TC 65/5/A, Report on Lewisham and Sydenham, 15 September 1940, LE; TC 23/9/H, Isle of Dogs, 13 September 1940; TC 65/5/D, 6 October 1940, CF; PRO ED, 50/206.
98 PRO ED, 50/206, Children's reactions to the War, H. R. V. Ball HMI, 13 November 1940.
99 PRO INF, 1/292, WHIR, 7–14 October 1940; PRO ED, 50/206, Nervous strain in children, not dated.
100 See for example, Mass-Observation, ES Diary 5420, 17–18 August 1940.
101 J. M. Bourne, *Britain and the Great War 1914–1918* (Edward Arnold, 1989), p. 220.
102 PRO INF, 1/292, 12–19 January 1943, Appendix.
103 PRO INF, 1/292, WHIR, 30 September–9 October 1940.
104 PRO INF, 1/292, WHIR, 11–18 November 1940.

105 Mass-Observation Archive, 9/T Air Raids. Shelter conditions in Stepney; 9/M Liverpool, City air raid shelters; Churchill College, Cambridge, Clementine Churchill papers, CSCT 3/37/71, J. P. L. Thomas, F. O. to Clementine Churchill.
106 PRO INF, 1/292, WHIR, 21–28 October 1940.
107 Mass-Observation Archive, TC, Air Raids, 9/M, Liverpool City air raid shelters.
108 PRO INF, 1/292, WHIR, 21–28 October 1940.
109 Sonia Orwell and Ian Angus, *The Collected Essays, Journalism and Letters of George Orwell. vol. II. My Country Right or Left 1940–1943*, p. 412, 15 March 1942.
110 Irving L. Janis, *Air War and Emotional Stress*, pp. 98, 99.
111 Sonia Orwell and Ian Angus, *The Collected Essays, Journalism and Letters of George Orwell. vol. II. My Country Right or Left 1940–1943*, p. 356, 25 June; p. 366, 16 August 1940. Also p. 367, 23 August.
112 Mass-Observation Archive, DR 492; Air Raids, TC, 23/9/B2, Exeter, woman teacher.
113 *British Medical Journal*, 21 September 1940.
114 Mass-Observation, Archive, FR 408.
115 For example, Colin Perry, *Boy in the Blitz* p. 91; Imperial War Museum 81/2/1, John Davies, 30 August 1940; PRO INF, 1/292, 7–14 October 1940, 7–14 May 1941.
116 PRO INF, 1/292, WHIR, 30 September–9 October 1940.
117 Mass-Observation Archive, Air Raids, 23/10/P, Sheffield.
118 *Croydon Times* 21 September 1940, 5 October 1940; *South London Press* 10 September 1940 and 13 September 1940. See also *Westminster and Pimlico News* 1 November 1940.
119 *Croydon Times* 21 September 1940.
120 *Mitcham News and Mercury* 15 November 1940.
121 PRO INF, 1/292, part 1, WHIR, 7–14 October 1940 (postal censorship reports).
122 PRO ADM, 1/12219, Letter from an anonymous army major, 5 December 1941.
123 Harold Nicolson, *Diaries and Letters 1939–1945* (Collins, 1967), p. 117.
124 Many examples include Kingston upon Thames Local History Room, Kingston ARP Committee, 3 September 1940.
125 There are numerous examples, including Teeside Record Office, DC/RE 2/10/2, Borough of Redcar Emergency Committee Diaries, 30 May 1941.
126 Tower Hamlets Library, Local History and Archives, MB [Metropolitan Borough of] Stepney, STE/878, Air Raid Precautions Committee, Book no. 1, 5 May 1938; 10 June 1940.
127 See, for instance, Teeside Record Office, DC/H/2/62, Hartlepool Borough Council Air Raid Precautions Committee, 30 July 1940.
128 Greenwich Heritage Centre, Woolwich Emergency Committee, 26 August 1940; 16 September 1940.

129 Teeside Record Office, DC/RE 2/10/2, Emergency Committee Diaries, 10 September 1940.

130 People complained about others carrying beds and chairs down to shelters and taking up so much space that there was no room for people caught in the street when the siren sounded: Merton Library, Merton and Morden Civil Defence Emergency Committee, 10 September 1940. In Redcar there were complaints about people taking prams 'and other vehicles' into shelters, and so causing congestion: Teeside Record Office Borough of Redcar Emergency Committee Diaries, DC/RE 2/10/2, 10 September 1940.

131 Sarah Fishman, *The Battle for Children: World War II, Youth Crime, and Juvenile Justice in Twentieth-Century France* (Harvard University Press, 2002), p. 1.

132 *Surrey Comet* 6 November 1940.

133 Edward Smithies, *Crime in Wartime: A Social History of Crime in World War II* (George Allen and Unwin, 1982), pp. 2–3, 171–6.

134 Edward Smithies, *Crime in Wartime*, pp. 26–39.

135 Wandsworth Local History Library, Wandsworth Civil Defence Control Committee, 18 May 1943; Lewisham Library, Lewisham Civil Defence Committee, 11 June 1940; 18 June 1940; 20 May 1941; 10 June 1941. Not far away in Woolwich, however, the council categorically stated that looting was not a problem: Greenwich Heritage Centre, Woolwich Emergency Committee 29 July 1940; *Mitcham and Tooting Advertiser* 30 May 1940; Merton Library, Merton and Morden Civil Defence Emergency Committee, 17 December 1940; Wimbledon, 9 April 1943. In 1943, Wimbledon Council offered a £5 reward (a very good week's wages) for information following damage to shelters.

136 Geoffrey Pearson, *Hooligan: A History of Respectable Fears* (Macmillan, 1983), p. 241.

137 PRO INF, 1/292, WHIR, 19–21 May 1941.

138 *Western Mail* 20 November 1940; Mass-Observation Archive, Air Raids, 23/9/M, Liverpool; Teeside Record Office, DC/ST/2/68, Stockton Borough Council, 23 May 1940.

139 Edward Smithies, *Crime in Wartime*, p. 161.

140 *Tooting, Balham, Mitcham and Colliers Wood Gazette* 26 October 1940; 21 December 1940.

141 Mass-Observation, TC, Air Raids, 9/M, Liverpool City air raid shelters.

142 Teeside Record Office, DC/H/2/62, Hartlepool Borough Council Air Raid Precautions Committee, 30 July 1940.

143 Imperial War Museum, 81/2/1, John Davies, 24 September 1940.

144 Colin Perry, *Boy in the Blitz*, p. 173.

145 Imperial War Museum, 86/5/1, Mrs M. L. C. Griffiths, in London, to Frances [no surname given], 11 October 1940.

146 Tower Hamlets, Local History and Archives, Bethnal Green, 603, 18 January 1941.

147 Kingston upon Thames Local History Room, Kingston ARP Committee, 3 December 1940; *Mitcham News and Mercury* 30 August 1940 reported cement shortages holding up work on shelters.
148 Greenwich Local History Library, Woolwich Emergency Committee, 26 August 1940.
149 Greenwich Local History Library, Greenwich ARP Emergency Committee, 10 April 1941.
150 Merton Library, Merton and Morden Civil Defence Emergency Committee, 10 September 1940. In Richmond upon Thames, however, shelter marshals could admit dogs, and the marshals even kept a supply of sleeping pellets for them. (They would not, however, allow smoking in their shelters.) Richmond upon Thames Local Studies Library, Richmond, Surrey Emergency Committee Report to Council, 10 September 1940.
151 Rosemary Pritchard and Saul Rosenzweig, 'The effects of war stress upon childhood and youth', *Journal of Abnormal Social Psychology*, 37 (1942), p. 332.
152 PRO INF, 1/292, WHIR, 14–21 October 1940; Tower Hamlets Local History and Archives, Bethnal Green, BG 701, General Emergency and Finance Committee, 3 October 1940. Lord Horder, 1871–1955, was a well-known doctor. He advised the Ministry of Labour and National Service on medical questions related to recruitment, and he chaired The Shelter Hygiene Committee of the Ministry of Home Security and Ministry of Health.
153 *British Medical Journal*, 28 September 1940, 5 April 1941. Old men suffered from retention of urine, mainly due to the lack of lavatories, although the cold and damp may have aggravated the problem. Sitting in shelters with bent knees on deck chairs for hours on end also led to thrombosis and oedema.
154 *Western Mail* 10 September 1940; Manchester Central Library Archive and Local Studies, City of Manchester Emergency Committee, 4 July, 3 October, 5 December 1940; Teeside Record Office, DC/ST/2/68, Stockton Borough Council Emergency Committee, 18 July 1940; *Glasgow Herald* 11, 14 October 1940.
155 PRO INF, 1/292, part 1, WHIR, 28 October–4 November 1940.
156 *Picture Post* 9 November 1940.
157 PRO INF, 1/292, WHIR, 7–14 October 1940.
158 *Western Mail* 16 November 1940. Cardiff's response was provided by the city engineer, who maintained that over the greater part of Cardiff the strata were unsuitable for deep shelters and that the cost of a few would be 'gigantic'.
159 PRO INF, 1/292, WHIR, 4–11 November 1940.
160 *Picture Post* 4 January 1941.
161 Mass-Observation Archive, Air Raids, 23/5/B, Public reactions to air raids in London, 18 August 1940.
162 Mass-Observation Archive, Air Raids, TC, 23/10/S, Swansea, 25 February 1941.

163 Mass-Observation Archive, Air Raids, TC, 23/9/A, Eastbourne, 16 August 1940.
164 Mass-Observation Archive, Air Raids, TC, 23/9/T, Stepney, 3 September 1940.
165 Edward Glover, 'Notes on the psychological effects of war conditions on the civilian population', *International Journal of Psychoanalysis*, 23:1 (1942), p. 19.
166 For example, Frank Robert Vivelo, *Cultural Anthropology: A Basic Introduction* (University Press of America, 1994), p. 193.
167 Graham Greene, *The End of the Affair* (Vintage, 2001), see especially pp. 71–2, 95. First published by William Heinemann in 1951.
168 In September 1940, Colin Perry noticed how many people on the London Underground were reading about God and religion. (Perry wrote that he had a strong faith but was not a churchgoer.) Colin Perry, *Boy in the Blitz*, p. 166.
169 Arthur Mee, *Nineteen-Forty: Our Finest Hour* (Hodder and Stoughton, 1941); Richard Weight, *Patriots: National Identity in Britain 1940–2000* (Pan, 2002), pp. 30–1.
170 Robert Currie, Alan Gilbert and Lee Horsley, *Churches and Churchgoers: Patterns of Church Growth in the British Isles Since 1700* (Clarendon Press, 1977), pp. 113–14; Mass-Observation Archive, FR 23, Church-religion in wartime, January 1940, and FR 1994, Religious instruction in schools, 5 January 1944.
171 PRO INF, 1/292, WHIR, 26 March–2 April 1914.
172 Sonia Orwell and Ian Angus, *The Collected Essays, Journalism and Letters of George Orwell. vol. II. My Country Right or Left 1940–1943* (Secker and Warburg, 1968), pp. 388–9.
173 PRO INF, 1/292, WHIR, 1–8 September 1942. In 1942, when the government asked people to join in a National Day of Prayer, Scottish shipyard workers thought that stopping work for a quarter of an hour was 'a farce', and workers' representatives on Production Committees refused to participate. A few expressed the view that 'war and religion do not mix'.
174 Mass-Observation Archive, FR 1607, Mass-Observation Fortnightly Bulletin, February 1943; file report 1566, Religion and the people, 5 January 1943.
175 Hugh Martin, *The British Churches in Wartime* (Ministry of Information, 1944), pp. 36–7.
176 Mass-Observation File Report 1607, Mass-Observation Fortnightly Bulletin February 1943.
177 Mass-Observation, *Puzzled People: A Study in Popular Attitudes to Religion, Ethics, Progress and Politics in a London Borough* (Victor Gollancz, 1947), pp. 56–9.
178 Mass-Observation Archive, FR 1566, Religion and the People, 5 January 1943.
179 Sian Nicholas, *The Echo of War* (Manchester University Press, 1996), pp. 126, 132.

180 Jeffrey Richards, *Films and British National Identity* (Manchester University Press, 1997), p. 85.
181 Jeffrey Richards, *Films and British National Identity*, pp. 106–9.
182 PRO BT, 64/4747.
183 Andrew Bergman, *We're in the Money: Depression America and its Films* (New York University Press, 1971); Charles J. Maland, *American Visions: The Films of Chaplin, Ford, Capra and Welles, 1936–41* (Arno, 1977).
184 Nicholas Reeves, *The Power of Film Propaganda: Myth or Reality?* (Cassell, 1999), pp. 136–204 and 239–40.
185 *Hackney Gazette* 26 August 1940.
186 *Croydon Times* 28 September 1940.
187 *Western Mail* 3 October 1940.
188 *Western Mail* 4 October 1940.
189 *Western Mail* 5 October 1940.
190 *The Times* 18 September 1940.
191 *The Times* 19 September 1940.
192 *The Times* 19 September 1940.
193 *The Times* 21 September 1940.
194 *The Times* 25 September 1940.
195 *The Times* 18 September 1940.
196 *Daily Herald* 18 September 1940.
197 Winston S. Churchill, *The Second World War. vol. 2. Their Finest Hour* (Cassell, 1949), p. 311.
198 *The Times* 7 September 1940.
199 *Southern Daily Echo* 17 October 1940.
200 *Westminster and Pimlico News* 18 October 1940.
201 Mass-Observation Archive, Air Raids, TC, 65/4/A, 6 September 1940; *The Times* 25 September 1940.
202 Mass-Observation Archive, Air Raids, TC, 23/5/B, 15 August 1940.
203 Birmingham Records Office, Birmingham City Council, BCC Emergency Committee, 11 September 1940, 17 October 1940.
204 Plymouth and West Devon Record Office, Plymouth Emergency Committee minutes, 1718/14, 30 October 1940.
205 Plymouth and West Devon Record Office, Plymouth Emergency Committee minutes, 1718/1, 19 July 1940.
206 *Bristol Evening Post* 2 October 1940.
207 *The Times* 31 October 1940.
208 Trade Union Congress, *Annual Report*, 1940, E. Athorn.
209 Respondents, who were contacted through personal knowledge, local newspapers and Brooklands, Weybridge, where Vickers and Hawker's had aircraft factories during the war are referred to in almost every case by initials and date of correspondence and/or interview. E. P., 8 October 2000.
210 G. E. R. 14 November 2000.
211 A. Seldon and J. Pappworth, *By Word of Mouth: Elite Oral History* (Methuen, 1983), p. 21.

212 F. B. 18 February 2001.
213 Marian Jones 7 October 2000.
214 G. E. R. 14 November 2000.
215 S. M. S. 23 January 2001.
216 E. G. 29 November 2000.
217 R. B. 5 October 1940.
218 Dr D. 7 February 2001.
219 W. M. 17 November 2000.
220 Dr D. 7 February 2001; M. W. B. 9 October 2000 and 16 October 2000.
221 D. T. 5 October 2000.
222 B. O'N. 2 and 17 November 2000.
223 W. R. 5 March 2001.
224 E. G. 29 November 2000; W. C. H. 7 October 2000.
225 O. J. D. 1 November 2000.
226 C. M. 15 December 2000.
227 B. O'N. 2 and 17 November 2000; J. C. 1 November 2000; D. C. 3 November 2000; P. W. 30 January 2001; Dr D. 7 February 2001; M. W. B. 9 and 16 October 2000.
228 B. O'N. 2 and 17 November 2000.
229 Southampton City Council Cultural Services, Oral History Archive, CO 124, female.
230 Southampton City Council Cultural Services, Oral History Archive, CO 139, male.
231 Dr D. 7 February 2001.
232 P. W. 30 January 2001; W. M. 17 November 2000.
233 P. T. 18 October 2000; E. W. 6 October 2000; Mrs G. 29 November 2000; N. D. 22 December 2000; B. T. 11 November 2000.
234 Imperial War Museum, 89/10/1, Miss Victoria Rayner.
235 A. S. 17 November 2000; O. J. D. 1 November 2000; M. J. 30 October 2000.
236 PRO HO, 45/196/2.
237 E. S. P. 8 October 2000; M. W. B. 16 October 2000; D. C. C. 16 November 2000; Marian Jones, 7 October 2000.
238 Churchill College, Cambridge, CSCT 3/31/41, 1 June 1968, Hambane to Chartwell.
239 Portsmouth Record Office, Oral History Archive, 2330A: Stanley Riddell (b. 1917) interviewed 1993.
240 Portsmouth Record Office, Oral History Archive, 2330A: Stanley Riddell; 2334A: Jack Price; 2333A: Dorothy Price.
241 A. S. 17 November 2000; P. W. 30 January 2001; E. G. 20 and 29 November 2000.
242 Southampton City Council Cultural Services, Oral History Archive, CO 128.
243 E. G. 20 and 29 November 2000; M. J. 30 October 2000.
244 Tony Malim and Ann Birch, *Introductory Psychology* (Macmillan, 1998), pp. 653–4.

245 This again fits in with what we know about group behaviour from psychology. Tony Malim and Ann Birch, *Introductory Psychology*, p. 679; David Sears, *Social Psychology* (Prentice Hall, 1985 edn), p. 362.

246 Brad Beaven and John Griffiths, 'Mass-Observation and civilian morale: working-class communities during the blitz 1940–41' Mass-Observation Archive Occasional Paper, No. 8, 1998.

247 Robert Mackay, *Half the Battle: Civilian Morale in Britain during the Second World War* (Manchester University Press, 2002).

248 S. J. Rachman, *Fear and Courage* (W. H. Freeman, 1978), p. 243.

7

Fall-out and conclusions

We have seen how people's reactions to the risks of aerial bombardment defied pre-war predictions of panic and a breakdown in public order. Culture and experience influenced people's behaviour in society at large and at work. Roof spotters acted as the eyes and ears of workers, and, as a result of the actual experience of air raids, people modified their standards of risk and danger. The general public gave a high priority to maintaining as normal a routine as possible; they felt safer when active and in the company of others, especially when they were responsible for them; they were sensitive to social pressures and the behaviour of others; some were driven by financial imperatives; and many disliked shelters for a host of reasons, which included a greater sense of helplessness when they were in them with nothing to do, and an awareness that shelters offered no protection from a direct hit. Experience of air raids fostered personal and local pride. The media and the messages conveyed were working with the grain of public opinion.

Media

The media performed varied roles. Sections of the media were icons of wartime work in air raids: newspapers were produced despite raids; the BBC broadcast in air raids; and cinemas, some theatres and live concert performances continued during them. The production, transmission or performance was a message, for it signified that people were carrying on, often in air raids. They were, moreover, part of a relationship with those consuming, listening or watching: performances required an audience for them to have (iconic) meaning. The existence of these various sections of the media contradicted the pre-war messages of novels, experts and newsreels. While politicians and the media made direct and explicit appeals to the public to work after the siren sounded, these were not a discrete sphere of propaganda; as we have seen, the message permeated society.

The media was a message in itself and, in addition, parts of the media were a conduit for an explicit message from politicians, journalists and film-makers. Politicians and print journalists transmitted their message through newspapers; the message was very occasionally explicit on the BBC and in newsreels. Feature films usually carried a more implicit message. Occasional references in films, novels or plays to continuing one's activities in air raids is not necessarily a message in the same way as politicians' and journalists' messages, which were conveyed with the hope or even the expectation of influencing behaviour. References to 'carrying on' in plays, films and novels were more likely to be a device for reinforcing their 'authenticity'. Thus, the same reference had different purposes.

The reception of the message is hard to judge; what we should not do is to fall into the trap of assuming that film reviewers or newspaper editors represented anyone other than themselves. The presence or absence of comment by a reviewer or editor cannot be taken as evidence of the wider reception. We do not know how far people responded to direct propaganda or were influenced by the portrayal of ideal British characteristics. It is on balance doubtful whether people in industrial and dock areas (the most heavily bombed areas), whose work was so vital to the war effort, would have been greatly influenced by official pressure to carry on at work if they had not wanted to do so. One wartime psychologist argued on the basis of his research that those who suffered most from bombing were less favourable to the 'official viewpoint' than others.[1] We can also draw on the insights of social psychologists.

Social psychologists now argue that for persuasive communication to be effective it requires a number of basic characteristics. First, those communicating must have certain qualities. They need to be credible, and this requires expertise and trustworthiness. By the summer of 1940, both Churchill and leading Labour politicians were credible: Churchill was believed to have been proved right over the wrong-headedness of appeasement; Labour politicians had for decades presented themselves as defenders of working-class interests, and so were unlikely to advocate a policy of working after the siren that could literally destroy the working class. It often helps if an audience can identify with the communicators and, in 1940 and 1941, Labour politicians and even Churchill had something in common with the public, as they were all bracing themselves for attempted invasion and defeat; Churchill's painted words also meant that his language was very powerful.

Second, the content and presentation of the message is important. All aspects of the media offered information about how best to work after the siren (with roof spotters), and presented values such as bravery, independence, intrinsic worth and purposefulness. The message was simple; it contained emotional appeal (Churchill and films were especially good at this); it worked in the self-interest of those hearing, reading or seeing the message; and it flattered the audience by creating an image of them to which they could aspire.

Third, the motives and abilities of the audience to respond are vital. People were not being asked to respond to hypothetical or abstract situations, but ones to which they related and that they experienced. Roof spotters and industrial alarm schemes provided practical and immediate support for workers to continue working after the public siren sounded. The closer a message is to the views of its recipients, the more likely it is that they will accept it. For a whole range of reasons that we have investigated, the message went with the grain.[2]

Age and air raids

Government and the media aimed their calls to continue after the air-raid siren sounded at those of working age, and it would seem that they were indeed the age group (along with children) who were most likely to want do so anyway. Younger people rather than older people were also likely to recover more quickly from the trauma of heavy raids. There was no cut-off age below which people stood up to raids well and over which they did not do so, but the ageing process across the life course played some part in people's behaviour in air raids. It is difficult to draw hard and fast conclusions from material that refers to 'old people', as perceptions of age are very much in the eye of the beholder, and the evidence is limited and patchy, but the evidence is fairly consistent that older people were more frightened by – and unsettled in – air raids, and more stressed and anxious than younger adults and children.[3]

Children appear to have stood up relatively well to the trials of air raids, a fact which contemporary commentators believed reflected parental influence. Many parents were loath for their children to be evacuated; many ensured that their children were quickly returned to them; and some parents never allowed their children to be evacuated. Other parents were keen for their children to be evacuated. In all these cases, the protection and care of children must have been uppermost in almost every parent's mind. Yet, at the same time official and unofficial attitudes towards the protection of children were ambiguous. By highlighting the way in which many young people were allowed or encouraged to take risks as roof spotters, this book has challenged historians' focus on protecting children in wartime. This positive contribution of young people to the war also contrasts with the wider publicity given to concerns about young people's and children's unruly and criminal behaviour, which again was thought to reflect parents' influence, although in this case their lack of control. One reason for parents' lack of control was that they were busy at work, which the government encouraged: government and the media heaped praise on workers who carried on after the siren sounded and who speedily returned to their normal work routine after heavy raids.

Despite transport and housing problems after raids (as other historians have already pointed out), most people returned to work quickly. Malcolm Smith suggests three broad reasons for this: the experience of the 1930s, which engendered a strong work ethic and fear of unemployment; people's desire to reassure those at work that they were safe; and a need to maintain the patterns of daily life.[4] This last point fits well with evidence in previous chapters of a wish to keep as much of a routine as possible.

Choices

When people managed to maintain their daily routines in the face of danger and under great stress, they saw it as a real personal achievement. Ordinary people who experienced air raids felt a great sense of pride, achievement and importance that was unrelated to the yardsticks of wealth, family relationships and a successful career by which society usually judges success. This sense of success may have contributed to the throwing off of old constraints.

One of the most striking contradictions of the war was that, despite all the new restraints on people: they could not move freely around the country; they could not move jobs without the Ministry of Labour's permission; most were subject to conscription; defence-of-the-realm regulations interfered with a host of daily activities; and rationing restricted food choice, nevertheless, in other respects people were faced with far more profound choices than in peacetime. Most people were relatively free to choose what they would do in an air raid. For the most part, people were not forced to take cover or to continue an activity if they did not wish to do so. This choice was in part a reflection of government fears of upsetting key workers in the war effort: however much the government would have liked to impose a blanket policy, it did not dare do so, for neither side of industry would have supported it, and it would have been well-nigh impossible to enforce. People also made surprising choices about their limited spending power. In 1940 and 1941, long before the full fruits of higher wartime wages, many people chose – through Spitfire funds – to hand over money to the government to buy aeroplanes. Choosing to run life-and-death risks at work for no financial gain, and giving money away to the government, were two of the most extraordinary aspects of wartime life. People were actively forging a quintessentially wartime relationship between themselves and the nation; it was a bond of their own making, and the result of their own direct choices.

The concept of the civilian in the front line

Between the retreat from Dunkirk in May 1940 and D-Day in June 1944, more civilians were on the receiving end of the enemy's attacks and more civilians died as a result of enemy fire than soldiers, many of whom were in training camps in Britain rather than fighting overseas: the term 'front-line civilian' was, therefore, an apt one, but the concept was a political and cultural construction, and it was polysemic and contested. When politicians used the term 'front-line civilian', they were expressing a bundle of ideas that included risk, danger and duty, but, above all, they were referring to those civilians who actively undertook work that carried a war-related risk. It was an allocution. They were not referring to civilians who were the passive victims of air raids in their own homes. The term was also used more widely but, for government and sections of the press, it had a very precise meaning. Language, like much else, was contested and developmental. The government's use of the term 'front line' meant more than being the passive victim of war, or of coping with the effects of war; it involved an active role, taking risks in order to prosecute the war. Politicians and journalists used the term not only to describe the role of civilians, but also to encourage them to behave in a particular way; the term was, therefore, used to influence behaviour. Politicians used the words to try to encourage people to behave as if they were in the front line, and also to encourage others to see them as if they were in the front line. It is a technique frequently used by parents – praising children for behaving in a certain way in order that they will indeed behave in that way; it is positive labelling and hopefully carries a self-fulfilling prophecy. The government's message was about the importance of people's actions, but, when the wider public used the term, they meant the wartime experience of risk and danger – irrespective of any action they may or may not have taken.

In 1941, Ritchie Calder described people in the blitzes on London as being in the front line.[5] *Picture Post* carried a photograph of a BBC basement, with two women on camp beds reading and a man studying. The caption ran 'A front line trench in the war of nerves. Tin-hatted Laurence Gilliam plans a drama programme'.[6] An illustrated survey of the Home Front, *Ourselves in Wartime*, carried the following caption to a photograph of an army officer addressing workers at an Ack-Ack factory:

> Their task: workers in this anti-aircraft gun factory hear from an Army officer what their skill and endurance mean to the men behind the guns. Total war ironed out the distinctions between soldier and civilian, the men who manned the weapons and those who made them were in the front line.[7]

Shelters too could be transformed into military language. One man used a military metaphor when describing in his diary the mass burial of civilians killed in an air raid; he wrote of them as 'unknown warriors'.8

The term 'front line' entered common usage beyond politicians and newspaper journalists. Colin Perry adopted the language of the media and used the term in a number of related ways in his diary. He first used the term on 3 August 1940 when cycling in Surrey and contemplating the possibility of invasion, 'I mused that my route was now in the front-line'. On 25 August, he was writing up his diary one evening after the siren had gone, and commented that 'I enjoyed the feeling of writing this front line report'. He used it on 23–24 September 1940 to express his physical closeness to death: 'we ride with death at our elbow. This is comparable with the front line in the last war'. Finally, he used it of London – of both the sights of London in wartime and of London's iconic status. On 7 October he wrote, 'this new London, this invincible "Front Line" citadel of freedom', and on 21 October after driving with his father back to London from St Albans, 'a drive to the Front Line in the heat of battle'.[9]

When politicians and newspaper journalists used the metaphor of civilians as front-line troops, it incorporated notions of discipline, hierarchy and unquestioning obedience to authority, and, as such, it was not a radical message. As we have seen, when people behaved as politicians encouraged them to behave, and when they withstood the onslaught of bombs, it enhanced people's sense of self-importance, which suggests that behaviour and actions encouraged by the government may have had some unintended consequences.

After the worst of the blitzes, in May 1941 the compilers of the Ministry of Information's Weekly Home Intelligence Reports drew parallels between civilians and troops in the field, and found similar factors affecting the behaviour of both. First, they thought it extremely important that people had a secure base. A safe refuge somewhere was important in enabling people to stand up to continuous night raiding. This is borne out by the way in which people actively sought ways of coping with blitzes, by for instance taking to shelters and the London Underground at night (or trekking out of cities at night and back in during the day to do their jobs). Many civilians in air raids were in familiar surroundings, unlike soldiers, who were often in unknown territory. Second, fatigue 'stunned' people and made key personnel less efficient. There was evidence that in heavily bombed cities, such as Plymouth, Portsmouth and Southampton, those with civil-defence duties became less efficient when they did not receive enough sleep. Third, conditioning was important. Those who experienced a gradual build-up in raids coped better than those who experienced a sudden heavy raid. Fourth, personal blitz experience inevitably affected people's feelings: the sight of badly wounded casualties or sudden death, loss of friends or relatives, 'near misses', temporary entombment or loss of one's home had a definite 'unnerving effect' on people, often delayed for a few hours or a day, and usually temporary.[10]

The Ministry of Information also thought that less-material factors affected both troops and civilians, although the compilers' comments seem more speculative, and it may be that they seized on those reports with which they agreed. First, the Ministry pointed to a belief in equality of sacrifice: as long as people believed that all classes and sections of society were suffering and enduring equally, they would put up with very great hardship, but people resented unfairness. In fact, many did not believe that everyone was suffering equally, but this does not appear to have affected people's willingness to continue after the siren. Second, the Ministry thought that people needed to be able to trust government – both central and local – and yet there is much evidence that although praise was lavished on civil-defence personnel, people had a low opinion of the organisation of after-raid services, such as rest centres and the Assistance Board. Third, the Ministry thought that people had to be sure of ultimate victory, and this does seem to have been the case. Finally, people had to believe that there would be a better world after the war. On this point the evidence is mixed.[11]

Politicians, journalists and ordinary civilians linked their behaviour and experiences to that of the Armed Forces by referring to themselves in a positive way as being in the front line. Indeed, on numerous occasions, civilians and members of the Armed Forces were caught in the same air raids, the latter assisted the civil-defence and rescue services, and some of the Forces lost their lives in air raids on civilian targets. These common experiences were more likely to occur in naval and garrison towns.[12] Elsewhere, many civilians during the period of the heavy raids in the early part of the war expressed a distinct hostility towards the army.[13]

How apt then were the military metaphors used of civilians? Influences on civilians were both distinctive from, and similar to, those which military analysts and autobiographical accounts identify as important factors in motivating the Armed Forces. In the Armed Forces, factors such as: selection; training; discipline; loyalty to the regiment, battalion, platoon, or crew members (i.e. primary group loyalty); leadership; group support; moral coercion and shame; drink; the inducements of the spoils of war; routine; political ideology; excitement; and the effects of activity and fatigue in reducing fear, have all been identified as factors affecting the willingness and ability of soldiers, sailors and airmen to carry on under fire or risk to their lives.[14]

There were some obvious differences between civilians and those in the Forces. For civilians caught in air raids, there had been little selection beyond the evacuation of certain vulnerable groups (although these included children, who actually stood up to the experience well). There was no training for civilians who did not have ARP/civil-defence duties – they learnt from experience. There was no discipline imposed on civilians, as the practice of carrying on after the siren was largely voluntary. There were no inducements from the spoils of war, and, although some may have gained Dutch courage from drink, there is no actual evidence of this happening. Loyalty to a group was not so much a motive as an outcome: after air raids and blitzes people felt a heightened sense of identification and pride in their city or area. How far political ideology or the broader aims of the war induced people to carry on is difficult to judge. Memory evidence suggests that it existed, but this does not come through in the contemporary material.

There were some similarities between civilians and the Armed Forces. It is impossible to assess the role of national leadership, but parents gave a lead to their children: most parents hid their fear and nervousness from their children, and children imitated their parents' behaviour. People gained strength from the presence of others, whether at work or at home, and from the presence of shelter officials. In some cases there was moral coercion to continue one's job during raids. Routine was extremely important to people. Some found it easier to cope if they were active and had their minds taken off the dangers. Those with ARP/civil-defence duties had at least some training. Some, especially young people, relished the excitement of dogfights, although the experience of direct raids and blitzes was extremely frightening, whatever one's age.

Local identity

Malcolm Smith, looking forward into the post-war years, has argued that the blitz 'made the community story a principal element in the interior monologue of the nation'.[15] During the war, that community was firmly rooted in a specific location. When air raids destroyed well-known local buildings, people often expressed shock. On 3 November 1940 a woman wrote in a letter, 'I am afraid I do mind frightfully about the loss of buildings and the shattering of London as a place that has grown. Just what you experience as vivid flashes of memory of the places you have known is what happens to me. Not memory but such a passion of affection for the odd corners I pass every day.'[16] When people recall air raids it is often the physical destruction of buildings in their city that they describe and recall. One Portsmouth man made an explicit link between himself and the damage to the Guildhall. 'Portsmouth man born . . . a Portsmouth family man . . . the end of the world. To see the Guildhall going you knew there was no hope, it was going to go. Never thought the outside part would stand up like it did.' A hairdresser whose clients worked in the Guildhall he felt that, 'The Guildhall was important to us'.[17]

There is a preoccupation among much recent history with constructions of the 'nation' in an imperial context, and many discussions of nationality ignore its local dimension.[18] Sonya Rose has argued that during the war the British empire was important to Britain's self-image as a virtuous, imperial power. Her evidence, however, relates to Whitehall strategies rather than to ordinary people's identity.[19]

After the war, few tears were shed as Britain gave up its empire. Despite the pre-war efforts of governments to create identities with the empire through the pomp and circumstance of imperial shows, such as officially designated days to celebrate the empire, and the imperial contribution to the war, what was important to most people was closer to home. During the war the BBC's efforts to promote the empire fell on stony home ground.[20] Moreover, those attempting to construct a national identity, had, since before the war, frequently used local rather than imperial images. Stanley Baldwin, the dominant Conservative politician for most of the inter-war years, constructed a vision of middle-class rural England with which the nation was invited to identify. Those on the left constructed an industrial Britain bound together by working-class values of solidarity and community. It was a small step for those in government in 1940 to appropriate this construct in order to reaffirm British solidarity and community, not in the dark satanic mills of Northern England, but in the bombed East End of London. The East Ender became the icon of British values. So, the location of national identity journeyed from the countryside, to the industrial North, to the East End of London, becoming more and more place-specific as it moved.

Historians of earlier periods have explored changing notions of national identity, including the ways in which meanings have been attached to landscapes and to some extent to regions, and geographers have also looked at the importance of place to people at a more local level, in the area of their home. They have argued that people's attachment to a place is vitally important to them.[21] Local and national press reports of aerial attacks on towns and cities, and the way in which people stood up to attacks at work and at home, enhanced people's attachment to these places: the physical and abstract, the material and the idealistic attributes of homes were reinforced, fitting the arguments of David Ley, who – drawing inspiration from French regional geographers of the early twentieth century – has argued that it is impossible to separate the 'real' and 'imagined' attributes of home. Anderson's notion of imagined communities is familiar to historians, but it is usually applied to national rather than local communities. As people were experiencing attacks on their homes and workplaces, so they were attaching meaning to these experiences; they were linking their personal experiences with their town or city, so reinforcing their attachment to, and pride in it, and at the same time giving meaning to their experiences. Geographers have already argued that places where day-to-day, mundane activities take place are 'saturated' with meaning;[22] this is also the case when the extraordinary happened in those places, for they then became drenched with further layers of meaning. What were those meanings?

These meanings were related to the role of people in their country's survival, the importance of their town or city to survival, and a sense of the significance of themselves and the area of their home in the country's history. Part of the current significance of wartime experiences for people is their contribution at their workplace to the war effort. Nowadays there is a sense of fellow-feeling with those with whom they shared the experience of air raids, whether at the workplace or away from it.[23] At a personal and at a local level, people felt that they were playing a part in their nation's history. The experience of war enhanced both local and national identity; they were two sides of the same coin, not contradictory or mutually exclusive identities (as can happen in other contexts).

Wartime media enhanced and reconstructed people's experiences in a multitude of ways. The media constructed local experiences and industries as national ones. Wartime experiences had a profound effect on people, because, as others have argued, when a place is imbued with meaning for people, they feel a sense of belonging to it; meaningful places become a part of who we are and how we see our place in the world; they are important in forming our identities.[24] Not everyone could have felt a strong attachment to, and identity with, a particular place, but the combined experiences and feelings of many, in conjunction with the media, were strong enough to transform the personal, particular and local experience into the public, the general and national history.

Air raids engaged all the senses. There were the sounds of the siren, of Ack-Ack gunfire, of planes, of bombs and of roof spotters' warnings. There were the sights of dogfights, of burning and destroyed buildings, of piles of rubble, of the injured and dead, of civil-defence workers, and of roof spotters. There were the smells of damp and dirty shelters and of burning. There were the physical feelings of dust up the nose, of inconveniences and pain, of flying glass and of shaking buildings. There were the emotions of apprehension, expectation, fear, excitement, boredom, and of intensified relationships with people and places, as well as a sense of living through momentous historical events. The combination of these sensual experiences helps to explain the lasting significance of air raids for those who lived through them. The experiences were added to by visual and written reconstructions at the time and since, and by the language used to explain the experiences. While politicians and sections of the media used the language of 'the front line' to denote specific *behaviour*, the wider public used the same language to express an inclusive *experience*, which heightened their feelings of belonging, contributing and enduring, and it is this meaning that has so far survived.

Notes

1 P. E. Vernon, 'A study of war attitudes', *British Journal of Medical Psychology*, 19 (1941–43), p. 290.

2 For current views on persuasive communication, there are a number of introductions: Ann L. Weber, *Social Psychology* (HarperPerennial, 1992), p. 137; Andrew Hart, *Understanding the Media* (Routledge, 1991), pp. 175–81.

3 Mass-Observation Archive, University of Sussex, Air Raids, TC, 23/8/A; TC, 65/4/A, 2 and 5 September 1940, LE; TC, Air Raids 12/C; PRO INF 1/292, Weekly Home Intelligence Reports (WHIR), 21–28 October 1940, 4–11 November 1940, 5–12 February 1941, 5–12 March 1941, 18–25 May 1943.

4 Malcolm Smith, *Britain and 1940* (Routledge, 2000), p. 77.

5 Ritchie Calder, *Carry on London* (The English Universities Press, 1941), p. xiv.

6 *Picture Post* 15 March 1941.

7 Anon., *Ourselves in Wartime* (Odhams Press), pp. 16–17.

8 Imperial War Museum 81/2/1 John Davies 4 December 1940.

9 Colin Perry, *Boy in the Blitz: The 1940 Diary of Colin Perry* (Sutton Publishing, 2000), pp. 37, 89, 152–3, 207. First published by Leo Cooper in 1972.

10 PRO INF 1/292, WHIR, 7–14 May 1941.

11 PRO INF 1/292, WHIR, 7–14 May 1941.

12 PRO HO 199/134. One incident alone shows the difficulty of distinguishing between the experiences of civilians and the Forces: in Plymouth on

11 September 1940 between the 'all clear' and a second air-raid warning, bombs killed thirteen pedestrians, of whom four were marines and one a soldier.

13 PRO INF 1/292, WHIR, 5–12 February 1941, 11–18 June 1941; 1–8 September 1942. They grumbled about soldiers' alleged bad driving, especially of lorries, the 'lavishness' of army rations and the supposed waste in army camps. In Sheffield grumbles were heard about the army driving out of the city as soon as the siren sounded; people thought that it was a waste of petrol and that the army should have stayed to help the civil defence. Jibes circulated, such as 'they're practising for when they meet Rommel' and 'there's the army, leaving the civilians to face the bombs'.

14 See, for instance, Baron Moran, *Anatomy of Courage* (Avery Publishing, 1987). First published in 1945 by Constable; John Keegan 'Towards a theory of combat motivation', in Paul Addison and Angus Calder (eds), *A Time to Kill 1939–45* (Pimlico, 1997), Huw Strachen, 'The soldiers' experience in two world wars: some historiographical comparisions', in Paul Addison and Angus Calder (eds), *A Time to Kill*; Nigel de Lee, 'Oral history and British soldiers' experiences', in Paul Addison and Angus Calder (eds), *A Time to Kill.*

15 Malcolm Smith, *Britain and 1940*, p. 120.

16 Imperial War Museum 85/45/1, Helen to Mrs W. C. Bowman, 3 November 1940.

17 Portsmouth City Record Office, Oral History 2345A, Harold Ellis (b. 1902) interviewed 1994.

18 Richard Weight, *Patriots: National Identity in Britain 1940–2000* (Pan, 2002); Anthony Smith, *Myths and Memories of the Nation* (Oxford University Press, 1999); Anthony Smith, *National Identity* (Penguin,1991); Geoffrey Cubitt, *Imagining Nations* (Manchester University Press, 1998); David Miller, *On Nationality* (Oxford University Press, 1975)

19 Sonya Rose, 'Race, empire and British wartime national identity, 1939–45,' *Historical Research*, 74 (2001), pp. 220–37.

20 Thomas Hajkowski, 'The BBC, the Empire, and the Second World War, 1939–1945', *Historical Journal of Film, Radio and Television*, 22 (2002).

21 Lewis Holloway and Phil Hubbard, *People and Place: the Extraordinary Geographies of Everyday Life* (Prentice Hall, 2001), p. 67.

22 Lewis Holloway and Phil Hubbard, *People and Place*, pp. 68, 76.

23 This is apparent in the interviews conducted for this study.

24 Lewis Holloway and Phil Hubbard, *People and Place*, p. 69.

Bibliography

Unpublished

Birmingham Central Library, Birmingham Record Office, Birmingham City Council, BCC Emergency Committee

Bristol Record Office, Bristol City Council Minutes Emergency Committee

British Library, National Sound Archive

Cambridge University Library, M. S. Vickers

Chelsea Library, Borough of Chelsea, War Emergency Committee Minute Book

Churchill College, Cambridge, Churchill Archives Centre, Clementine Churchill papers

Cornwall Record Office, Truro, CC/1/23/1, Cornwall County Council, Emergency Committee Minutes; DPP 62/24/2, St Ewe Parish Invasion Book

Coventry City Record Office, CCA/1/4/48/1, National Emergency Committee

Glamorgan Record Office, City of Cardiff, vol. 11, BC/C/6/78, Proceedings of ARP committee; vol. 12, BCC/C/6/79, Civic Buildings and Markets' Committee; Proceedings of the Libraries Committee

Greenwich Heritage Centre, Borough of Woolwich Emergency Committee; Borough of Greenwich, ARP Emergency Committee

House of Lords Record Office, Beaverbrook papers, BBK

Imperial War Museum, London, Department of Art; Department of Documents; Department of Printed Books; Film and Video Archive; Photograph Archive; Sound Archive

Kensington Central Library, Kensington Emergency Committee

Kingston upon Thames Local History Room, Kingston ARP Committee

Leeds Central Library, City of Leeds, Air Raids Precautions and Civil Defence Committee Reports to the Council

Lewisham Library, Lewisham Civil Defence Committee

Liverpool Record Office, Civil Defence Emergency Committee Minute Book, 352/MIN/DEF/1/6

Manchester Central Library Archives and Local Studies, City of Manchester Emergency Committee

Merton Library, Merton and Morden Civil Defence Emergency Committee

National Archives, Kew (formerly Public Record Office), ADM; AIR; BT; CAB; ED; HO; INF; MH; RAIL

Plymouth and West Devon Record Office, Plymouth, 1561/CD/IU/1; Plymouth Emergency Committee Minutes

Portsmouth City Record Office, CCM40A/3, War Emergency Committee; Oral History Archive
RAF Museum, Hendon, Aviation Records Department, AC 70/10/80
Richmond upon Thames Local Studies Library, Borough of Richmond, Surrey Emergency Committee Report to Council; Borough of Barnes Town Council meetings
The Royal Aeronautical Society Library, London
Southampton City Council, Cultural Services, Oral History Archive; Southampton City Council, SC/T Acc 3749 SC/T9/73
Surrey Record Office, Woking, Dennis Specialist vehicles, 1463/WN 1
Teeside Record Office, Middlesbrough, DC/ST/2/68-9, Stockton Borough Council Emergency Committee; Borough of Redcar, DC/RE/2/10/2, Emergency Committee Diaries; Emergency Committee, Borough of Middlesbrough, CB/M/C/2/111; Borough of West Hartlepool, Minutes of the Emergency Committee; DC/H/2/62, Hartlepool Borough Council ARP Committee
Tower Hamlets, Local History and Archives, Bethnal Green General Emergency and Finance Committee, BG 603, 701; SN/EMER/2, Stoke Newington Emergency Committee; Metropolitan Borough of Shoreditch, S/A/2 ARP (Civil Defence) Committee Minutes; MBS Stepney, STE/878, Air Raid Precautions Committee Book
University of Leeds, Liddle Collection 1939–45
University of Sussex, Mass-Observation Archive
University of Warwick Library, Modern Records Centre, FBI, TUC
Wandsworth Local History Library, Wandsworth Civil Defence Control Committee

Published before 1945

Hansard books

Parliamentary Papers (PP), 1940–41, vol. iv, Annual Report of the Chief Inspector of Factories for 1939 and 1940
PP 1945–46, vol. xii, Annual Report of the Chief Inspector of Factories for 1944
PP 1946–47, vol. xi, Annual Report of the Chief Inspector of Factories for 1945
Air Training Corps Gazette, *Aircraft Recognition Test* (1942)
Anon. *Aircraft Recognition Tests: What is it?* (The Aeroplane, 1940)
Anon. *Ourselves in Wartime* (Odhams Press, 1944)
Balchin, Nigel *Darkness Falls from the Air* (Collins, 1942)
Calder, Ritchie *Carry on London* (The English Universities Press, 1941)
Churchill, Randolph S. (compiler), *Into Battle: Speeches by the Rt. Hon. Winston S. Churchill PC, MP* (Cassell, 1941)
Farrer, David *The Sky's the Limit: The Story of Beaverbrook at MAP* (Hutchinson, 1943)
Green, Henry *Caught* (Hogarth Press, 1943)

Griffith, C. (compiler) *Raid Spotters Note Book* (Charles Petts, not dated)
Holden, Inez *It Was Different at the Time* (The Bodley Head, 1943)
Idle, E. Doreen *War Over West Ham* (Faber and Faber, 1943)
Kimble, P. *Newspaper Reading in the Third Year of the War* (George Allen and Unwin, 1942)
Langdon, David *Home Front Lines* (Methuen, 1942)
MacRoberts, N. de P. *ARP Lessons from Barcelona* (Eyre and Spottiswoode, 1938)
Martin, Hugh *The British Churches in Wartime* (Ministry of Information, 1944)
Mee, Arthur *Nineteen-Forty: Our Finest Hour* (Hodder and Stoughton, 1941)
Moss, Louis and Box, Kathleen *Newspapers: An Inquiry into Newspaper Reading Amongst the Civilian Population* (Wartime Social Survey for Ministry of Information, June–July 1943)
Pratt Boorman, H. R. *Hell's Corner: Kent Becomes the Battlefield of Britain* (Kent Messenger, 1942)
Priestley, J. B. *Postscripts* (Heinemann, 1940)
Priestley, J. B. *Daylight on Saturday* (Heinemann, 1943)
Robbins, Gordon *Fleet Street Blitzkrieg Diary* (Ernest Benn, January 1944)
Scott, Peggy *They Made Invasion Possible* (Hutchinson, 1944)
Shipley, Rev. S. Paul (compiler) *Bristol Siren Nights: Diaries and Stories of the Blitzes* (Rankin Bros, Undated, but probably 1943)
Shute, Nevil *What Happened to the Corbetts* (Heinemann, 1939)
Shute, Nevil *Most Secret* (Heinemann, 1945)
Strachey, John *Post D: Some Experiences of an Air Raid Warden* (Victor Gollancz, 1941)
TUC, *The TUC in Wartime: An Informal Record of Three Months' Progress* (TUC, January 1941)

Journals

The Aeroplane Spotter
British Medical Journal
Communist Party of Great Britain *Party Organiser*
League of Coloured People *Newsletter*
The Listener
Ministry of Labour *Gazette*
Monthly Film Bulletin
Picture Post
Today's Cinema
Trades Union Congress *Annual Report* 1940

Journal articles

Anon., 'The Jim Crow spotter's chair', *Labour Management* (March 1941)
Glover, Edward 'Notes on the psychological effects of war conditions on the civilian population', *International Journal of Psychoanalysis*, 23:1 (1942)

Pritchard, Rosemary and Rosenzweig, Saul 'The effects of war stress upon childhood and youth', *Journal of Abnormal Social Psychology*, 37 (1942)

Schmideberg, Melitta 'Some observations on individual reactions to air raids', *International Journal of Psychoanalysis* 23:3 and 4 (1942)

Thouless, Dr Robert H. 'Psychological effects of air raids', *Nature* 148:3746 (16 August 1941)

Vernon, P. E. 'Psychological effects of air raids', *Journal of Abnormal Psychology*, 36 (1941)

Vernon, P. E. 'A study of war attitudes', *British Journal of Medical Psychology*, 19 (1941–43)

Newspapers

Bristol Evening Post
Catholic Herald
City Press
Croydon Times
Daily Express
Daily Herald
Daily Mail
Daily Mirror
Evening Standard
Express and Echo (Exeter)
Glasgow Herald
Guardian
Hackney Gazette
Lewisham Borough News
Liverpool Post
Mitcham News and Mercury
Mitcham and Tooting Advertiser
New Statesman and Nation
Observer
Oxford Mail
Southern Daily Echo
South London Press
Sunday Times
Surrey Comet
Thames Valley Times
The Times
Tooting, Balham, Mitcham and Colliers Wood Gazette
Wandsworth Borough News
Western Evening Herald (Plymouth)
Western Mail
Westminster and Pimlico News
Wimbledon Borough News
Yorkshire Post

Published since 1945

Books

Addison, Paul *The Road to 1945: British Politics and the Second World War* (Pimlico, 1994)

Addison, Paul and Calder, Angus (eds), *Time To Kill: The Soldier's Experience of War in the West, 1939–1945* (Pimlico, 1997)

Addison, Paul and Crang, Jeremy (eds), *The Burning Blue: A New History of the Battle of Britain* (Pimlico, 2000)

Aldgate, Anthony *Cinema and History: British Newsreels and the Spanish Civil War* (Scolar Press, 1979)

Aldgate, Anthony and Richards, Jeffrey *Britain Can Take It: The British Cinema in the Second World War* (Edinburgh University Press, 1994)

Allen, Robert C. and Gomery, Douglas *Film History: Theory and Practice* (Knopf, 1985)

Andrews, Julian *London's War: The Shelter Drawings of Henry Moore* (Lund Humphries, 2002)

Barnett, Correlli *The Audit of War* (Macmillan, 1986)

Beardmore, George *Civilians at War: Journals 1938–1946* (John Murray, 1984)

Belfrage, Bruce *One Man in His Time* (Hodder and Stoughton, 1951)

Bergman, Andrew *We're in the Money: Depression America and its Films* (New York University Press, 1971)

Berwick Sayers, W. C. *Croydon and the Second World War* (Croydon Corporation, 1949)

Bourne, J. M. *Britain and the Great War 1914–1918* (Edward Arnold, 1989)

Branston, Gill and Stafford, Roy *The Media Student's Handbook* (Routledge, 1996)

Briggs, Adam and Cobley, Paul (eds), *The Media: An Introduction* (Longman, 1998)

Briggs, Asa *The History of Broadcasting in the United Kingdom. vol. 3. The War of Words* (Oxford University Press, 1995)

Broad, Richard and Fleming, Suzie (eds), *Nella Last's War: A Mother's Diary 1939–45* (Falling Wall Press, 1981)

Bromley, Roger *Lost Narratives: Popular Fictions, Politics and Recent History* (Routledge, 1988)

Brooke, Stephen *Labour's War: The Labour Party During the Second World War* (Clarendon, 1992)

Bullock, Alan *The Life and Times of Ernest Bevin. vol. 2. Minister of Labour 1940–1945* (Heinemann, 1967)

Calder, Angus *The People's War, Britain 1939–1945* (Panther, 1971)

Calder, Angus *The Myth of the Blitz* (Pimlico, 1991)

Chamberlain, Mary and Thompson, Paul (eds), *Narrative and Genre* (Routledge, 1998)

Chapman, James *The British at War: Cinema, State and Propaganda, 1939–45* (I. B. Tauris, 1998)

Chisholm, Anne and Davie, Michael *Beaverbrook: A Life* (Hutchinson, 1992)

Churchill, Winston S. *The Second World War. vol. 2. Their Finest Hour* (Cassell, 1949)

Croucher, Richard *Engineers at War* (Merlin Press, 1982)

Cubitt, Geoffrey *Imagining Nations* (Manchester University Press, 1998)

Curran, James and Seaton, Jean *Power Without Responsibility* (Routledge, 1997)

Currie, Robert, Gilbert, Alan and Horsley, Lee *Churches and Churchgoers: Patterns of Church Growth in the British Isles Since 1700* (Clarendon, 1977)

Darwin, Bernard *War on the Line: The Story of the Southern Railway in Wartime* (The Southern Railway Co., 1946)

Donnelly, Peter (ed.), *Mrs Milburn's Diaries: An Englishwoman's Day-to-Day Reflections* (Harrap, 1979)

Douglas, Mary *Risk: Acceptability According to the Social Sciences* (RKP, 1986)

Doyle, Brian (compiler and editor) *The Who's Who of Children's Literature* (Hugh Evelyn, 1968)

Ellis, Peter Berresford and Schofield, Jennifer *Biggles! The Life Story of Capt. W. E. Johns* (Veloce Publishing, 1993)

Fishman, Sarah *The Battle for Children: World War II, Youth Crime, and Juvenile Justice in Twentieth-Century France* (Harvard University Press, 2002)

Gilbert, Martin (ed.), *The Churchill War Papers. vol. II. Never Surrender, May 1940–December 1940* (Heinemann, 1994)

Goodman, Philomena *Women, Sexuality and War* (Palgrave, 2000)

Greene, Graham *The End of the Affair* (Vintage, 2001) First published by William Heinemann in 1951

Griffiths, Dennis *The Standard* (Macmillan, 1996)

Hamilton, Tim *Identification Friend or Foe: Being the Story of Aircraft Recognition* (HMSO, 1994)

Harrisson, Tom *Living Through the Blitz* (Penguin, 1978)

Hart, Andrew *Understanding the Media* (Routledge, 1991)

Hollis, Patricia *Jennie Lee: A Life* (Oxford University Press, 1997)

Holloway, Lewis and Hubbard, Phil *People and Place: The Extraordinary Geography of Everyday Life* (Prentice Hall, 2001)

Hunt, Peter *An Introduction to Children's Literature* (Oxford University Press, 1994)

Jackson, Mick *Five Boys* (Faber and Faber, 2001)

Janis, Irving L. *Air War and Emotional Stress: Psychological Studies of Bombing and Civil Defense* (The Rand Corporation, 1951)

Jefferys, Kevin *The Churchill Coalition and Wartime Politics 1940–45* (Manchester University Press, 1991)

Jones, Helen *Health and Society in Twentieth-Century Britain* (Longman, 1994)

Kracauer, Siegfried *From Caligari to Hitler: A Psychological History of the German Film* (Princeton University Press, 1947, republished 2004)

Lane, Tony *The Merchant Seamen's War* (Manchester University Press, 1990)

Lee, Jennie *My Life With Nye* (Jonathan Cape, 1980)

McCooey, Chris *Despatches from the Home Front: The War Diaries of Joan Strange 1939–1945* (Monarch Publications, 1989)

McCulloch, Art (compiler), *The War and Uncle Walter: The Diary of an Eccentric* (Doubleday, 2003)
Mackay, Robert *Half the Battle: Civilian Morale in Britain During the Second World War* (Manchester University Press, 2002)
McLaine, I. *Ministry of Morale: Home Front Morale and the Ministry of Information in World War II* (Allen and Unwin, 1979)
Maland, Charles J. *American Visions: The Films of Chaplin, Ford, Capra and Welles, 1936–41* (Arno, 1977).
Malim, Tony and Birch, Ann *Introductory Psychology* (Macmillan, 1998)
Marwick, Arthur *Britain in the Century of Total War: War, Peace and Social Change, 1900–1967* (Penguin, 1970)
Marwick, Arthur *War and Social Change in the Twentieth Century: A Comparative Study of Britain, France, Germany, Russia and the US* (Macmillan, 1974)
Mass-Observation, *Puzzled People: A Study in Popular Attitudes to Religion, Ethics, Progress and Politics in a London Borough* (Victor Gollancz, 1947)
Middlemas, Keith *Politics in Industrial Society: The Experience of the British System Since 1911* (André Deutsch, 1979)
Miller, David *On Nationality* (Oxford University Press, 1975)
Millgate, Helen D. (ed.), *Mr Brown's War: A Diary of the Second World War* (Sutton Publishing, 2003)
Monaco, Paul *Cinema and Society* (Elsevier, 1976)
Moran, Charles McMoran Wilson, Baron *Anatomy of Courage* (USA: Avery Publishing, 1987). First published in 1945 by Constable.
Munton, Alan *English Fiction in the Second World War* (Faber, 1989)
Murphy, Robert *British Cinema in the Second World War* (Continuum, 2000)
Nicholas, Sian *The Echo of War: Home Front Propaganda and the BBC* (Manchester University Press, 1996)
Nicolson, Harold *Diaries and Letters 1939–1945* (Collins, 1967)
Nixon, Barbara *Raiders Overhead: A Diary of the London Blitz* (Scolar Press, London, 1980), first published in 1943
Noakes, Lucy *War and the British: Gender, Memory and National Identity* (I. B. Tauris, 1998)
Orwell, Sonia and Angus, Ian *The Collected Essays, Journalism and Letters of George Orwell. vol. II. My Country Right or Left 1940–1943* (Secker and Warburg, 1968)
Pearson, Geoffrey *Hooligan: A History of Respectable Fears* (Macmillan, 1983)
Pelling, Henry *Winston Churchill* (Pan, 1977)
Perks, Robert and Thomson, Alastair (eds), *The Oral History Reader* (Routledge, 1998)
Perry, Colin *Boy in the Blitz: The 1940 Diary of Colin Perry* (Sutton Publishing, 2000)
Piette, Adam *Imagination at War: British Fiction and Poetry, 1939–1945* (Papermac, 1995)
Ponting, Clive *1940: Myth and Reality* (Hamish Hamilton, 1990)
Rachman, S. J. *Fear and Courage* (W. H. Freeman, 1978)

Rattigan, Neil *This is England: British Film and the People's War, 1939–1945* (Associated University Presses, 2001)
Rattigan, Terence *The Collected Plays of Terence Rattigan. vol. 1* (Hamish Hamilton, 1968)
Reeves, Nicholas *The Power of Film Propaganda: Myth or Reality?* (Cassell, 1999)
Richards, Jeffrey *Films and British National Identity* (Manchester University Press, 1997)
Richards, W. L. *Pembrokeshire under Fire: The Story of the Air Raids of 1940–41* (J. W. Hammond, 1965)
Roberts, John *The Art of Interruption: Realism, Photography and the Everyday* (Manchester University Press, 1998)
Rose, Sonya *Which People's War? National Identity and Citizenship in Britain 1939–1945* (Oxford University Press, 2003)
Rowlinson, Frank *Contribution to Victory: An Account of Some of the Special Work of the Metropolitan-Vickers Electrical Co. Ltd. in the Second World War* (Vickers, 1947)
Rumpf, Hans *The Bombing of Germany* (White Lion Publishers, 1975 edn)
Sacks, Oliver *Uncle Tungsten: Memoirs of a Chemical Boyhood* (Macmillan, 2001)
Saunders, Hilary St George *Ford at War* (Ford, 1946)
Scott, J. D. *Vickers: A History* (Weidenfeld and Nicholson, 1962)
Sears, David *Social Psychology* (Prentice Hall, 1985 edn)
Seldon, A. and Pappworth, J. *By Word of Mouth: Elite Oral History* (Methuen, 1983)
Shawn, William (ed.), *Mollie Panter-Downes London War Notes 1939–1945* (Farrer, Straus and Giroux, 1971)
Sheridan, Dorothy (ed.), *Wartime Women: A Mass-Observation Anthology 1937–45* (Phoenix Press, 2000)
Sheridan, Dorothy, Street, Brian and Bloome, David *Writing Ourselves: Mass-Observation and Literary Practices* (Hampton Press, 2000)
Sillitoe, Alan *Life Without Armour: An Autobiography* (HarperCollins, 1995)
Slovic, Paul *The Perception of Risk* (Earthscan, 2000)
Smith, Anthony *National Identity* (Penguin, 1991)
Smith, Anthony *Myths and Memories of the Nation* (Oxford University Press, 1999)
Smith, Harold L. *Britain in the Second World War* (Manchester University Press, 1996)
Smith, Malcolm *Britain and 1940* (Routledge, 2000)
Smithies, Edward *Crime in Wartime: A Social History of Crime in World War II* (George Allen and Unwin, 1982)
Stevenson, John *British Society 1914–1945* (Penguin, 1984)
Summerfield, Penny *Women Workers in the Second World War: Production and Patriarchy in Conflict* (Croom Helm, 1984)
Summerfield, Penny *Reconstructing Women's Wartime Lives* (Manchester University Press, 1998)

Taylor, John *A Dream of England: Landscape, Photography and the Tourist's Imagination* (Manchester University Press, 1994)

Thoms, David *War, Industry and Society: The Midlands 1939–45* (Routledge, 1989).

Thomson, George P. *Blue Pencil Admiral* (Sampson Low, Marston & Co., 1947)

Titmuss, Richard *Problems of Social Policy* (HMSO, 1950)

Tory, Peter *Giles: A Life in Cartoons* (Headline, 1992)

Trussler, Simon *British Theatre: Cambridge Illustrated History* (Cambridge University Press, 2000)

Twyford, H. P. *It Came to Our Door: The Story of Plymouth Throughout the Second World War* (Underhill, first published 1945, revised 1949)

Vivelo, Frank Robert *Cultural Anthropology: A Basic Introduction* (University Press of America, 1994)

Weber, Ann L. *Social Psychology* (HarperPerennial, 1992)

Weight, Richard *Patriots: National Identity in Britain 1940–2000* (Pan, 2002)

Wood, Derek *Attack Warning Red: The Royal Observer Corps and the Defence of Britain, 1925 to 1975* (Macdonald and Jane's, 1976)

Zweiniger-Bargielowska, Ina *Austerity in Britain: Rationing, Controls and Consumption, 1939–1953* (Oxford University Press, 2000)

Chapters in books

Ceadel, Martin 'Popular fiction and the next war, 1918–39', in Frank Gloversmith (ed.), *Class, Culture and Social Change: A New View of the 1930s* (Harvester Press, 1980)

Chapman, James 'Cinema, propaganda and national identity: British film and the Second World War', in Justine Ashby and Andrew Higson (eds), *British Cinema, Past and Present* (Routledge, 2000)

Harper, Sue 'The representation of women in feature films, 1939–45', in Philip Taylor (ed.), *Britain and the Cinema in the Second World War* (Macmillan, 1988)

Lewis, Adrian 'Henry Moore's "Shelter Drawings": memory and myth', in Pat Kirkham and David Thoms (eds), *War Culture: Social Change and Changing Experience in World War Two* (Lawrence and Wishart, 1995)

Macnicol, John 'The evacuation of schoolchildren', in Harold L. Smith (ed.), *War and Social Change: British Society in the Second World War* (Manchester University Press, 1986)

Mellor, David Alan 'Mass-Observation: the intellectual climate', in Jessica Evans (ed.), *The Camerawork Essays: Context and Meaning in Photography* (River Orams Press, 1997)

Thoms, David 'The blitz, civilian morale and regionalism, 1940–1942', in Pat Kirkham and David Thoms (eds), *War Culture: Social Change and Changing Experience in World War Two* (Lawrence and Wishart, 1995)

Thorpe, Andrew 'Britain', in Jeremy Noakes (ed.), *The Civilian in War* (Exeter University Press, 1992)

Journal articles

Beaven, B. and Thoms, D. 'The blitz and civilian morale in three northern cities, 1940–42', *Northern History Journal*, 32 (1996)

Browne, R. C. 'A conception of industrial health', *British Medical Journal* 1 (1947)

Eley, Geoff 'Finding the People's War: film, British collective memory, and World War II', *American Historical Review*, 1063 (2001)

Gregor, Neil 'A *Schicksalsgemeinschaft*? Allied bombing, civilian morale and social dissolution in Nuremberg, 1942–1945', *Historical Journal*, 43:4 (2002)

Hajkowski, Thomas 'The BBC, the Empire, and the Second World War, 1939–1945', *Historical Journal of Film, Radio and Television*, 22 (2002)

Portelli, Alessandro 'The peculiarities of oral history', *History Workshop Journal*, 12 (1981)

Rose, Sonya 'Race, empire and British wartime national identity, 1939–45', *Historical Research*, 74 (2001)

Sokoloff, Sally 'The home front in the Second World War and local history', *The Local Historian*, 32 (2002)

Summerfield, Penny and Peniston-Bird, Corinna 'Women in the firing line: the Home Guard and the defence of gender boundaries in Britain in the Second World War', *Women's History Review*, 9 (2000)

Unpublished papers

Beaven, B. and Griffiths, J. 'Mass-Observation and civilian morale: working-class communities during the blitz 1940–41'. Mass-Observation Archive Occasional Paper no. 8, 1998, University of Sussex Library

Webb, D. Le P. 'Never a Dull Moment: A Personal History of Vickers Supermarine 1926–60. Part II', Unpublished typescript, University of Cambridge Library

Index

Note: 'n' after a page reference indicates the number of a note on that page.